A PRIORI JUSTIFICATION

A PRIORI JUSTIFICATION

Albert Casullo

OXFORD
UNIVERSITY PRESS

2003

OXFORD
UNIVERSITY PRESS

Oxford   New York
Auckland   Bangkok   Buenos Aires   Cape Town   Chennai
Dar es Salaam   Delhi   Hong Kong   Istanbul   Karachi   Kolkata
Kuala Lumpur   Madrid   Melbourne   Mexico City   Mumbai   Nairobi
São Paulo   Shanghai   Taipei   Tokyo   Toronto

Copyright © 2003 by Albert Casullo

Published by Oxford University Press, Inc.
198 Madison Avenue, New York, New York 10016

www.oup.com

Oxford is a registered trademark of Oxford University Press

Library of Congress Cataloging-in-Publication Data
Casullo, Albert.
A priori justification / Albert Casullo.
   p.   cm.
Includes bibliographical references.
ISBN 0-19-511505-8
1. A priori.   I. Title.
BD181.3 .C38 2002
121'.4—dc 21   2002025253

9 8 7 6 5 4 3 2 1

Printed in the United States of America
on acid-free paper

For Becky

O sogno d'or
poter amar così!

Giacomo Puccini
La Rondine, Act One

Preface

Many colleagues, friends, and students provided helpful comments and sound advice on various aspects of this project. I am deeply grateful to all of them, more so than I can adequately express. Panayot Butchvarov, Heimir Geirsson, and David Hunter read the entire manuscript and gave me many valuable suggestions that greatly improved the final version. I have benefited enormously from the comments of Tony Anderson, George Bealer, Larry BonJour, David Chalmers, Alvin Goldman, Robin Jeshion, Philip Kitcher, Kirk Ludwig, Penelope Maddy, Paul Moser, Alvin Plantinga, Ernie Sosa, and Kadri Vihvelin. My colleagues and students at the University of Nebraska–Lincoln, including Robert Audi, Edward Becker, Bryan Belknap, Tim Black, Nancy Brahm, Harry Ide, Joe Mendola, Thad Metz, Peter Murphy, David Pitt, Guy Rohrbaugh, and Mark van Roojen, provided fruitful discussions on countless occasions. Tim Black proofread the manuscript and helped prepare the index. Peter Ohlin and Cynthia Read, of Oxford University Press, were supportive through all phases of the project and patient when it required more time than originally anticipated.

I am particularly indebted to three individuals who contributed in other ways: Panayot Butchvarov, who for thirty years has been a constant source of inspiration, insight, constructive criticism and sound judgment; Larry Hardin, who recognized and nourished my interest in philosophy when I was an undergraduate student at Syracuse University; and Philip Kitcher, whose support and encouragement during the early stages of this project were instrumental in bringing it to fruition.

For financial support, which made the timely completion of this project possible, I thank the University of Nebraska–Lincoln. The Research Council provided a research fellowship in the summer of 1997, and the College of Arts and Sciences and the Philosophy Department supported a reduction in my teaching load for the fall of 2000.

This book is dedicated to my wife, Becky, with love, as a small token of gratitude for all that she has given to me.

Acknowledgments

I wish to thank the original publishers for granting permission to use portions of some of my previously published articles:

"Necessity, Certainty, and the A Priori," *Canadian Journal of Philosophy* 18 (1988): 43–66.

"Revisability, Reliabilism, and A Priori Knowledge," *Philosophy and Phenomenological Research* 49 (1988): 187–213.

"Causality, Reliabilism, and Mathematical Knowledge," *Philosophy and Phenomenological Research* 52 (1992): 557–584.

"Analyticity and the A Priori," *Canadian Journal of Philosophy*, supp. vol. 18 (1993): 113–150.

"The Coherence of Empiricism," *Pacific Philosophical Quarterly* 81 (2000): 31–48.

"Modal Epistemology: Fortune or Virtue?" *Southern Journal of Philosophy* 38, supp. (2000): 17–25.

"Experience and A Priori Justification," *Philosophy and Phenomenological Research* 63 (2001): 665–671.

"A Priori Knowledge," in *The Oxford Handbook of Epistemology*, ed. Paul Moser (New York: Oxford University Press, 2002).

Contents

A PRIORI JUSTIFICATION

Introduction

1 The Contemporary Divide

The major divide in contemporary epistemology is between those who embrace and those who reject the a priori. The importance of the issue, however, extends beyond the boundaries of epistemology to virtually every other area of philosophy. To a large extent, one's views about the a priori determine how one goes about answering other philosophical questions. Current opinion is deeply divided and radically polarized. Proponents of the a priori frequently allege that rejecting it is tantamount to rejecting philosophy as a respectable intellectual discipline. Opponents respond that no intellectually respectable theory of knowledge can accommodate the a priori.

My goal is to provide a systematic treatment of the primary epistemological issues associated with the a priori that is sensitive to recent developments in the field of epistemology. Assessing the status of the a priori within contemporary epistemology requires distinguishing the requirements of the a priori from traditional assumptions about the nature of knowledge and justification. Freeing the a priori from those assumptions allows us to view it from a fresh perspective, which yields three major insights. First, the concept of a priori justification is minimal: it is simply the concept of nonexperiential justification. Second, the basic question that must be addressed to resolve the controversy over the existence of a priori knowledge is whether there are nonexperiential sources of justified beliefs. Third, and most important, articulating the concept of nonexperiential justification and establishing that there are nonexperiential sources of justified belief require empirical investigation. Hence, epistemologists must both acknowledge and embrace the role of empirical evidence in resolving these fundamental issues.

3

2 The Kantian Background

The contemporary discussion of a priori knowledge is shaped by Kant's introduction to the *Critique of Pure Reason*. There, in a remarkably short compass, he offers a definition of a priori knowledge, provides criteria for such knowledge that forge a close relationship between the a priori and the necessary, argues that some of our knowledge is indeed a priori, introduces the distinction between analytic and synthetic propositions, and maintains that there are clear examples of synthetic a priori knowledge.

Kant's treatment of the a priori involves a conceptual framework, a series of questions posed within it, and responses to those questions. The framework consists of three distinctions: the *epistemic* distinction between a priori and empirical knowledge, the *metaphysical* distinction between necessary and contingent propositions, and the *semantic* distinction between analytic and synthetic propositions. Within this framework, he addresses four primary questions:

(1) What is a priori knowledge?
(2) Is there a priori knowledge?
(3) What is the relationship between the a priori and the necessary?
(4) What is the relationship between the a priori and the analytic?

The contemporary discussion proceeds largely within Kant's framework, addressing the questions he raises and taking his answers as a starting point.

3 Synopsis

Kant's four questions provide the general structure for this study. Part I, consisting of three chapters, addresses the concept of a priori justification. Chapter 1 provides a taxonomy of widely endorsed conditions on a priori justification. The conditions fall into two broad categories: epistemic and nonepistemic. I argue for two major claims. First, nonepistemic conditions\ are neither necessary nor sufficient for a priori justification. Second, if a theory imposes epistemic conditions on the a priori that differ from those it imposes on the a posteriori, they must be supported by independent argument or rejected as ad hoc. Two defensible conditions on a priori justification emerge: (1) justification by a nonexperiential source, and (2) justification that is not defeasible by experience.

Chapter 2 examines two conceptions of a priori justification. The first alleges that condition (1) is both necessary and sufficient for such justification, and the second maintains that condition (2) is also necessary. Two criteria are introduced to evaluate them: continuity with historical precedent and coherence with generally accepted principles about justification and knowledge. I argue that although the former favors neither, the latter favors the weaker conception, which allows for the possibility of experientially justified defeaters.

Chapter 3 articulates the requirements of fallible a priori justification. I distinguish two senses of fallibility, justification that does not guarantee truth and justification that is defeasible, and argue that, although these senses are logically independent of one another, there are some significant relations between them. This investigation allows me to show that several fallibilist accounts of a priori justification face difficulties that are avoided by the account defended in chapter 2.

Part II, also consisting of three chapters, addresses the existence of a priori knowledge. Chapter 4 examines arguments in favor of such knowledge. I identify three types of argument. The first offers an analysis of the concept of a priori knowledge and maintains that some knowledge satisfies the conditions in the analysis. The second offers criteria of the a priori and contends that some knowledge meets the criteria. The third maintains that radical empiricist theories of knowledge are deficient in some respect. I contend that the arguments fail. The conceptual arguments involve implausible conceptions of a priori knowledge. The criterial arguments involve false epistemic premises. The deficiency arguments fail because theories endorsing the a priori suffer from the same deficiencies.

Chapter 5 addresses arguments against the existence of a priori knowledge. I identify three types of argument. The first offers an analysis of the concept of a priori knowledge and maintains that no cases of knowledge satisfy the conditions in the analysis. The second offers radical empiricist accounts of knowledge of propositions alleged to be knowable only a priori. The third maintains that the a priori is incompatible with epistemic naturalism. I contend that the negative arguments also fail. The conceptual arguments impose implausible conditions on a priori knowledge. The radical empiricist accounts do not establish that the propositions in question are not also known a priori. Finally, I distinguish two varieties of epistemic naturalism and argue that neither is incompatible with the a priori.

Chapter 6 argues that proponents of the a priori face two major challenges: articulating the experiential/nonexperiential distinction and providing supporting evidence for the claim that there are nonexperiential sources of justification. I argue that the most promising approaches to addressing both involve empirical investigation. Concerning the first, I propose viewing experience as a natural kind whose underlying nature must be uncovered by empirical investigation. Concerning the second, I contend that providing compelling support for the a priori involves two related projects. The first, which is philosophical, involves more fully articulating the claim that there are nonexperiential sources of justification. The second involves providing empirical supporting evidence for the articulated claim.

Part III, consisting of two chapters, addresses Kant's third and fourth questions. My primary goal is to argue that, although these questions are intrinsically interesting, resolving them is not necessary to answer the two prior questions concerning the concept and existence of a priori knowledge. In chapter 7, I argue that the relationship between the a priori and the necessary takes on prominence against the background of two views: the traditional rationalist conception of a priori knowledge and Kant's claim that necessity is a criterion of the a priori. Since I offer independent grounds for rejecting both views, resolving the disputes over the relationship is not necessary to answer the two prior questions.

Chapter 8 addresses two questions. Is there synthetic a priori knowledge? Is the analytic/synthetic distinction cogent? The epistemic significance of the first derives from the assumption that synthetic a priori knowledge raises difficult explanatory problems that are circumvented by analytic a priori knowledge. The epistemic significance of the second derives from the assumption that if the analytic/synthetic distinction is not cogent then the cogency of the a priori/a posteriori distinction is also doubtful. I argue that both assumptions are false and, as a consequence, resolving the controversies surrounding the two questions is not necessary to answer the two prior questions.

My presentation of the issues proceeds largely within the Kantian framework. In particular, I take for granted the distinction between necessary and contingent truths but offer no account of the distinction beyond the intuitive formulation presented earlier. I also take for granted the traditional view that belief is an attitude directed toward propositions. Once again, I offer no account of the nature of propositions or a defense of their existence. There are two reasons for this beyond the fact that I have nothing original to offer here. First, the arguments I offer do not turn on any particular view of the nature of the attitudes or their objects. Second, by not committing myself on these issues, I hope to present results whose cogency does not depend on particular views about these issues.

PART I

WHAT IS A PRIORI KNOWLEDGE?

1

The Leading Proposals

1.1 Introduction

Questions about a priori knowledge are among the most controversial in the field of epistemology. The traditional disputes have been centered around the content and extent of such knowledge. More recently, disputes over the existence of a priori knowledge have come to the fore. One question that naturally arises in the face of such controversy is whether all parties share a common conception of what is at issue. Even a cursory examination of the recent literature indicates that they do not.[1] Consequently, the first step is to clarify the concept at the center of the controversy.

The assumption that there is a coherent concept of a priori knowledge is itself controversial. The only answer to those who claim that there is none is to provide one. My contention is that, given the framework of concepts traditionally utilized in discussions of empirical knowledge, there is no significant obstacle. To those who reject the framework of concepts of traditional epistemology, I offer no argument. If they have an alternative framework, let them provide it, and we will see whether there is room within it for the a priori. If that framework is merely forthcoming, then we patiently await its arrival. Working within our present conceptual framework, we face two challenges. The first is to bring some order to the vast number of alternative analyses that have been proposed. The second is to evaluate systematically the proposed analyses to bring to the fore those that have most merit.

---

1. For a bibliography of recent literature on the a priori, see Casullo, "A Priori Knowledge Appraised."

Before turning to the proposed analyses, I introduce two methodological caveats. First, accounts of a priori knowledge are developed within a broader epistemological context involving assumptions about the requirements of knowledge and the nature of epistemic justification. Many traditional accounts, for example, were developed in a context dominated by Cartesian standards of knowledge and foundationalist assumptions about justification. It would be quite surprising if the resulting accounts of a priori knowledge did not incorporate at least some of those broader epistemological assumptions. Consequently, when examining conceptions of a priori knowledge, it is critical to distinguish between the requirements of the a priori as opposed to the requirements of the background theory of knowledge or justification.

Second, it is important to be clear about the primary target of an analysis of the concept of a priori knowledge. There are two approaches to analyzing it. The first, the *reductive* approach, analyzes the concept of a priori knowledge in terms of the concept of a priori justification. According to the reductive approach, S knows a priori that *p* just in case (1) S's belief that *p* is justified a priori and (2) the other conditions for knowledge are satisfied. The primary target of analysis is the concept of a priori justification. The second, the *nonreductive* approach, provides an analysis of the concept of a priori knowledge that does not include any conditions involving the concept of the a priori. Its primary target is the concept of a priori knowledge.

There are compelling reasons in favor of the reductive approach. First, an analysis of a priori knowledge must address the Gettier problem. The goal of an analysis of a priori knowledge, however, is not to solve that problem. Its goal is to mark the difference between a priori and a posteriori knowledge, but it is not very likely that this difference resides in the details of the solution to the Gettier problem. Second, it is uncontroversial that knowledge entails truth. The view that justification entails truth is quite controversial and widely rejected. If a priori justification does not entail truth, the possibility of a priori justified false beliefs emerges. Focusing on the question of a priori knowledge often results in overlooking this possibility and, as a consequence, offering accounts of the a priori incompatible with it.

Although I maintain that the primary target of analysis should be the concept of a priori justification, I propose to identify and evaluate analyses of the concept of a priori knowledge, as well as analyses of the concept of a priori justification. For economy of expression, I shall refer to conditions proposed in an analysis of either concept as "conditions on a priori justification," and to an analysis of either concept as an "analysis of a priori justification."

1.2   Two Taxonomies

The conditions on a priori justification proposed in the literature span a wide gamut. They can be divided initially into two broad categories: (I) epistemic and (II) nonepistemic. Those in the former category essentially involve at least one epistemic concept; those in the latter do not. Epistemic conditions themselves fall into two broad categories: (A) justification and (B) defeasibility. Those in the former category appeal to the justification of the belief in question; those in the latter appeal to the defeasibility of justification. Justification conditions fall into two broad categories: (1) source and (2) strength. Those in the former category appeal to the source of the justification; those in the latter appeal to the strength of the justification. Conditions appealing to the source of justification fall into two broad categories: (a) negative and (b) positive. Conditions in the first category specify sources incompatible with a priori justification; conditions in the second specify sources providing such justification. Defeasibility conditions also fall into two broad categories: (1) strong and (2) weak. Those in the former exclude all defeaters; those in the latter exclude only some. Nonepistemic conditions fall into two categories: (A) necessity and (B) analyticity. Those in the first invoke the concept of necessity; those in the second invoke the concept of analyticity. Both categories further divide into two categories: (1) necessary and (2) sufficient. Conditions falling into the former invoke necessity (analyticity) as a necessary condition for the a priori; those in the latter invoke the relevant concept as a sufficient condition. Table 1.1 provides a taxonomy of conditions on a priori justification.

Analyses of a priori justification invoke either one or more of the above conditions. Simple analyses consist of only a single condition; complex analyses consist of more than one. Nonepistemic analyses consist of only nonepistemic conditions. Pure epistemic analyses consist of only epistemic conditions; impure epistemic analyses include, in addition, some nonepistemic condition. The prevalent nonepistemic analyses assert either that necessity or that analyticity provides both necessary and sufficient conditions for a priori justification. Impure epistemic analyses commonly combine necessity with some epistemic condition.[2] The most prevalent analyses, however, are pure epistemic. Simple pure epistemic analyses invoke either the source of justification[3] or a strong defeasibility condition.[4] Complex pure epistemic analyses combine a negative characterization of the source of justification with a weak defeasibility condition.[5] Some add to those conditions a guarantee of truth.[6] Table 1.2 provides a taxonomy of analyses of a priori justification.

---

2. Chisholm, *Theory of Knowledge*, 3rd ed., analyzes the concept of an axiom, the basic concept in his analysis of the a priori, in terms of the concepts of necessary truth and certainty. Plantinga, *Warrant and Proper Function*, chap. 6, offers an analysis of a priori belief in terms of the source of justification and conviction that p is necessarily true.

3. See Butchvarov, *The Concept of Knowledge*, pt. one, sec. 9; BonJour, *The Structure of Empirical Knowledge*, app. A; BonJour, *In Defense of Pure Reason*, chap. 1; and Moser, "Introduction."

4. See, for example, Putnam, "'Two Dogmas' Revisited."

5. See Hale, *Abstract Objects*, chap. 6.

6. See, for example, Kitcher, *The Nature of Mathematical Knowledge*, chap. 1.

Table 1.1. Taxonomy of Conditions on
A Priori Justification

I. Epistemic	II. Non-epistemic
A. Justification	A. Necessity
1. Source	1. Necessary
a. Negative	2. Sufficient
b. Positive	B. Analyticity
2. Strength	1. Necessary
B. Defeasibility	2. Sufficient
1. Strong	
2. Weak	

1.3   Nonepistemic Analyses

Nonepistemic analyses maintain that either necessity or analyticity provides both necessary and sufficient conditions for a priori justification. There is a general reason for regarding them with suspicion. The analysandum in question is epistemic. It is a type of justification. An informative analysis, however, should highlight what is distinctive about such justification. An analysis in terms of necessity or analyticity highlights what is distinctive about the propositions so justified rather than the justification itself. Hence, it will fail to be informative.

Nonepistemic analyses typically involve the expression "a priori truth" or "a priori proposition." This introduces a complication since these expressions do not have a fixed meaning. Some authors introduce them as shorthand for "truth (proposition) that can be known a priori."[7] In this sense "a priori" remains an epistemic predicate, one whose primary application is to knowledge or justification rather than truth. There is, however, another sense in which "a priori" has its primary application to truth rather than to knowledge or justification. For example, Anthony Quinton maintains that "'*A priori*' means either, widely, 'non-empirical' or, narrowly, following Kant, 'necessary.'"[8]

The narrow sense of a priori is clearly nonepistemic since "necessary" is a predicate whose primary application is to truth. Quinton's characterization of the wide sense of a priori in terms of the nonempirical suggests that this sense is epistemic since "empirical" is typically an epistemic predicate. The appearances, however, are deceiving because, according to Quinton, "The idea of the empirical is a development of the contingent. It aims to explain how a

---

7. See Moser, "Introduction," and Swinburne, "Analyticity, Necessity, and Apriority."

8. Quinton, "The *A Priori* and the Analytic," 90.

Table 1.2. Taxonomy of Analyses of A Priori Justification

I. Epistemic	II. Nonepistemic

A. Pure
  1. Source
  2. Strong defeasibility
  3. Source + weak defeasibility
  4. Source + weak defeasibility + strength
B. Impure
  1. Source + necessity
  2. Source + analyticity
	A. Necessity (necessary and sufficient)
	B. Analyticity (necessary and sufficient)

statement can owe its truth to something else, what conditions the something else must satisfy if it is to confer truth on a statement."[9] Since Quinton alleges that the primary application of "empirical" is to truth conditions, his wide sense of a priori is also nonepistemic. Quinton's goal is to defend the thesis that all a priori statements are analytic. He maintains however, that "the essential content of the thesis is that all *necessary* truths are analytic."[10] Hence, Quinton's thesis is not directed toward the epistemic concept of the a priori.

The upshot is that there are two senses of a priori: one whose primary application is to knowledge or justification and one whose primary application is to truth conditions. Hence, a nonepistemic analysis of the a priori can have either as its target. If its target is the latter, then the analysis is not open to my initial argument because the analysis is not directed toward the epistemic concept. It is directed toward a nonepistemic concept pertaining to truth conditions. My concern, however, is with the analysis of the epistemic concept.

Are there nonepistemic analyses of the epistemic concept? R. G. Swinburne defends the following thesis:

(S1) A proposition is a priori if and only if it is necessary and can be known to be necessary.[11]

Unlike Quinton, Swinburne maintains that "a priori" has its primary application to knowledge. An a priori proposition is one that can be known a priori. Hence, it appears that he is proposing a nonepistemic analysis for an epistemic concept.

Closer examination reveals that Swinburne is not proposing (S1) as an analysis of the concept of a priori knowledge. Instead, he endorses Kant's

9. Ibid., 92.
10. Ibid., 93.
11. Swinburne, "Analyticity, Necessity, and Apriority," 186–187.

analysis of a priori knowledge as absolutely independent of all experience, maintaining that Kant meant by this "knowledge which comes to us through experience but is not contributed by experience."[12] Swinburne's concern, however, is with the question of how we *recognize* such knowledge. He proposes (S1) as capturing Kant's answer to this question.

The upshot here is that not every biconditional of the form

(AP) A proposition is a priori if and only if . . . ,

where "a priori" is an epistemic predicate, provides an analysis of the concept of a priori knowledge. Biconditionals of this form may be proposed in response to different questions. Swinburne's question

(Q1) How do we identify the items satisfying some analysis of a priori knowledge?

is different from the question

(Q2) What is the analysis of a priori knowledge?

Indeed an answer to (Q1) presupposes, rather than provides, an answer to (Q2). An answer to (Q1) provides a way of ascertaining whether an item of knowledge satisfies the conditions in the analysis. Biconditionals of the form (AP) are often presented in response to a third question:

(Q3) What is the distinctive feature of propositions knowable a priori?[13]

This question differs from (Q1) in that it does not seek conditions useful for purposes of identifying propositions knowable a priori. Instead, it seeks characteristics common to all and only those propositions, whether or not those characteristics are readily identifiable. An answer to (Q3) could provide an answer to (Q1) but need not. Furthermore, an answer to (Q2) need not and should not provide an answer to (Q3). If it did, the answer would be trivial. It would state that the distinctive feature of all truths knowable a priori is that they satisfy the conditions of a priori knowability.

Apparent nonepistemic analyses of the a priori must be scrutinized along two dimensions. What is the target of the analysis? What question is being asked of the target? My target is the concept of a priori justification as opposed to the concept of a priori truth. My contention is that a nonepistemic analysis of the former cannot succeed. Since the concept is fundamentally epistemic, any satisfactory analysis must identify the salient *epistemic* feature of such justification. This requires invoking at least some epistemic concepts. My contention does not entail that there are no nonepistemic features common to all and only propositions justifiable a priori. It only entails that it is not by virtue of having those features that such propositions are justifiable a priori.

---

12. Ibid., 186.
13. See Moser, "Introduction," 7–8.

My contention that an adequate analysis of the concept of a priori justification must include an epistemic condition leaves open the possibility that it also includes some nonepistemic condition. We now turn to the question of whether some nonepistemic condition is necessary for a priori justification. My focus is on conditions involving the concept of necessity since they are the most common. Moreover, conditions involving the concept of analyticity are usually parasitic upon those involving necessity. As we shall see in chapter 8, analyticity is usually introduced to provide an analysis of the concept of necessity.

1.4   Nonepistemic Conditions

Analyses of the concept of a priori justification that include the concept of necessity fall into two categories. Some include necessity as a component of an epistemic condition. Others include it as an independent condition. We begin by considering two examples that fall into the first category. Laurence BonJour offers the following version of the traditional rationalist conception of the a priori: "a proposition is justified *a priori* when and only when the believer is able, either directly or via some series of individually evident steps, to intuitively 'see' or apprehend that its truth is an invariant feature of all possible worlds, that there is no possible world in which it is false."[14] The traditional rationalist conception consists of a single condition with two components: the source of a priori justification, or intuitive apprehension, and the content of such apprehensions, or necessary truths.

Assessing the implications of the analysis is tricky since it involves a metaphorical sense of "see": S's belief that p is justified a priori if and only if S intuitively "sees," either directly or indirectly, that p is true in all possible worlds. Taken literally, "S sees that p" (for example, that there is a rabbit in the garden) entails "S believes that p."[15] If we assume that the metaphorical sense of "see" preserves the logical features of the literal, "S intuitively 'sees' that p is true in all possible worlds" entails "S believes that p is true in all possible worlds." Hence, on the traditional rationalist conception, "S's belief that p is justified a priori" entails "S believes that necessarily p."

The conception faces five objections. The first is due to *conceptual deficiency*. Many, including some mathematicians, are not conversant with the metaphysical distinction between necessary and contingent propositions. Consider a mathematician, S, who believes a theorem T on the basis of a generally accepted proof. S's belief that T is justified. Suppose that S lacks the concept of necessity and, as a consequence, does not believe that necessarily T. It is implausible to maintain that S's belief that T is not justified a

14. BonJour, *The Structure of Empirical Knowledge*, 192. BonJour no longer endorses this conception.

15. See, for example, Chisholm, *Theory of Knowledge*, 3rd ed., 41.

priori merely because S lacks a concept that is not even a constituent of the content of S's belief.

One way to avoid the conceptual deficiency problem is to weaken the rationalist conception and to maintain that "S's belief that p is justified a priori" entails "S believes that necessarily p" only if S possesses the concept of necessity. The weakened conception faces the remaining objections. The second objection, then, is the problem of *modal skepticism*. Among philosophers conversant with the concept of necessary truth, some deny (let us suppose erroneously) its cogency. They are familiar with the standard examples of necessary truths, they understand the intuitive ways of marking the distinction between necessary and contingent truths, and they know the philosophical motivations for marking the distinction along with the supporting arguments. Yet they remain unconvinced. Hence, although they believe that many mathematical propositions, such as that $2 + 2 = 4$, are true, they do not believe that any are necessarily true. But it is implausible to maintain that none of their mathematical beliefs are justified a priori merely because they have an erroneous metaphysical belief.

The problem is exacerbated when we consider modal beliefs. Among the propositions that we can know a priori, according to traditional rationalists, are modal propositions such as "Necessarily $2 + 2 = 4$." Suppose that S believes that necessarily $2 + 2 = 4$. For S's belief to be justified a priori, S must intuitively "see" and, hence, believe that necessarily necessarily $2 + 2 = 4$. But here we face the third problem, *modal ignorance*. Not everyone who believes that necessarily $2 + 2 = 4$ has considered the status of iterated modal propositions. It is implausible to deny that they have a priori justification that necessarily $2 + 2 = 4$ solely on the grounds that they have not considered and, hence, do not believe the modal principle that if necessarily p then necessarily necessarily p. In addition, we face the fourth problem, *modal agnosticism*. The modal principle that if necessarily p then necessarily necessarily p is controversial. Not all who have considered it believe that it is true.[16] Suppose that S believes that necessarily $2 + 2 = 4$ on the basis of not being able to conceive a counterfactual situation in which $2 + 2 = 4$ is false. It is implausible to maintain that S's belief that necessarily $2 + 2 = 4$ is either unjustified or justified a posteriori solely on the basis of the fact that S is agnostic about the status of the iterated modal proposition that necessarily necessarily $2 + 2 = 4$. After all, the iterated modality is not part of the content of the belief whose justificatory status is in question.

Finally, the conception faces a *regress*, the fifth problem. According to the traditional rationalist, S's belief that p is justified a priori only if S believes that necessarily p. Must S's belief that necessarily p be justified or not? If not, then it is hard to see why it is a necessary condition for the a

---

16. See, for example, Chandler, "Plantinga and the Contingently Possible," and Salmon, "The Logic of What Might Have Been."

priori justification of S's belief that *p*. If so, then presumably its justification must be a priori. But, in order for its justification to be a priori, S must
see that necessarily *p* is true in all possible worlds, which in turn requires
believing that necessarily necessarily *p*. But now a regress threatens since
we can once again ask the question: Must S's belief that necessarily necessarily *p* be justified or not? Hence, the rationalist can avoid a regress only
by endorsing the implausible view that a priori justified belief that *p* requires
unjustified belief that necessarily *p*. The requirement is doubly implausible.
First, the concept of necessity is not part of the content of the belief that *p*,
and, second, the belief on which the belief that *p* depends for its a priori
justification is itself unjustified.

Alvin Plantinga provides a more fully articulated version of an epistemic
condition on a priori justification that includes necessity. He maintains that
S knows a priori that *p* if and only if S believes a priori that *p* and the other
conditions for knowledge are satisfied. What is it for S to believe a priori
that *p*? The distinctive element of believing a priori that *p* is *seeing* that *p* is
true. Seeing that *p* is true, in turn, consists in finding yourself convinced
that *p* is true and could not have been false.[17] Such conviction, however,
can occur in the absence of seeing that *p* is true. It could, for example, be
based solely on testimony. What more is required? To see that *p* is true is

(1) to form the belief that *p* is true and indeed necessarily true (when it
is necessarily true, of course), (2) to form this belief immediately, rather
than as a conclusion from other beliefs, (3) to form it not merely on the
basis of memory or testimony (although what someone tells you can
certainly get you to see the truth of the belief in question), and (4) to
form this belief with that peculiar sort of phenomenology with which
we are well acquainted, but which I can't describe in any way other than
as the phenomenology that goes with seeing that such a proposition is
true . . . [and (5)] the relevant cognitive module is functioning properly.[18]

Some a priori beliefs are based on others. In such cases, S does not see
that *p* is true but, instead, sees that *p* follows from some other proposition
that S sees is true. Hence, either seeing that *p* is true or seeing that *p* follows
from something one sees to be true is sufficient for believing a priori that *p*.
This condition, however, is not necessary. Since Plantinga acknowledges
that there are *false* a priori beliefs, the final step in the analysis is to drop
the references to truth: "Take the conditions severally necessary and jointly
sufficient for seeing that *p* is true; to believe *p* *a priori* is to meet the set of
those conditions minus the *truth* conditions—that is, the condition that *p*
be true (in the case of seeing directly that *p* is true) and the condition that *p*
follow from *q* (in the case of seeing indirectly that *p* is true)."[19] Plantinga's

17. Plantinga, *Warrant and Proper Function*, 105.
18. Ibid., 106.
19. Ibid.

analysis is rich and complex. My concern, at this juncture, is solely with his first condition on believing a priori that *p*: believing not only that *p* is true but also that *p* is necessarily true.

Plantinga expresses some reservations about the condition. He allows that God could make creatures who know contingent truths but not on the basis of experience. Suppose that these creatures form powerful convictions that certain contingent statements are true. Moreover, suppose that these convictions are independent of experience in the requisite sense and satisfy the other conditions on seeing that a proposition is true *except* for the conviction that the proposition is *necessarily* true. Would such knowledge be a priori? According to Plantinga,

> Whether it would be *a priori* knowledge, then, depends upon whether that notion includes having that conviction. More exactly, the question here is whether the term '*a priori* knowledge' expresses the concept of knowledge independent (in the right way) of experience, or whether it expresses a stronger concept: the concept of knowledge independent of experience accompanied by the conviction that what is known is necessary. This is the sort of question to which there may be no answer; the thing to do is to note both concepts but bracket the question which concept is expressed by the term.[20]

Presumably, his reluctance to choose between the two concepts is based on the belief that there is no compelling reason that favors one over the other. My contention is that the stronger concept is open to the five objections presented against the traditional rationalist conception.

Suppose that two cognizers, S and S*, both believe that $2 + 1 = 3$ and do so independently (in the right way) of experience. Moreover, suppose that although S* believes that necessarily $2 + 1 = 3$, S does not because S lacks the concept of necessity. It is implausible to maintain that S's *conceptual deficiency* deprives S of a priori knowledge of a mathematical proposition with no modal content. If one weakens the requirement to apply only to those who have the concept and have considered the issue, we run into the problem of *modal skepticism*. Suppose that both S and S* have some philosophical sophistication but disagree on the cogency of the distinction between necessary and contingent propositions. S* believes that some propositions, including mathematical propositions, are necessary. S, on the other hand, regards the distinction between necessary and contingent propositions with suspicion and, as a consequence, refrains from modal beliefs. Finally, suppose that mathematical propositions are necessary and S is in the grip of a false philosophical theory. In this scenario, S* knows a priori that $2 + 1 = 3$ but S does not. It is implausible, however, to hold that S's false beliefs about a controversial metaphysical issue affects the justificatory status of S's belief that $2 + 1 = 3$. The latter belief is mathematical and has no modal content.

20. Ibid., 107.

Analogous problems arise in the case of modal knowledge. Consider a modal proposition such as that necessarily 2 + 1 = 3. For someone to believe it a priori, that person must be convinced that necessarily necessarily 2 + 1 = 3. Here the problem of *modal ignorance* arises. It is not obvious that traditional proponents of the a priori entertained iterated modal propositions. It is implausible, however, to maintain that such traditional proponents failed to have a priori knowledge that necessarily 2 + 1 = 3 solely on the basis of the fact that they did not entertain iterated modal propositions. Moreover, there is *modal agnosticism* among those who have entertained the modal principle that if necessarily *p* then necessarily necessarily *p*. Not all are convinced that it is true. Some don't fully understand it, some who understand it don't know what to think about it, others who understand it think that it is false, and some who think that it is true are not fully convinced that it is true. Yet, it seems that one can believe and know a priori that necessarily 2 + 1 = 3 without having convictions about difficult issues in the philosophy of modal logic. But if one can believe a priori that necessarily 2 + 1 = 3 without being convinced that necessarily necessarily 2 + 1 = 3, why shouldn't one be able to believe a priori that 2 + 1 = 3 without being convinced that necessarily 2 + 1 = 3?

Finally, the conviction requirement threatens to lead to a *regress*. To believe a priori that *p*, one must believe that *p* is necessarily true. But must this latter belief also be a priori? If so, then to believe it, one must believe that necessarily necessarily *p*. The very same question, of course, arises with respect to this belief, and a regress threatens. If one attempts to stop the regress at the first step by maintaining that the belief that *p* is necessarily true need not be a priori, then one is in the position of endorsing the paradoxical view that a necessary condition of believing a priori that *p* is that one believe a posteriori that necessarily *p*. This clearly violates the condition that a priori beliefs must be independent of experience.

R. M. Chisholm provides an analysis of the a priori in which necessity is offered as an independent necessary condition. Consider the following definitions:

D1   h is an axiom = Df   h is necessarily such [that] (i) it is true and (ii) for every S, if S accepts h, then h is certain for S.[21]
D2   h is *axiomatic* for S = Df   (i) h is an axiom and (ii) S accepts h.[22]
D3   h is known *a priori* by S = Df   There is an *e* such that (i) *e* is axiomatic for S, (ii) the proposition, *e* implies *h*, is axiomatic for S, and (iii) S accepts *h*.[23]

A priori knowledge is restricted to axioms and their axiomatic consequences. To be an axiom, a proposition must satisfy two *independent* conditions: it

21. Chisholm, *Theory of Knowledge*, 3rd ed., 28.
22. Ibid.
23. Ibid., 29.

must be necessarily true and certain for everyone who accepts it. These conditions are independent, for neither entails the other. Since axioms are necessary truths and axiomatic consequences of axioms follow necessarily from axioms, all a priori knowledge is of necessary truths.

What support does Chisholm offer for his analysis? He opens his discussion of the a priori with the following remarks:

> There are propositions that are necessarily true and such that, once one understands them, one *sees* that they are true. Such propositions have traditionally been called *a priori*. Leibniz remarks, "You will find a hundred places in which the scholastic philosophers have said that these propositions are evident, from their terms, as soon as they are understood."[24]

This passage involves two claims: (1) some propositions have both the metaphysical property of being necessarily true and the epistemic property of being such that if one understands them, then one *sees* that they are true; and (2) such propositions have traditionally been called a priori. The key question, however, is not addressed: In virtue of which feature are they a priori? The quotation from Leibniz, which invokes the authority of the scholastics, mentions only the second. There is no mention of the metaphysical property. In a footnote to this passage, Chisholm invites us to compare the scholastic analysis with one offered by Ambrose and Lazerowitz: "A proposition is said to be true *a priori* if its truth can be ascertained by examination of the proposition alone or if it is deducible from propositions whose truth is so ascertained, and by examination of nothing else. Understanding the words used in expressing these propositions is sufficient for determining that they are true."[25] Once again, only the epistemic condition is mentioned. Hence, if Chisholm is indeed following his chosen predecessors, he should offer an analysis of the a priori in terms of the epistemic property alone.

He does go on to consider such an analysis:

> One cannot *accept* a proposition, in the sense in which we have been using the word "accept," unless one also *understands* that proposition. We might say, therefore, that an *a priori* proposition is one such that, if you accept it, then it becomes certain for you. (For, if you accept it, then you understand it, and, as soon as you understand it, it becomes certain for you.)[26]

But he then rejects it on the grounds that it

> would be at once too broad and too narrow. It would be too broad in that it also applies to what is self-presenting, and what is self-presenting

<hr />

24. Ibid., 26. The quoted passage is from Leibniz, *New Essays Concerning Human Understanding*, bk. IV, chap. 7.

25. Chisholm, *Theory of Knowledge*, 3rd ed., 26, n. 1. The quoted passage is taken from Ambrose and Lazerowitz, *Fundamentals of Symbolic Logic*, 17.

26. Chisholm, *Theory of Knowledge*, 3rd ed., 27.

is not necessarily true. It would be too narrow in that it does not hold
of all *a priori* propositions. We know some *a priori* propositions on
the basis of others, and these propositions are not themselves such that,
once they are understood, then they are certain.[27]

The claim that the analysis is too narrow is uncontroversial, but the problem
it raises is not resolved by restricting a priori propositions to necessary truths.
It is the claim that the analysis is too broad that motivates the restriction.

The claim that the analysis is too broad is puzzling in two respects. First,
it is false by Chisholm's lights:

Self-presenting properties are a source of certainty. If you think about
riding a bicycle, then you have all the justification you need for *believing* that you are thinking about riding a bicycle. The example
illustrates a more general principle:

M1   If the property of being F is self-presenting, if S is F, and
      if S believes himself to be F, then it is certain for S that
      he is F.[28]

Clearly, there is a difference between the conditions that must be satisfied
in order for one to be justified in believing that one instantiates a self-
presenting property and the conditions that must be satisfied in order for
one to be justified in believing an a priori proposition. Accepting an a priori
proposition is sufficient for certainty, whereas accepting that one instantiates a self-presenting property is necessary but not sufficient for certainty.
One must also instantiate the self-presenting property. Chisholm is confus-
ing the claim that S's belief that p, where p is some a priori proposition, and
S's belief that he is F, where F is some self-presenting state, are both certain
with the stronger claim that the conditions under which they are certain are
the same. The latter claim is false, and this difference is sufficient to exclude
knowledge of self-presenting states from being a priori.

Moreover, and more important, even if one concedes the truth of Chisholm's claim, its relevance is not apparent. For, if S's accepting that he is F,
where F is self-presenting, were sufficient for it to be certain for S that he is
F, then it would follow that one's knowledge of self-presenting states and
simple necessary truths are on a par epistemically. Restricting the a priori
to necessary truths would be arbitrary and unmotivated. To make this point
more concrete, let us briefly compare Chisholm's position with that of BonJour.
Both maintain that a priori knowledge is based in intellectual apprehension
and that such apprehension is intimately connected with one's understanding of the proposition apprehended. Their positions also differ in a significant respect. For Chisholm, when one understands a proposition in the
requisite manner, one apprehends that it is true, whereas for BonJour one

27. Ibid.
28. Ibid., 19.

apprehends that it is *necessarily* true. Hence, in BonJour's case, there is a rationale for restricting a priori knowledge to necessary truths. The epistemic condition requires the restriction. In Chisholm's case the restriction is either arbitrary or superfluous. If all propositions that satisfy the epistemic condition must be necessary, then it is superfluous. If propositions that satisfy the condition need not be necessary, it is arbitrary. So Chisholm is faced with a choice: either incorporate the necessity condition into the epistemic condition or provide an alternative rationale for its inclusion.

1.5   Strength and Defeasibility Conditions

Justification comes in degrees. For example, one's belief that there is a cardinal on the trellis is justified to a higher degree if one gets a good look at the bird than if one just catches a glimpse of it. Moreover, one is justified to a higher degree if one is knowledgeable about the distinctive features of cardinals than if one is not. Most, if not all, justified beliefs are defeasible. One's perceptually justified belief that there is a cardinal on the trellis is defeated by one's remembering that one frequently misidentifies other birds as cardinals. The defeasibility of a justified belief is related to the strength of its justification. At a very crude first approximation, the weaker the justification for a belief the more susceptible it is to being defeated.[29] Most contemporary theorists agree that knowledge in general does not require justification that either provides a guarantee of truth or is indefeasible. The requirements of a priori knowledge are more controversial.

For a condition on a priori justification to fall into the strength category, it must satisfy two criteria: (CR1) it must require of beliefs justified a priori a degree of justification greater than that required for knowledge in general, and (CR2) this requirement must not be a consequence of some more general requirement on epistemic justification. Our concern is with the analysis of the concept of a priori justification. Such an analysis articulates conditions distinctive of the a priori, that is, conditions that differentiate between a priori and a posteriori justification. Analyses of a priori justification are often embedded within a more general theory that includes standards for knowledge and an account of epistemic justification. Consequently, we must distinguish the requirements of the a priori from the more general requirements on knowledge and justification.

My two criteria differentiate between these requirements. If an account of a priori knowledge includes a condition that requires some high degree of justification, but that degree of justification is not greater than the degree of justification the account requires for knowledge in general, then the condition is not distinctive of the a priori. All cases of knowledge, a priori and a posteriori alike,

---

29. This issue is discussed in more detail in chapter 3.

must satisfy the requirement. (CR1) eliminates such conditions. Conditions that satisfy (CR1) fall into two broad categories. In some cases, the condition is a consequence of some more general requirement on epistemic justification. Once again, such conditions are not distinctive of the a priori. A posteriori justified beliefs must also satisfy the condition. (CR2) eliminates such conditions.

Some theorists have imposed high standards on the degree of justification necessary for a priori knowledge. Consider, for example, the following remarks by Panayot Butchvarov:

> Both primary a priori and primary a posteriori knowledge consist in the unthinkability of mistake in belief, and this unthinkability is due, in both cases, to the incompatibility of the falsehood of the belief with the context of the belief. And knowledge falls into two kinds, for the context of a belief consists of two kinds of elements: experiences and concepts.[30]

The standard Butchvarov imposes on a priori justification is quite high indeed: for one's belief that p to be a priori justified, one must find it unthinkable that one's belief that p be mistaken. Two points, however, need to be noted here. First, he imposes the same high standard on a posteriori justification. Second, the standard follows straightforwardly from his conception of primary knowledge as consisting in the unthinkability of mistake. Hence, despite the high standard, Butchvarov's condition on primary a priori justification does not fall into the strength category. Since it is a consequence of general requirements on knowledge, it fails to satisfy (CR1).

R. M. Chisholm provides an analysis of noninferential a priori justification that satisfies (CR1) but not (CR2).[31] He maintains that there are six degrees of positive justification, ranging from the probable to the certain. The fourth degree, the evident, is minimally sufficient for knowledge. Recall again the three definitions that articulate Chisholm's conception of the a priori.[32] A priori knowledge falls into two categories: the axiomatic and the axiomatic consequences of the axiomatic. The axiomatic consists of those propositions known a priori but not on the basis of any other propositions. The axiomatic propositions provide the foundation for all a priori knowledge. In addition to the unique structural role they play, axiomatic propositions have another distinctive epistemic property: they must be certain. Certainty, however, is not a necessary condition for knowledge: "We may assume that what is thus known a priori is evident. But the a priori, unlike the axiomatic, need not be certain."[33] Hence, noninferential a priori knowl-

30. Butchvarov, The Concept of Knowledge, 94–95.
31. Chisholm offers an account of a priori knowledge but not of a priori justification. I assume in the subsequent discussion that condition (ii) in his definition of axiom is also a necessary condition for noninferential a priori justification.
32. See section 1.4.
33. Chisholm, Theory of Knowledge, 3rd ed., 29.

edge, or the axiomatic, must have a degree of justification two degrees higher than the minimal requirement for knowledge.

Chisholm requires of axiomatic propositions a degree of justification greater than that minimally necessary for knowledge. What is the basis for this requirement? There are two possibilities: it may be a consequence of general requirements on justification or a consequence of requirements distinctive of the a priori. Chisholm is not explicit on this point, but there is evidence that it is a consequence of the former. He initially defines the various degrees of epistemic justification in terms of the primitive relational predicate "at least as justified as," but he goes on to introduce five axioms, or epistemic principles, that are intended to delineate the content of the primitive predicate. The fourth principle states

(A4) If anything is probable for S, then something is certain for S.[34]

Chisholm offers no elaboration or defense of this principle. His only comment is that "this type of principle is one feature of what is called 'foundationalism' in the theory of knowledge."[35] In subsequent remarks, as he initiates his account of empirical knowledge, Chisholm maintains, "In pursuing traditional epistemology, we begin by sorting out those of our beliefs that are *certain*. We begin here since the application of each of our material epistemic principles requires that we appeal to something that is certain. It is mainly because of this fact that the present view may be called 'foundational.'"[36] It is not clear whether Chisholm views this requirement as a consequence of (A4) or as an independent claim.

Chisholm's claims about the requirements of foundationalism are controversial. My concern here is not to assess their cogency but to draw attention to a consequence of them. If Chisholm is committed to foundationalism as a general thesis about the structure of epistemic justification and if his brand of foundationalism requires that basic beliefs be certain, then, a fortiori, a priori justification requires that basic a priori beliefs be certain. The degree-of-justification condition on basic a priori justification is not a consequence of the requirements of the a priori but a consequence of the requirements of his foundationalist conception of justification. Hence, it does not satisfy my second criterion for inclusion in the strength category.

The views of Butchvarov and Chisholm differ markedly from those of Philip Kitcher, whose analysis of a priori justification also requires a high degree of justification: "Our goal is to construe a priori knowledge as knowledge which is independent of experience, and this can be achieved . . . by supposing that, in a counterfactual situation in which an a priori warrant produces belief that p, then p. On this account, a priori warrants are ultra-

---

34. Ibid., 14.
35. Ibid.
36. Ibid., 62.

reliable; they never lead us astray."[37] Although he maintains that a priori justification requires ultra-reliability, Kitcher denies that this requirement extends to a posteriori justification. It is not a consequence of the general requirements of justification or knowledge. It is a requirement distinctive of the a priori. Hence, it satisfies both criteria for inclusion in the strength category.

Let us briefly take stock before drawing some final conclusions. We have looked at three accounts of a priori knowledge that include a condition requiring a high degree of justification. These conditions are of three sorts: one is a consequence of the general requirements on knowledge, one is a consequence of the general requirements on epistemic justification, and one is distinctive of a priori justification. Conditions of the first two sorts need not be addressed. Since they follow from the general requirements of knowledge or justification, their tenability depends on the tenability of the general theory of knowledge or justification from which they follow. They are not requirements imposed by the a priori. Only conditions of the third sort, which are consequences of the underlying conception of the a priori, must be addressed. Concerning such conditions, I have one contention. Either some independent argument is provided to underwrite the claim that conditions on a priori justification must be stronger than those on a posteriori justification or not. If the former, then the tenability of the condition depends on the tenability of the supporting argument. If the latter, then the requirement should be rejected as ad hoc.

Kitcher's condition falls into the strength category. His supporting argument, however, is not compelling: "To generate *knowledge* independently of experience, a priori warrants must produce warranted *true* belief in counterfactual situations where experiences are different."[38] Kitcher is correct in pointing out that knowledge requires truth. But the relevance of this claim is unclear since his concern here is with the requirements of a priori *warrant*. Furthermore, he concedes that, in the case of a posteriori knowledge, the truth requirement is compatible with warrant that is not ultra-reliable.

Kitcher offers an additional consideration in support of his ultra-reliability condition. He claims that it rests on an intuition that can be supported by an independent argument:

> The intuition is that a priori warrants must be ultra-reliable: if a person is entitled to ignore empirical information about the type of world she inhabits then that must be because she has at her disposal a method

---

37. Kitcher, *The Nature of Mathematical Knowledge*, 24. A note on terminology: Kitcher endorses a psychologistic conception of knowledge, according to which S knows that *p* if and only if S believes that *p* and S's belief that *p* is produced by a process that is a warrant for it. "Warrant" refers to those processes that produce beliefs in the manner appropriate for knowledge. Kitcher does not offer an account of warrants.

38. Ibid.

of arriving at belief which guarantees *true* belief. (This intuition can be defended by pointing out that if a method which could produce false belief were allowed to override experience, then we might be blocked from obtaining knowledge which we might otherwise have gained.)[39]

Kitcher's supporting argument is not transparent. My first goal is to offer a reconstruction of it. I then show that the argument does not support the ultra-reliability condition.

The supporting argument seems to go as follows. Suppose that some nonexperiential belief-forming process, say, intuition, justifies the belief that *p*. Moreover, suppose that some experiential process, say, perception, justifies the belief that not-*p*. Suppose we allow both (1) S's belief that *p*, which is justified by intuition, overrides S's justified belief that not-*p*, which is justified by perception, and (2) intuition is not an ultra-reliable belief-forming process; that is, some beliefs produced by intuition are false. We are now faced with the prospect that a *false* belief that *p*, justified by intuition, overrides a *true* belief that not-*p*, justified by perception, with the consequence that we are blocked from obtaining the perceptual knowledge that not-*p* that we might have otherwise obtained.

Two points should be noted in response to Kitcher's argument. First, the argument applies with equal force to experiential sources of justification. It can be employed to show that if beliefs justified by some experiential belief-forming process, say, memory, are allowed to override beliefs justified by perception, then memory must be an ultra-reliable belief-forming process. Second, if we restrict our attention to the domain of experientially justified beliefs, we don't find the consequence that we are sometimes blocked from obtaining knowledge that we might have otherwise gained either controversial or problematic. The following example illustrates both points.

Suppose that I remember leaving my pen on the coffee table just a few seconds ago, but when I glance over at the coffee table, I don't see it. Suppose that my recollection is quite vivid and firmly convinces me that I did indeed leave the pen on the coffee table. Moreover, suppose that I have reasonably good short-term memory. Finally, suppose that there were a number of objects on the coffee table and that my glance was rather quick. Here it is plausible to maintain that my belief warranted by memory that my pen is on the coffee table overrides my belief warranted by perception that my pen is not on the coffee table. Now suppose that, despite my reasonably good memory, I in fact left my pen on the end table adjacent to the coffee table and that my perceptual belief was in fact true. Here we have a situation in which one process justifies a false belief, another justifies a true belief, and the former belief overrides the latter. As a consequence, I am blocked from having knowledge that my pen is not on the coffee table that I might have

39. Ibid., 30.

otherwise gained, knowledge that I might have gained in the absence of the errant recollection. This consequence does not even tempt us, much less lead us to the conclusion that memory must be an ultra-reliable process if it is to override perception. Moreover, the consequence that I am blocked from knowledge that I might have otherwise gained is not at all counterintuitive. It is a manifestation of a familiar epistemic phenomenom: justified false belief. Hence, given that we don't find this consequence problematic in the case of experiential belief-forming processes, the burden falls on Kitcher to explain why we should regard it as problematic in the case of nonexperiential belief-forming processes.

My observations about strength conditions also apply to defeasibility conditions. Analyses of the a priori that impose a defeasibility condition are of three sorts: those in which the condition is a consequence of general requirements on knowledge, those in which it is a consequence of general requirements on justification, and those in which it is distinctive of the a priori. As in the case of strength conditions, our concern is solely with conditions of the third sort, for conditions of the first two sorts are not a consequence of the requirements of the a priori.

Consider again Butchvarov's analysis of a priori knowledge in terms of the unthinkability of mistake. If I find mistake in a certain belief that p unthinkable, then it follows that I find it unthinkable that any future circumstances could provide me with a reason to revise my belief that p. If I were to find it thinkable that anomalies in quantum theory could provide a reason to revise arithmetic, with the result that $2 + 2 \neq 4$, then I would find mistake in my belief that $2 + 2 = 4$ thinkable. Similarly, if I were to find it thinkable that cognitive superscientists could have wired my brain so that I am convinced upon reflection that $2 + 2 = 4$ even though it is not, I would find mistake in my belief that $2 + 2 = 4$ thinkable. Hence, Butchvarov's account of a priori justification requires, minimally, the unthinkability of defeaters for the belief that p. Whether it also requires the impossibility of such defeaters is a complex matter since it raises difficult issues about the relationship between unthinkability and impossibility.[40] But let us suppose that it does. We would then have an analysis of the first sort. Since the defeasibility condition on a priori knowledge is a consequence of a general requirement on knowledge, it is not a condition distinctive of a priori knowledge. Hence, its tenability depends on the tenability of Butchvarov's conception of knowledge. Of course if his conception of knowledge is untenable, his conception of a priori knowledge is also untenable. But its untenability is not due to the requirements of the a priori.

By contrast, consider the following remarks of Hilary Putnam, the primary proponent of a strong defeasibility condition:

40. See Butchvarov, *The Concept of Knowledge*, 76–88, for a challenging discussion of this question.

If there are indeed statements which have the maximum degree of confirmation in all circumstances, then these are simply truths which it is *always rational to believe*, nay, more, truths which it is never rational to even begin to doubt. Many philosophers have believed that there are such truths. Perhaps this is what Aristotle thought a *first principle* was like; more likely it is what Descartes thought a *clear and distinct* idea was like. On the face of it, then, the concept of a truth which is confirmed no matter what is not a concept of *analyticity* but a concept of *apriority*.[41]

Putnam maintains that strong indefeasibility is a consequence of maximal confirmation in all circumstances and then goes on to identify the concept of a truth that is strongly indefeasible with the concept of the a priori. Strong indefeasibility is not a general requirement of either knowledge or justification. It is characteristic of the a priori. Hence, Putnam's condition is of the third sort.

Defeasibility conditions on a priori justification should be evaluated in a manner analogous to strength conditions. Conditions imposed by the general theory of knowledge or justification in which the analysis is embedded must be distinguished from those imposed by the a priori. If the condition falls into the former category, then its tenability depends on the account of knowledge or justification in which the theory of the a priori is embedded. Such conditions are not the province of the a priori and need not be considered. If the condition is imposed solely by the requirements of the a priori, then the following question arises: Is some independent argument provided to support the contention that a priori justification and a posteriori justification differ with respect to defeasibility conditions? If such an argument is provided, the tenability of the condition depends on the tenability of the argument. In the absence of such an argument, the condition should be rejected as ad hoc.

Putnam's supporting argument is not compelling. There is some plausibility to the claim that truths it is always rational to believe are akin to first principles or clear and distinct ideas. But both of these concepts are broader than the concept of the a priori. A first principle is one that is justified (or known) but not on the basis of other principles. First principles are not justified (or known) on the basis of others for no others are more justified (or "better known") than they. Such principles are first in the order of justification. But this leaves open the question of whether they are justified a priori or otherwise. Leibniz, for example, maintains that there are both a priori and a posteriori first principles: "The immediate awareness of our existence and of our thoughts furnishes us with the first *a posteriori* truths, or truths of fact, i.e., *the first experiences*, while identical propositions embody the first *a priori* truths, or truths of reason, i.e., *the first illuminations*. Neither admits of proof, and each may be called *immediate*."[42] Similarly, for Descartes, clarity and

41. Putnam, "'Two Dogmas' Revisited," 90.
42. Leibniz, *New Essays Concerning Human Understanding*, bk. IV, chap. 7; quoted in Chisholm, *Theory of Knowledge*, 3rd ed., 27.

distinctness are criteria of knowledge in general rather than criteria of the a priori. Hence, there is little basis for Putnam's further claim that the concept in question is a concept of apriority.

The defeasibility condition proposed by Putnam is an example of a strong defeasibility condition. It maintains that a priori justification excludes the possibility of *any* defeaters. Philip Kitcher, on the other hand, maintains that a priori justification excludes only the possibility of *experiential* defeaters. Moreover, he denies that a posteriori justification excludes the possibility of such defeaters. Hence, he endorses a weak defeasibility condition on a priori justification that is not a consequence of the general requirements on justification. Since the requirement is distinctive of a priori justification, the primary issue is whether there is independent support for its inclusion.

Kitcher maintains that it is a consequence of Kant's characterization of a priori justification as absolutely independent of all experience: "If alternative experiences could undermine one's knowledge then there are features of one's current experience which are relevant to the knowledge, namely those features whose *absence* would change the current experience into the subversive experience."[43] Given that Kitcher's argument ties the weak defeasibility condition to the central idea that a priori justification be independent of experience, it cannot be rejected as ad hoc. Instead, we must explore more carefully the requirements of justification that is independent of experience.

1.6 Source Conditions

The most common analyses of a priori justification are in terms of source conditions. They draw their inspiration from Kant's claim that a priori knowledge, which is independent of all experience, must be distinguished from empirical knowledge, "which has its sources a posteriori, that is, in experience."[44] These analyses fall into two broad camps, depending on whether they involve a negative source condition or a positive source condition. The most familiar negative analysis is

> (N1) S's belief that *p* is justified a priori if and only if S's justification for the belief that *p* does not depend on experience.

Critics of negative analyses maintain that they are not sufficiently informative.[45] At best, they specify what a priori justification is not rather than what it is. Moreover, the relevant sense of *experience* needs articulation.

43. Kitcher, *The Nature of Mathematical Knowledge*, 89.
44. Kant, *Critique of Pure Reason*, 43.
45. See Butchvarov, *The Concept of Knowledge*, pt. 1, sect. 9, and Pollock, *Knowledge and Justification*, chap. 10.

There is a broad sense of experience, in which it includes any occurrent conscious state of a cognizer. This sense, however, includes alleged a priori sources of justification, such as intuitively apprehending the truth of some proposition or following a proof. There is a narrower sense of experience, in which it includes only sense experience in its various forms, that is, only the experiences associated with the five senses. This sense, however, excludes other alleged a posteriori sources of justification, such as introspection and memory.

The critics maintain that these problems can be circumvented by opting for a positive analysis having the form

> (P1) S's belief that *p* is justified a priori if and only if S's belief
>   that *p* is justified by Φ,

where "Φ" designates some specific source of justification. For example, according to Butchvarov, it designates finding the falsehood of a belief unthinkable in any circumstances.[46] But according to BonJour, it designates apparent rational insight into the necessary features of reality.[47]

There are two dimensions of difference between (N1) and (P1). First, (N1) characterizes a priori justification in terms of the sources on which it does not depend, whereas (P1) characterizes it in terms of the sources on which it does depend. Second, (N1) specifies the relevant source in general terms, whereas (P1) does so by enumeration. I address the second dimension first.

An analysis of the concept of a priori justification that enumerates the sources of such justification is too theory dependent. One cannot reject the *source* of a priori justification proffered by such an analysis without rejecting the *existence* of a priori justification. Disagreement about the source of a priori justification is disagreement about the existence of a priori justification. For example, given Butchvarov's analysis, one cannot reject (as BonJour does) the claim that finding the falsehood of a belief unthinkable in any circumstances is the source of a priori justification without rejecting the existence of the a priori since, according to this analysis, a priori justification is justification based on such findings. It should, however, be possible for proponents of the a priori to disagree over the source of a priori justification without thereby disagreeing over the existence of such justification. Moreover, even if some particular version of the positive analysis is extensionally adequate, the analysis is uninformative. It tells us that Φ is an a priori source of justification but gives no indication of *why* Φ is an a priori source. It does not highlight the features by virtue of which Φ qualifies as an a priori source.

There is a general positive analysis of the a priori that avoids the problem of theory dependence:

---

46. Butchvarov, *The Concept of Knowledge*, 93.
47. BonJour, *In Defense of Pure Reason*, 106–110.

(P2) S's belief that p is justified a priori if and only if S's belief
that p is justified by *some* nonexperiential source.[48]

(P2) allows proponents of the a priori to agree that there is a priori justification despite disagreeing about its source. Furthermore, it identifies the feature of sources of justification by virtue of which they qualify as a priori.

One motivation for offering a positive analysis of the a priori is to bypass
the problem of articulating the relevant sense of experience. (P2), which I
have argued is the superior version of the positive analysis, does not circumvent the problem since the relevant sense of nonexperiential also requires articulation. There is, however, another reason for preferring (P2) over
its negative competitor: (N1) conceals a critical ambiguity. The condition

(C1) S's justification for the belief that p does not depend on
experience

does not specify the *respect* in which S's justification must be independent
of experience. There are, however, two possibilities: the source of *justification* for S's belief that p and the source of potential *defeaters* for S's justification. As a consequence, some maintain that (C1) is equivalent to

(C2) S's belief that p is nonexperientially justified.

Others maintain that it is equivalent to the conjunction of (C2) and

(C3) S's justified belief that p cannot be defeated by experience.

Hence, we must distinguish between two different versions of (C1) and, a
fortiori, two different versions of the negative analysis:

(N2) S's belief that p is justified a priori if and only if S's belief
that p is nonexperientially justified, and
(N3) S's belief that p is justified a priori if and only if S's belief
that p is nonexperientially justified and cannot be defeated
by experience.

We have now arrived at a happy coincidence. The condition in (N3),

(C4) S's belief that p is nonexperientially justified and cannot be
defeated by experience,

is not a *pure* source condition. It involves both a source condition and a weak
defeasibility condition. Only (C2) is a pure negative source condition. (C2),
however, is equivalent to

---

48. It is common to distinguish between those a priori justified beliefs that are
directly justified and those that are *indirectly* justified by nonexperiential sources.
Those that are justified indirectly are justified exclusively by other beliefs that are
either directly justified by nonexperiential sources or justified exclusively by other
beliefs that are directly justified by nonexperiential sources. For ease of exposition,
I do not introduce this distinction into my formulations. The reader should regard it
as implicit in this and subsequent formulations.

(C5) S's belief that p is justified by *some* nonexperiential source.

Since the pure negative source condition, (C2), and the general positive source condition, (C5), are equivalent, it follows that the pure negative source analysis of a priori justification, (N2), is equivalent to the general positive source analysis of a priori justification, (P2).

1.7   Conclusion

We are left with two analyses of a priori justification. One, (N2), or equivalently, (P2), is a pure source analysis. The other, (N3), combines a source condition with a weak defeasibility condition. Both draw their inspiration from Kant's characterization of a priori knowledge as absolutely independent of all experience. Both have strong support among contemporary epistemologists. The goal of chapter 2 is to adjudicate between these two competing analyses.

2

Two Conceptions of A Priori Justification

2.1 Introduction

Chapter 1 surveyed a wide range of proposed conditions on a priori justification. Most, including nonepistemic conditions, strength conditions, and strong defeasibility conditions, were rejected. Once analyses involving those conditions were eliminated, only two remained:

> (AP1) S's belief that p is justified a priori if and only if S's belief that p is nonexperientially justified, and
>
> (AP2) S's belief that p is justified a priori if and only if S's belief that p is nonexperientially justified and cannot be defeated by experience.

I now turn to the assessment of these two analyses.

My goal in chapter 2 is to argue that (AP1) is the superior analysis. In section 2.2, I introduce two parameters of evaluation: continuity with historical precedent and coherence with generally accepted concepts and principles in the theory of knowledge. I argue that historical precedent does not favor either analysis. In section 2.3, I develop a framework of accepted principles in the general theory of knowledge and utilize this background, in section 2.4, to introduce the intuitions behind (AP1) and (AP2). I argue, in section 2.5, that several theoretical considerations favor (AP1) over (AP2). (AP1) coheres better with the standard treatment of related epistemic concepts. (AP1) highlights, whereas (AP2) obscures, the central epistemic question raised by the theory of a priori knowledge. Finally, (AP1), but not (AP2), satisfies a plausible criterion of adequacy regarding a priori justification. Section 2.6 addresses objections to (AP1). Finally, in section 2.7, I introduce a third conception of a priori justification, which represents a compromise between (AP1) and (AP2), although I reject it because it inherits the shortcomings plaguing (AP2).

2.2   Two Competing Demands

A viable conception of the a priori must satisfy two competing demands: sensitivity to historical precedent and compatibility with contemporary assumptions about knowledge and justification. The contemporary discussion of the a priori is largely a response to a series of questions initially posed by Kant and subsequent attempts to answer them. If the concept is to be relevant in addressing these issues, its analysis must respect historical precedent. We must also recognize, however, that traditional conceptions of the a priori may reflect broader assumptions about the requirements of knowledge and the nature of epistemic justification that are no longer generally accepted. If the concept is to play a role in contemporary epistemology, it must cohere with other generally accepted concepts and principles. Hence, we need a concept that preserves the traditional requirements of the a priori but frees them from traditional views about the nature of knowledge and justification.

Kant's characterization provides the core of the traditional conception of the a priori. Our initial task is to determine whether either (AP1) or (AP2) provides a better account of that conception. Interpreting Kant's characterization presents a number of difficulties. On the one hand, it cannot be taken literally. He allows that a priori knowledge can depend on experience in at least two ways: it may be necessary to entertain the proposition in question or to acquire concepts involved in the proposition. Yet he is not explicit about the respect in which a priori knowledge must be independent of experience. There is general agreement that the relevant respect is justification. Hence, on the traditional conception,

> (APK) S knows a priori that p if and only if S knows that p and
> S's justification for the belief that p does not depend on
> experience.

There is indirect evidence for attributing (APK) to Kant since his primary argument for the existence of a priori knowledge appears to presuppose it. In maintaining that necessity is a criterion of the a priori, he argues, "Experience teaches us that a thing is so and so, but not that it cannot be otherwise."[1] Presumably, the claim here is not merely the psychological claim that experience does not convince us that p cannot be otherwise but the epistemic claim that it does not justify the belief that p cannot be otherwise.

---

1. Kant, *Critique of Pure Reason*, 43.

The controversial issue is whether condition

(C1) S's justification for the belief that p does not depend on experience

entails only

(C2) S's belief that p is nonexperientially justified

or also

(C3) S's justified belief that p cannot be defeated by experience.

Kant, however, never directly addresses this issue. Since his arguments in support of the existence of a priori knowledge proceed indirectly via criteria, he does not explicitly articulate the requirements of (C1). So there is ample room for dispute.

One might argue that there is indirect evidence favoring (AP1) since Kant's arguments in support of a priori knowledge never refer to the defeasibility of justification. He never attempts to show, for example, that experience cannot defeat justified belief in necessary propositions. His focus is exclusively on the role of experience in justifying such beliefs. Although this observation has merit, it is not conclusive because, if his underlying conception of knowledge entailed that justification sufficient for knowledge is indefeasible, then it would have been otiose to explicitly mention (C3) since it is a consequence of the general requirements for knowledge. Alternatively, if he held that a justified belief is defeasible by experience only if it is justified by experience, then he would have taken for granted that (C3) is a consequence of (C1).

Kant's characterization of the a priori is suggestive yet not fully articulated. In particular, Kant never articulates the sense of independence relevant to his conception of the a priori. Although both (AP1) and (AP2) draw their inspiration from Kant's remarks, those remarks are too sketchy to favor one interpretation over the other. Both interpretations are historically respectable, but historical precedent does not favor either. We now examine each from a contemporary perspective.

2.3   General Epistemology

Let us begin with a primer of contemporary epistemology. It is common to divide human knowledge into categories, each involving a unique source and a class of beliefs with a distinctive content: (1) perception and knowledge of the external world, (2) memory and knowledge of the past, and (3) introspection and knowledge of one's psychological states. The primary epistemological question within each category is whether the source justifies the beliefs in the target class to a degree sufficient for knowledge. Skeptical arguments purport to establish that these sources either do not provide any justification or provide justification that is insufficient for knowledge.

Justification comes in degrees. It is generally granted that the degree of justification minimally sufficient for knowledge (hereafter referred to simply as "justified") does not entail either truth or indefeasibility. The following questions frequently arise about alleged sources of knowledge. Is it a source of incorrigibly justified beliefs? Is it a source of indefeasibly justified beliefs? Although these questions are significant, a negative answer to either one does not entail that the source in question is *not* a source of knowledge.

Sources of justification interact with themselves and with other sources in different ways. Defeasibility provides the most familiar example. Beliefs justified by one source can defeat the justification conferred on a belief by a different source. For example, perceptually justified beliefs can defeat the justification conferred on a belief by memory. If I believe on the basis of memory that I left the shopping list on the coffee table a few minutes ago, but when I go to retrieve it I see that there is nothing on the coffee table, then my perceptually justified belief defeats the justification conferred on my belief by memory. Defeasibility is not limited to sources that are different. Beliefs justified by a particular source can be defeated by subsequent beliefs justified by the same source. If I believe on the basis of memory that I left the shopping list on the coffee table and, subsequently, remember that it was the kitchen table rather than the coffee table, then my latter belief justified by memory defeats the justification conferred on my former belief by memory.

A source of justification can also corroborate the justification conferred on a belief by a different source. For example, a belief justified by memory can also be justified by perception. If I remember that the shopping list is on the coffee table but, in order to be sure, walk into the living room and see that it is there, my belief that the list is on the coffee table is justified by both memory and perception. Here we have a case of epistemic overdetermination. My belief is justified by two sources, each of which is alone sufficient to justify that belief. Had I decided not to walk into the living room, my belief that the list is on the coffee table would have been justified by my remembering that it was there. Corroboration, and the resulting epistemic overdetermination, is not limited to sources that are different. For example, if prior to a vacation, I check to see if the toaster is unplugged and, later, check again to make sure that it is unplugged, each inspection justifies my belief that the toaster is unplugged. Once again, my justification for that belief is overdetermined. Either inspection is alone sufficient to justify the belief that the toaster is unplugged.

The relationship between the source of possible defeaters for a justified belief and the source of justification for that belief is not straightforward. In particular, the *Source Defeasibility Thesis* is false:

> (SD) If S's belief that p is justified by source A then it is not the case that S's justified belief that p is defeasible by beliefs justified by a source other than A.

As we saw earlier, my perceptually justified belief that there is nothing on the coffee table can defeat the justification conferred by memory on the belief that the shopping list is on the coffee table. In the case of corroborating sources of justification for a belief, the *Source Corroboration Thesis* is false:

> (SC) If S's belief that *p* is justified by source *A* then it is not the case that S's justified belief that *p* is corroborated by a source other than *A*.

In an earlier example, my belief that the shopping list is on the coffee table, which was initially justified by memory, was later corroborated by my seeing the list on the coffee table.

Our discussion highlights one respect in which one's justification for a belief can be independent of a particular source. Suppose that I believe that the shopping list is on the coffee table solely on the basis of remembering that it is there. There is a clear sense in which my justification for that belief does not depend on perception but does depend on memory. This sense of independence, called *Source Independence*, can be articulated as follows:

> (SI) S's justification for the belief that *p* does not depend on source *A* if and only if S's belief that *p* is justified by a source other than *A*.

Matters become more complex when my original justification is corroborated by seeing that the shopping list is on the coffee table. Here we have a case of epistemic overdetermination. I have two justifications for the belief that *p*, remembering that *p* and seeing that *p*, each of which is sufficient to justify that belief. In cases of epistemic overdetermination, we must distinguish between S's *overall* justification for the belief that *p* and the *component* justifications that constitute S's overall justification. My overall justification for believing that the shopping list is on the coffee table depends on both memory and perception since my belief is justified by both memory and perception. Nevertheless, neither of the component justifications that constitute my overall justification depends on both memory and perception. My original justification depends solely on memory, and my corroborating justification depends solely on perception. Hence, in cases of overdetermination, "S's justification for the belief that *p*" in (SI) refers to each component of S's overall justification minimally sufficient to justify the belief that *p*.

2.4   The Supporting Intuitions

Virtually all traditional epistemologists would regard our earlier list of sources of knowledge as deficient in an important respect. They would insist that, in addition to experiential sources, there are some nonexperiential sources of knowledge and that associated with each source is a class of beliefs with a distinctive content. There are differences within the tradition over the number of sources and the associated target class of beliefs. For our purposes, let us assume that there is a single nonexperiential source, intuition, and that its associated target class includes logic and mathematics.

All the points made with respect to the experiential sources apply to it. The primary epistemological question is whether intuition justifies logical and mathematical beliefs to a degree sufficient for knowledge. The primary obstacle to a positive answer is the skeptic who maintains that the logical and mathematical beliefs alleged to be justified by intuition are not so justified. Skepticism about the a priori comes in two forms: radical skepticism maintains that logical and mathematical beliefs are not justified to a degree sufficient for knowledge; moderate skepticism maintains that such beliefs are justified to a degree sufficient for knowledge but not by intuition. Some in the tradition maintain that intuition is not only a source of justified beliefs but also a source of incorrigibly or indefeasibly justified beliefs. If the latter claims are unfounded, it does not follow that intuition is *not* a source of knowledge.

Suppose that intuition interacts with perception in much the same manner that memory interacts with perception. It follows that beliefs justified by perception can defeat the justification conferred on some beliefs by intuition. Moreover, it also follows that some beliefs justified by intuition can also be justified by perception. If S's justification for the belief that p derives exclusively from intuiting that p, then S's justification does not depend on perception. In cases in which S's belief that p is justified both by intuiting that p and by seeing that p, S's overall justification for the belief that p depends on both sources. The component of S's overall justification that consists in intuiting that p does not depend on perception, and the component that consists in perceiving that p does not depend on intuition.

Consider now

(C1) S's justification for the belief that p does not depend on experience.

Proponents of (AP1) maintain that (SI) captures the relevant sense of "does not depend on experience" in (C1). More specifically, they maintain that the following version of (SI) captures that sense:

(SI*) S's justification for the belief that p does not depend on experience if and only if S's belief that p is justified by some nonexperiential source.

Hence, they conclude that (C1) should be analyzed as

(C2) S's belief that p is nonexperientially justified.

Moreover, since (SD) is false, (C2) does *not* entail

(C3) S's justified belief that p cannot be defeated by experience.

Finally, since (SC) is false, (C2) does not entail

(C6) S's justified belief that p is not corroborated by experience.

Since (C2) does not entail (C3), proponents of (AP1) conclude that (C1) does not entail (C3).

Proponents of (AP2), however, deny that (C1) should be analyzed as (C2). They maintain that (SI*), which underwrites (C2), does not capture the relevant sense of "does not depend on experience" in (C1), and they offer the following argument in support of their contention. Suppose S's belief that p is justified by intuition. Furthermore, suppose that although S's justification is defeasible by experiential evidence, it is not defeated. According to (SI*), S's justification for the belief that p does not depend on experience. However, the argument continues, S's justification for the belief that p does depend on experience. If S had possessed the relevant experiential evidence, S's belief that p would not have been justified. Hence, S's justification depends on the *absence* of the defeating experiential evidence. Proponents of (AP2) conclude that an adequate analysis of (C1) must entail (C3).

2.5   The Case for (AP1)

At this juncture, we have not uncovered any basis for preferring either (AP1) or (AP2). Each has respectable historical credentials and each is motivated by a plausible intuition. Moreover, the two analyses are not completely divergent. Both entail that if S's belief that p is justified a priori, then it is justified nonexperientially. They diverge over

(A) If S's belief that p is justified nonexperientially, then S's belief that p is justified a priori.

According to (AP1), (A) is trivially true. According to (AP2), it is possibly false since its antecedent leaves open the possibility of experientially justified defeaters for S's justified belief that p. Alternatively, according to (AP2),

(B) If S's belief that p is justified a priori, then S's belief that p cannot be defeated by experience

is trivially true. According to (AP1), it is possibly false since it is possible that S's belief that p is justified by a nonexperiential source but defeasible by experience. The remaining question is whether there are any further considerations that favor one analysis over the other.

One response is to maintain that the disagreement is purely verbal. We are faced with a choice between two different ways of stipulatively defining the locution "S's belief that p is justified a priori," and it is just a matter of deciding which to employ. The "facts" about justification remain unchanged whatever the choice, and all the relevant facts can be stated given either choice. The translation manual in table 2.1 removes any apparent disagreement.

Table 2.1. Translation Manual

(AP1)		(AP2)
Justified a priori	=	Justified nonexperientially
Justified nonexperientially and indefeasible by experience	=	Justified a priori

According to (AP1), (B) is trivially true if "justified a priori" is replaced by "justified nonexperientially and indefeasible by experience." Similarly, according to (AP2), (A) is trivially true if "justified a priori" is replaced with "justified nonexperientially." Despite the attraction of the stipulative approach, I believe that four theoretical considerations favor (AP1) over (AP2).

First, the questions formulated with (AP1) are more continuous with those raised in the realm of empirical knowledge. Compare the questions

(A1) Is the belief that p justified introspectively?
(A2) Is the belief that p justified experientially?

with the questions

(B1) Is the belief that p justified intuitively?
(B2) Is the belief that p justified a priori?

It is uncontroversial that (A1), (A2), and (B1) are questions about the *source* of justification for the belief that p. They are equivalent, respectively, to

(A1*) Does introspection justify the belief that p?
(A2*) Does some experiential source justify the belief that p?
(B1*) Does intuition justify the belief that p?

If "a priori" in (B2) is analyzed as recommended by (AP1), then (B2) raises a parallel question since it is equivalent to

(B2*) Does some nonexperiential source justify the belief that p?

If "a priori" in (B2) is analyzed as recommended by (AP2), then (B2) raises a different question since is equivalent to

(B2+) Does some nonexperiential source provide justification for the belief that p that is indefeasible by experience?

Hence, (AP2) introduces an ambiguity into the locution "justified Φ-ly." It has one meaning when "Φ-ly" is replaced by expressions such as "perceptually," "intuitively," "introspectively," and "experientially" but a different meaning when replaced by "a priori."

Second, (AP1) highlights the distinctive role of the concept of nonexperiential justification within the theory of a priori knowledge. (AP1) identifies the concept of a priori justification with the concept of nonexperiential justification. The analysis provided by (AP2), on the other hand, is reducible to the concept of nonexperiential justification and other concepts available from the theory of empirical knowledge. Hence, on both analyses, the only novel concept introduced into epistemology by the theory of a priori knowledge is the concept of nonexperiential justification. Both agree that the essential and distinctive concept of the theory of a priori knowledge is the concept of nonexperiential justification. By identifying a priori justification with this concept, (AP1) highlights its centrality and makes it the focus of investigation into the a priori.

Third, by embedding the central concept of nonexperiential justification in a broader analysis, (AP2) shifts the focus of investigation into the a priori to questions about defeasibility, with the consequence that important questions about justification are overlooked. Consider the questions

(Q1) Are there nonexperiential sources of justified beliefs?
(Q2) Are there nonexperiential sources of justified beliefs that are indefeasible by experience?

A negative answer to (Q2) does not entail a negative answer to (Q1). There are two possible explanations of the negative answer: (1) there are *no* nonexperientially justified beliefs, or (2) there *are* nonexperientially justified beliefs but they are defeasible by experience. (2), but not (1), is compatible with a positive answer to (Q1). Proponents of (AP2), however, typically focus exclusively on (Q2), arguing that the answer is negative. They do not go on to address (Q1) since, on their account, it is not a question about *a priori* justification. But the question is important no matter how it is formulated. If the answer to (Q2) is indeed negative, then we need an explanation of this important fact. Such an explanation must address (Q1).

The tendency to overlook (Q1) is reinforced by the ambiguity in the expression "justified Φ-ly" which (AP2) introduces. That ambiguity leads to the following seductive line of reasoning:

(P1) S's belief that *p*, which is alleged to be justified a priori, is defeasible by experience.
(P2) Hence, S's belief that *p* is not justified a priori.
(P3) Hence, S's belief that *p* is justified experientially.

Proponents of (AP2) must be careful to resist the inference from (P2) to (P3) and recognize that what follows from (P2) is this:

(P4) Either S's belief that *p* is experientially justified or it is nonexperientially justified but defeasible by experience.

Furthermore, to get from (P4) to (P3), an additional premise is necessary:

(P5) It is not the case that S's belief that *p* is nonexperientially justified but defeasible by experience.

Proponents of (AP2) who endorse (P3), however, rarely address (P5), and this oversight, I suggest, is due to a failure to recognize that "justified Φ-ly" changes its meaning in the transition from (P2) to (P3).

Philip Kitcher, the most articulate proponent of the weak defeasibility condition, provides an example of a quick dismissal of (Q1) on the grounds that it is not a question about a priori knowledge. Kitcher endorses an analysis of a priori warrant that includes the following condition:

> (K2) If a is an a priori warrant for X's belief that p then a is a process such that, given any life e, sufficient for X for p, if a process of the same type were to produce in X a belief that p, then it would warrant X in believing that p.[2]

X's *life* at t is the totality of X's experiences up to time t and a life *sufficient* for X for p is one that is sufficient for X to have the belief that p. Hence, (K2) requires of an a priori warrant that the beliefs it produces remain justified in any experiential setting sufficient for X to believe that p. For X's belief that p to remain justified in such settings, the justification that the process confers on S's belief that p must not be defeated by those experiences.

Having argued that the sources traditionally alleged to justify beliefs a priori do not meet condition (K2), Kitcher acknowledges that his arguments leave open the possibility that these sources do indeed justify the beliefs in question, although not a priori.[3] He does not, however, take this possibility very seriously:

> For all that has been said so far, it would be possible to maintain that one of the sources attributed with the power of engendering a priori mathematical knowledge could actually produce our mathematical knowledge—although, in the light of my criticisms, the claims about apriority would have to be retracted. I think that this approach is implausible. Why would anybody want to adopt the theories about the basic warrants for mathematical beliefs which have been reviewed above? Two answers occur to me: because of a desire to defend apriorism

---

2. Kitcher, *The Nature of Mathematical Knowledge*, 24. I refer to this condition as (K2) since it is the second of the three conditions in Kitcher's analysis of a priori warrant. Kitcher's analysis is discussed in more detail in my "Revisability, Reliabilism, and A Priori Knowledge."

3. Although Kitcher's analysis of a priori warrant involves three conditions, his rejection of traditional apriorism rests primarily on the claim that it fails to satisfy (K2), as the following passage (from Kitcher, *The Nature of Mathematical Knowledge*, 88) indicates:

> The charge that my argument against apriorism presupposes too strong a notion of apriority is relatively easy to rebut. Previous chapters have shown, systematically, that the processes which apriorists take to generate our mathematical beliefs would be unable to warrant those beliefs against the background of a suitably recalcitrant experience. If apriorists are to escape this criticism on the grounds that the analysis of apriority is too strong, then they must allow that it is not necessary for an a priori warrant to belong to a type of process members of which could warrant the belief in question given any sufficient experience. To make this concession is to abandon the fundamental idea that a priori knowledge is knowledge which is independent of experience.

and out of sheer desperation. *With the collapse of apriorism the first motive disappears.* The source of the second answer is the apparent difficulty of giving *any* account of mathematical knowledge.[4]

If Kitcher's analysis of a priori warrant is correct and his arguments cogent, then the sources traditionally alleged to engender a priori knowledge do not engender *a priori* knowledge. But from this it does not follow that they do not engender *knowledge*. And it is hard to see why the fact that such sources are not sanctioned as a priori by Kitcher's analysis makes their existence any less plausible.

Fourth, (AP2) is incompatible with a widely endorsed criterion of adequacy. Saul Kripke puts the point as follows: "Something may belong in the realm of such statements that *can* be known *a priori* but still may be known by particular people on the basis of experience."[5] Kitcher, echoing this point, maintains that "A clearheaded apriorist should admit that people can have empirical knowledge of propositions which can be known a priori."[6] According to the criterion of adequacy, an analysis of the concept of a priori justification should allow for the following possibility:

(CA) S knows empirically that p and S can know a priori that p.

(AP2), however, precludes this possibility, or so I shall argue.

Before presenting the argument, I must stress one point: (AP2) does *not* involve a strength condition. It does not require of a priori knowledge a degree of justification greater than that minimally required for knowledge in general. Another way of putting the same point is that (AP2) does not require of a priori knowledge a degree of justification greater than that required for a posteriori knowledge. Let us state this point explicitly as the *Equality of Strength Thesis*:

(ES) The degree of justification minimally sufficient for a priori knowledge equals the degree of justification minimally sufficient for knowledge in general.

To keep the point explicit in the course of the argument, let us call a belief justified to the degree minimally sufficient for knowledge a *justified$_k$* belief. We now turn to the argument. Let us begin by assuming that

(A) S knows empirically some mathematical proposition that p and S can know a priori that p.

From the left conjunct of (A), it follows that

(1) S's belief that p is justified$_k$ empirically.

4. Ibid., 91 (First emphasis mine; second, Kitcher's).
5. Kripke, *Naming and Necessity*, 35.
6. Kitcher, *The Nature of Mathematical Knowledge*, 22. The plausibility of Kitcher's criterion derives from the observation that the following argument is intuitively invalid: S knows that p. It is possible that S knows a priori that p. Therefore, S knows a priori that p.

Several empirical sources have been alleged to justify beliefs in mathematical propositions: counting collections of objects, reading textbooks, consulting mathematicians, and computer results. Let us grant that each can justify S's mathematical belief that p. Each of these sources is fallible in an important respect. The justification each confers on a belief that p is defeasible by an empirically justified *overriding* defeater, that is, by an empirically justified belief that not-p. Suppose that S's belief that p is justified by counting a collection of objects and arriving at a particular result. It is possible that S recounts the collection and arrives at a different result. If S were to do so, S's original justification would be defeated by an empirically justified overriding defeater. Suppose that S's belief that p is justified by a textbook (mathematician or computer result) that states that p. It is possible that S encounters a different textbook (mathematician or computer result) that states that not-p. In each case, if S were to do so, S's original justification would be defeated by an empirically justified overriding defeater. Hence, given the fallible character of empirical justification, it follows that

> (2) S's empirical justification$_k$ for the belief that p is defeasible
> by an empirically justified belief that not-p,

where "justification$_k$" abbreviates "justification to the degree minimally sufficient for knowledge."

A difficult question arises at this juncture. What are the conditions under which S's justified belief that p is defeated by S's justified belief that not-p? Suppose, to revert to one of our earlier examples, that S believes on the basis of memory that the shopping list is on the coffee table, but upon walking through the living room S does not see the list on the coffee table. How strongly must S's belief that the list is not on the coffee table be justified in order to defeat the justification conferred by memory on the belief that the list is on the coffee table? Would the degree of justification conferred by a passing glance do? Would a higher level of justification be required, say, that conferred by carefully inspecting the table? One suggestion is that S's justified belief that p is defeated by S's justified belief that not-p if and only if S's belief that not-p is justified to at least the same degree as S's justified belief that p.[7] This principle entails

> (D) S's justified belief that not-p defeats (can defeat) S's justified$_k$
> belief that p if and only if S's belief that not-p is at least
> justified$_k$ (justifiable$_k$).

The issues here, however, are complex, and I am not in a position to defend (D) as opposed to some alternative proposal.

---

7. Plantinga appears to endorse such a principle in *Warrant: The Current Debate*, 217–218; see especially n. 4.

Fortunately, the question need not be answered for our present purposes. It is sufficient to note that the conditions under which S's justified belief that not-p defeats S's justification for the belief that p is a function of the relative degree of justification each enjoys. We need not adjudicate between competing accounts of the minimal degree of justification that S's belief that not-p must enjoy in order to defeat S's justified$_k$ belief that p. Let us introduce "d" to stand for that degree of justification, whatever it is, and call a belief justified to degree d a *justified$_d$* belief. We can now replace (D) with the more neutral principle:

(D*) S's justified belief that not-p defeats (can defeat) S's justified$_k$ belief that p if and only if S's belief that not-p is at least justified$_d$ (justifiable$_d$).

Returning now to the argument, we see that the conjunction of (D*) and (2) entails

(3) S's belief that not-p is at least justifiable$_d$ empirically.

Furthermore, the conjunction of (AP2) and the right conjunct of (A) entails

(4) It is not the case that S's nonexperiential justification$_k$ for the belief that p is defeasible by S's empirically justified belief that not-p.[8]

The conjunction of (4) and (D*) entails

(5) It is not the case that S's belief that not-p is at least justifiable$_d$ empirically.

The conjunction of (3) and (5) is a contradiction. Hence, (AP2) does not satisfy the proposed criterion of adequacy. (AP1), on the other hand, does satisfy the criterion since it does not preclude the possibility of defeaters of any kind.

My argument against (AP2) highlights an important difference between overriding and undermining defeaters. It is not in general true that if S's justified belief that q defeats the justification conferred on S's belief that p by source A, it also defeats the justification conferred on S's belief that p by source B. For example, although S's justified belief that he suffers from double vision defeats the justification conferred on his belief that $2 + 2 = 4$ by the process of counting objects, it does not affect the justification conferred on that belief by intuition or testimony. More generally, undermining defeaters for S's justified belief that p are *source sensitive*. They defeat by providing evidence that the alleged source of justification is not likely to generate true beliefs. Typical undermining defeaters show either that the source itself is defective in some way (as in the example of double vision)

---

8. I follow Kitcher, *The Nature of Mathematical Knowledge*, 22, here in assuming that the modalities collapse.

or that the source is operating in an environment for which it is not well adapted (poor lighting, for example, in the case of visually justified beliefs).

Overriding defeaters, however, are *source neutral*. If S's justified$_d$ belief that not-p defeats the justification$_k$ conferred on S's belief that p by source A, then it also defeats the justification$_k$ conferred on S's belief that p by *any other* source. For example, suppose that S's belief that the shopping list is on the coffee table is justified$_k$ by memory, but a subsequent perceptual experience, which justifies$_d$ S's belief that the list is not on the coffee table, defeats S's original justification. Had S's belief that the shopping list is on the coffee table been originally justified$_k$ by testimony, S's perceptually justified$_d$ belief that it is not on the coffee table would still have defeated S's original justification. The source neutrality of overriding defeaters underwrites two important features of our epistemic practices: (1) the corroboration and correction of the deliverances of one source by comparison to the deliverances of other sources and (2) the evaluation of the reliability of sources by comparing the deliverances of one to those of others.[9]

In conclusion, it is important to be clear about what my argument does and does not prove. One who is sympathetic to the weak defeasibility condition ensconced in (AP2) can satisfy the criterion of adequacy by denying (ES). Suppose, for example, that we add to (AP2) the condition that a priori knowledge requires certainty, or justification$_c$, but retain the position that a posteriori knowledge requires only the lower degree of justification, justification$_k$. On the modified theory, the requirement that S's a priori justified belief be indefeasible by empirically justified beliefs does not entail that S's belief that not-p is not empirically justified$_d$. S's empirically justified$_d$ belief that not-p does not enjoy a high enough degree of justification to defeat S's nonexperiential justification$_c$ for the belief that p. If we return to our original argument, from the assumption that S can know a priori that p and the modified version of (AP2), it follows that

(4*)   It is not the case that S's nonexperiential justification$_c$ for the belief that p is defeasible by S's empirically justified belief that not-p.

9. Vihvelin, "A Defense of a Reliabilist Account of A Priori Knowledge," rejects my argument on the grounds that an empirically justified defeater for S's empirically justified belief that p need not be a defeater for S's a priori justified belief that p. She offers the following example. Suppose that S is justified in believing that p on the basis of testimony but later learns a proof for p. An empirical *undermining* defeater for S's testimonial justification for the belief that p, discovering that the testifier is incompetent or untrustworthy, is not a defeater for S's proof-based justification for the belief that p. My argument, however, does not invoke the general principle that *any* empirical defeater for S's empirically justified belief that p is also a defeater for S's a priori justified belief that p. It invokes the weaker principle that empirical *overriding* defeaters for S's empirically justified belief that p are also defeaters for S's a priori justified belief that p. Hence, her counterexample does not affect my argument.

The conjunction of (4*) and (D*), however, does not entail

> (5) It is not the case that S's belief that not-p is at least justifiable$_d$ empirically,

and the reductio is blocked.

Having made this point, I offer three additional observations. First, the goal of my argument is to establish that (AP2) cannot satisfy a widely endorsed criterion of adequacy on a priori justification. The fact that (AP2) can be modified to satisfy the criterion has no bearing on the cogency of my argument. Second, the point of arguing that (AP2) cannot satisfy the criterion of adequacy is to show that (AP2) does not provide an adequate analysis of the concept of a priori justification. The maneuver of adding a strength condition to (AP2) to satisfy the criterion concedes that (AP2) is inadequate. Third, one cannot salvage the weak defeasibility condition in (AP2) merely by adding a strength condition. Unless one offers some independent reason for imposing differential standards on a priori and a posteriori knowledge, the strength condition is ad hoc.

Philip Kitcher's analysis is instructive in this respect. He endorses the criterion of adequacy that (AP2) fails to satisfy. Does his analysis fare any better? I noted in section 1.5 that he does endorse a strength condition on a priori warrants:

> (K3) If a is an a priori warrant for X's belief that p then a is a process such that, given any life e, sufficient for X for p, if a process of the same type were to produce in X a belief that p, then p.[10]

This condition requires that a priori warrants be ultra-reliable: that they not produce any false beliefs in relevant counterfactual situations. The implications of (K3) are difficult to assess since Kitcher is not explicit about the relationship between the reliability of a process and the degree of justification that the process confers on the beliefs that it produces. But let us make the intuitively plausible assumption that the degree of justification that a process confers on the beliefs that it produces is roughly proportional to its degree of reliability. Given this assumption, (K3) ensures that a priori warrants confer a higher degree of justification on the beliefs they produce than empirical warrants confer on the beliefs they produce since the latter warrants are not ultra-reliable. As a consequence, Kitcher's analysis does satisfy the criterion of adequacy.

There are, however, two problems with (K3). First, as I argued in section 1.5, the supporting arguments he offers for (K3) are not compelling. Consequently, if (K3) is retained solely on the grounds that it allows the analysis to meet the criterion of adequacy, the condition is ad hoc. Second, (K3)

---

10. Kitcher, *The Nature of Mathematical Knowledge*, 24.

commits Kitcher to the strong defeasibility condition, which, as I argued in section 1.5, is also ad hoc. It is a consequence of (K3) that if S's belief that p is justified a priori then S's belief that not-p cannot be justified a priori since a priori warrants, according to (K3), cannot produce false beliefs. Hence, there are no a priori justified *overriding* defeaters for S's a priori justified belief that p. On the other hand, potential *undermining* defeaters would call into question the reliability of alleged a priori warrants. Since it is a consequence of (K3) that such warrants are ultra-reliable, any potential undermining defeater would be false and, hence, not justified a priori. Kitcher is faced with a dilemma. Either he can drop (K3) from his analysis, in which case he cannot satisfy a criterion of adequacy that he endorses, or he can retain (K3), in which case he is open to the charge that the condition is ad hoc.

2.6   Objections to (AP1)

(AP1) provides a weaker, more minimal conception of a priori justification than (AP2). I have argued that the weakness of (AP1) is an advantage since it yields a concept that coheres better with concepts and principles in other areas of the theory of knowledge. Conversely, the stronger conditions imposed by (AP2) introduce disanalogies between a priori and a posteriori justification for which there is no apparent justification. Philip Kitcher, however, disputes these contentions. He suggests that (AP1) is *too* weak, and he offers a rationale for imposing conditions on a priori justification that are more stringent than those on a posteriori justification. In this section, I argue that (AP1) can accommodate his concerns.

Kitcher's initial worry is that (AP1) may be too weak: "I suspect that it may make *a priori* knowledge come too cheap. If we relegate the contributions of benign experience to the background, treating experience as playing no role in the generation of belief when people construct and follow proofs, why should we not do just the same when they engage in various kinds of thought-experiments?"[11] This concern raises two issues that must be clearly distinguished: the requirements of *justification* and the requirements of *a priori* justification. An account of the latter is part of a more general theory of knowledge and justification. Any adequate analysis of the concept of a priori justification must entail that beliefs justified a priori satisfy the conditions on justification endorsed by the more general theory in which it is embedded. Addressing the epistemic status of particular sources, such as thought experiments, is difficult in the absence of a general theory of epistemic justification. Hence, we need to fix our background epistemic assumptions in order to address Kitcher's concern.

11. Kitcher, "Aprioristic Yearnings," 402–403.

Let us adopt the psychologistic perspective on knowledge that Kitcher favors and assume that the epistemic justification of a belief is a function of the reliability of the processes that produce the belief. Let us also assume that the thought experiments in question are all produced by processes of the same type and that such processes are nonexperiential. Either the type of process involved in thought experiments is sufficiently reliable to justify the beliefs it produces or it is not. If not, then those beliefs are not justified. If so, then those beliefs are justified. Whether those beliefs are *justified* does not turn on the differences between (AP1) and (AP2). It turns on the general requirements of justification. Assume now that the beliefs produced by thought experiments are justified. Either that justification is empirically defeasible or it is not. If not, then both (AP1) and (AP2) sanction them as justified a priori. If so, then (AP1), but not (AP2), sanctions them as justified a priori. Whether those justified beliefs are justified *a priori* does turn on the differences between (AP1) and (AP2).

Once we distinguish between the requirements of justification and the requirements of a priori justification, Kitcher's charge that (AP1) cheapens a priori knowledge is difficult to sustain. If thought experiments are not sufficiently reliable, neither (AP1) nor (AP2) will sanction beliefs produced by them as justified. If they are sufficiently reliable, then both will sanction the beliefs produced by them as justified. Given a fixed background theory of justification, the standards for justification are the same for both. The only difference between (AP1) and (AP2) is over the classification of beliefs that are justified by thought experiments but defeasible by experience. (AP1) classifies them as justified a priori. Although (AP2) does not classify them as justified a priori, it does classify them as justified empirically. Hence, (AP1) makes a priori justification as expensive as (AP2) makes empirical justification. The claim that (AP1) makes a priori justification too cheap can be sustained only against the background assumption that a priori justification should be *more expensive* than empirical justification. Putting this point less metaphorically, the claim that the standards (AP1) imposes on a priori justification are too weak can be sustained only if one denies the Equality of Strength Thesis:

(ES) The degree of justification minimally sufficient for a priori knowledge equals the degree of justification minimally sufficient for knowledge in general.

And, as I argued in section 1.5, this move is ad hoc unless it is supported by independent argument. As we shall see shortly, Kitcher does go on to offer some considerations that are alleged to support the differential treatment.

Before turning to those considerations, let us consider a critical issue concerning thought experiments that Kitcher does not explicitly address. He compares thought experiments to following proofs. The analogy is apt. It is useful to think of thought experiments as arguments. In both cases one moves from premises to a conclusion by a process of reasoning. Let us grant, for present purposes, that reasoning is a nonexperiential process. The fact that one believes a conclusion on the basis of reasoning from a set of premises is not sufficient to ensure that one's justification for believing the conclusion is nonexperiential. It is also necessary that one's justification for believing all the premises be nonexperiential. Kitcher, however, does not articulate the premises of his thought experiments or their epistemic status. But, if any of those premises are either justified on the basis of experience or not justified at all, then (AP1) does not yield the result that belief in their conclusion is justified a priori.

Kitcher's second criticism of (AP1) is directed at the contention that a priori warrants and empirical warrants should be treated on a par. Proponents of (AP1) allege that perception can justify beliefs despite the fact that the beliefs it justifies are defeasible by experience. Hence, they contend, there is no reason to hold nonexperiential sources, such as pure reflection, to a higher standard. Kitcher, however, counters that the two cases are different. In the case of perception, we have an impressive track record. Most of us are pretty good at discriminating between situations in which we can reliably form beliefs about medium-sized physical objects and those situations in which we should withhold belief. On the other hand,

> a sober look at the history of mathematics reveals that the deliverances of pure reflection—or by any of the processes that a friend of apriority might take to yield the new mathematical knowledge—do not have an impressive track record. . . . Thus, instead of thinking that beliefs can be produced by processes whose normal power to warrant is well-sustained, as in the standard perceptual cases, we should view our situation with respect to the apriorist's favored knowledge-generating processes as one in which there is ample antecedent reason for doubt, so that we cannot ignore the contributions from experience.[12]

Kitcher's remarks suggest two points of disanalogy between the two cases: (1) the deliverances of pure reflection are not reliable: they don't have "an impressive track record," and (2) we have evidence that the process of pure reflection is not reliable: "there is ample antecedent reason for doubt."

I agree with Kitcher that if either of these points is true, then the process of pure reflection does not generate a priori justification. Nevertheless, agreement here does not provide a basis for favoring (AP2) over (AP1) for, if either point is true, (AP1) does not sanction the beliefs produced by pure reflection as justified a priori. Concerning the first point, if pure reflection is not a reliable process, the beliefs it generates do not satisfy the general conditions on justification. If such beliefs are not justified, then, a fortiori, they are not justified a priori. Concerning the second point, if one has reason to doubt the reliability of the process of pure reflection, then one has an undermining defeater for the justification conferred on any belief by that process.

12. Ibid., 403.

Hence, once again, beliefs produced by that process do not satisfy the general conditions on justification.

Kitcher's case against (AP1) fails. His claim that (AP1) is too weak depends on the assumption that the requirements of a priori justification should be higher than those of empirical justification. But the case he makes for that assumption, based on alleged disanalogies between perception and nonexperiential processes such as pure reflection, fails to support it. My suspicion here is that in his efforts to discredit mathematical apriorism, Kitcher is needlessly concerned that (AP1) provides his opponents with the resources to deflect his criticisms. As I have shown, if his observations about nonexperiential processes such as pure reflection are correct, then (AP1) also discredits mathematical apriorism. Hence, his concerns are misplaced.[13]

2.7   A Third Conception of A Priori Justification

The taxonomy of conditions on a priori justification offered in chapter 1 distinguishes among source, strength, and defeasibility conditions. I also pointed out in section 1.6 that although

(C2) S's belief that p is nonexperientially justified

is a pure source condition,

(C4) S's belief that p is nonexperientially justified and cannot be defeated by experience

is not since it involves a defeasibility condition. The implication here is that source and defeasibility conditions are logically independent of one another and, in particular, that source conditions do not entail defeasibility conditions. The observations made in section 2.5 about the defeasible character of empirical sources of justification provide the resources to articulate more clearly the relationship between source and defeasibility conditions. In this section, I introduce a third conception of a priori justification: one that is stronger than (AP1) but weaker than (AP2). Its theoretical interest lies in the fact that although it involves only source conditions, it nevertheless entails a weak defeasibility condition.

In section 2.5, I noted that beliefs justified by experiential sources are defeasible by experientially justified overriding defeaters. The examples that were offered in support of this claim highlight another important feature of experiential sources of justification. In each case, the overriding defeater is justified by the *same* source as the belief whose justification it defeats. Moreover, it is a general feature of experiential sources that they can justify

13. For an alternative discussion of Kitcher's concerns, see Manfredi, "The Compatibility of A Priori Knowledge and Empirical Defeasibility."

overriding defeaters for the beliefs that they justify. For example, if my belief that my neighbor's new car is black is justified by perception but when I look again I realize that it is dark blue, then the justification conferred on my belief by perception is defeated by a perceptually justified overriding defeater. If I remember that I left the shopping list on the coffee table but later remember that it was actually on the kitchen table, then the justification conferred by memory on my initial belief is defeated by an overriding defeater justified by memory. Although the case of introspection is more controversial, the situation appears to be analogous. If my doctor asks me whether I feel a sharp pain when he prods my abdomen in a particular spot and I initially respond that I do but subsequently realize that it wasn't sharp after all, my introspectively justified belief that I feel a sharp pain is defeated by an introspectively justified overriding defeater.[14]

This feature of experiential sources can be articulated more precisely as follows:

> (SR) A is a *self-revisable* source of justified beliefs if and only if for every belief that p which A can justify for S, A can also justify for S the belief that not-p.

Self-revisable sources of justification satisfy the following version of the Source Defeasibility Thesis:

> (SD*) For any self-revisable source A, S's belief that p is justifiable by A if and only if A can justify overriding defeaters for S's justified belief that p.

If A is self-revisable and can justify S's belief that p, then A can justify for S the belief that not-p, which is an overriding defeater for S's justified belief that p. Alternatively, if a self-revisable source A can justify S's belief that not-p, which is an overriding defeater for S's justified belief that p, then it can also justify S's belief that p.

Consider now the following analysis of a priori justification, which consists only of source conditions:

> (AP3) S's belief that p is justified a priori if and only if S's belief that p (a) is justified by a nonexperiential source and (b) cannot be justified by experiential sources.

The conditions in (AP3) are obviously stronger than those in (AP1). The former entail, but are not entailed by, the latter. The conditions in (AP3), however, are weaker than those in (AP2). Consider condition (b) in (AP3):

> (3b) S's justified belief that p cannot be justified by experiential sources.

---

14. The subsequent arguments don't depend on the claim that introspection is a self-revising source of justified beliefs since it is not a source of justification or potential defeaters for those beliefs traditionally alleged to be justified nonexperientially.

Given that experiential sources of justification are self-revisable, the conjunction of (3b) and (SD*) entails

(c) S's justified belief that p cannot be defeated by experientially justified overriding defeaters.

Condition (c), however, does not entail condition (b) in (AP2),

(2b) S's justified belief that p cannot be defeated by experientially justified beliefs,

since (c) does not entail

(d) S's justified belief that p cannot be defeated by experientially justified *undermining* defeaters.

Hence, (3b), which is a source condition, entails (c), which is a defeasibility condition.

To see that (c) does not entail (d), consider the following example. Suppose that Sal forms a number of justified beliefs on the basis of intuition. Moreover, assume that experiential sources cannot justify overriding defeaters for any of those beliefs. Suppose that Sal uncovers via intuition a number of errors in her earlier mathematical work. Disturbed by the unusual lapses, Sal searches for an explanation and soon realizes that she began taking a new medication at the time the lapses began and that they occurred shortly after taking her daily doses. To evaluate her suspicion that the lapses are due to the new medication, Sal begins to keep records, which subsequently provide confirming evidence. Finally, suppose that Sal forms a mathematical belief that p, justified by intuition, but shortly thereafter realizes that she has just taken her daily dose of the new medication. Sal's justification for the belief that p is defeated by her justified belief that she is prone to error shortly after taking the medication. Moreover, the undermining defeater in question is experientially justified. Even though Sal's beliefs about her mathematical errors are justified by intuition, her observations about the conditions under which the errors occurred are justified experientially. Her discovery and confirmation of the fact that the errors occurred shortly after taking her daily doses of the medication are based on experience. Since Sal's justification for believing the undermining defeater involves some beliefs justified by experience, her justification for believing the defeater is also experiential.

I have shown that source conditions and defeasibility conditions on a priori justification are not fully independent of one another. Although the source condition in (AP1) does not entail any defeasibility conditions, the stronger source conditions in (AP3), together with (SD*), do entail a weak defeasibility condition. Apart from its theoretical interest, this result may also allow us to explain why many think that the traditional Kantian conception of a priori justification involves a weak defeasibility condition. When Kant argues that knowledge of mathematical propositions is a priori, he claims that "they carry with them necessity, which *cannot* be derived from experience."[15] This suggests that Kant endorses (AP3). If one takes (AP3) to be the Kantian conception of a priori justification, then that conception does indeed involve a defeasibility condition, although one weaker than that endorsed by (AP2).

One might contend at this point that, given the choice between (AP1) and (AP2), (AP3) represents a reasonable compromise with good historical credentials. Unfortunately, it faces two serious problems. (AP2) derives its initial support from the intuition that the requirement of independence from experience demands that a priori justification not be subject to empirical defeasibility. (AP3) violates that intuition. On the other hand, (AP3) inherits the four problems presented against (AP2). In particular, it rules out the possibility of empirically justified beliefs that are justifiable a priori. Hence, like many compromise positions, (AP3) inherits the disadvantages of both extreme positions but enjoys the advantages of neither.

2.8   Conclusion

My goal in this chapter is to adjudicate between two analyses of the concept of a priori justification:

(AP1) S's belief that *p* is justified a priori if and only if S's belief that *p* is nonexperientially justified, and

(AP2) S's belief that *p* is justified a priori if and only if S's belief that *p* is nonexperientially justified and cannot be defeated by experience.

I begin by introducing two parameters of evaluation: continuity with historical precedent and coherence with concepts and accepted principles in other domains in the theory of knowledge. Both analyses have respectable historical credentials. Both attempt to articulate Kant's idea that a priori knowledge is knowledge that is independent of experience. Kant's remarks, although suggestive, are not fully articulated and, as a consequence, do not provide a basis for favoring either. The burden of the decision falls on theoretical considerations. Here I argue that (AP1) introduces a conception of a priori justification that coheres with related concepts in the theory of empirical knowledge and focuses attention on the central question of whether there are nonexperiential sources of justified belief. (AP2), on the other hand, introduces a crucial ambiguity into the locution "justified Φ-ly," which results in drawing attention away from questions about nonexperiential justification to questions about defeasibility. Moreover, (AP1), but not (AP2), satisfies a widely endorsed criterion of adequacy on the concept of a priori justification: that it allow for the possibility of empirical knowledge of propo-

---

15. Kant, *Critique of Pure Reason*, 52 (emphasis mine).

sitions knowable a priori. I go on to consider objections to (AP1) and, in particular, the concern that the resulting conception of a priori justification is too weak. Closer examination of the cases that motivate the concern reveals that they are not sanctioned as justified by (AP1). Finally, I introduce a third conception of a priori justification, (AP3), which is weaker than (AP2) but stronger than (AP1). (AP3) is of primarily theoretical interest in that it allows me to show that source and defeasibility conditions on a priori justification are not fully independent of one another. Since (AP3) is less plausible than either (AP1) or (AP2), I conclude that (AP1) offers the superior analysis of the concept of a priori justification.

There is, however, a residual issue in the background: (AP1) essentially involves the distinction between experiential and nonexperiential sources of justification. As I noted in section 1.6, the distinction is not fully transparent. There are two relatively clear senses of experience, neither of which is adequate for drawing the distinction between a priori and a posteriori justification. Hence, the cogency of the latter distinction ultimately depends on the cogency of the distinction between experiential and nonexperiential sources of justification. I return to this issue in chapter 6.

3

Fallible A Priori Justification

3.1 Introduction

One of the most striking results of our examination of proposals about a priori justification is a tendency to treat a priori and a posteriori knowledge differently. Although most contemporary epistemologists deny that a posteriori knowledge requires justification that is indefeasible or that provides a guarantee of truth, it is common to find such conditions imposed upon a priori knowledge. I argued against such conditions in chapter 1 and, in chapter 2, defended a concept of a priori justification that treats it on a par with a posteriori justification. Several other authors also reject these stronger conditions and offer accounts of fallible a priori justification. Although I am sympathetic with their goal, I believe that their accounts are flawed because they do not fully understand the implications of rejecting the stronger conditions. My purpose in this chapter is to explore the requirements of fallible a priori justification and to expose some of these flaws.

The chapter consists of two parts. The first, comprising sections 3.2 and 3.3, is more theoretical. The notion of fallibility has been heavily utilized by post-Cartesian epistemologists, but often in different senses with no clear exposition of the relations among them. My goal in section 3.2 is to identify two important senses of infallibility, and to argue that neither entails the other. In section 3.3, I identify corresponding senses of fallibility. Once again, I argue that neither entails the other, but my main goal is to explore whether there are any interesting epistemic premises that link the two. The second part of the chapter, comprising sections 3.4 and 3.5, focuses on the work of several proponents of fallible a priori justification. My goal is to uncover some errors that stem from a failure to understand fully the requirements of fallibilism. Since the concept of fallible a priori justification that I defend in chapter 2 is free of these errors, my results provide indirect support for it by demonstrating its superiority over some competing accounts.

3.2   Two Senses of Infallibility

There are two different senses of infallibility that have played a prominent role in recent discussions of the a priori. The first is *Cartesian* infallibility (or c-infallibility). S's belief that *p* is *strongly* c-infallibly justified by source *A* if and only if S's belief that *p* is justified by source *A* and it is not logically possible that S's belief that *p* is justified by source *A* and *p* is false.[1] S's belief that *p* is *weakly* c-infallibly justified by source *A* if and only if S's belief that *p* is justified by source *A* and it is not the case that *p* is false. There are other senses of c-infallibility. All entail some connection between justification and *truth*.

The second is Peircian infallibility (or p-infallibility). S's belief that *p* is *strongly* p-infallibly justified by source *A* if and only if S's belief that *p* is justified by source *A* and indefeasible by any evidence. S's belief that *p* is *weakly* p-infallibly justified by source *A* if and only if S's belief that *p* is justified by source *A* and indefeasible by any experiential evidence. There are other senses of p-infallibility. All entail some connection between justification and *defeasibility*.

Although c-infallibility and p-infallibility are frequently associated with each other, they are different concepts. All concepts of c-infallibility entail a connection between justification and truth, whereas all concepts of p-infallibility entail a connection between justification and defeasibility. Since defeasibility and truth are different concepts, p-infallibility and c-infallibility are different concepts. The fact that these concepts are different does not entail that there are no important connections between them. What it does show is that such a connection cannot be assumed. My goal in section 3.2 is to argue that neither concept entails the other.

Consider first the entailment from c-infallibility to p-infallibility. From

(SC) S's belief that *p* is strongly c-infallibly justified by source *A*,

---

1. My definition of strong c-infallibility is the standard one, which has the unfortunate consequence that it is trivially satisfied by any necessary truth. For example, if S justifiably believes some necessary truth on the basis of testimony, S's belief is not infallibly justified since testimony does not provide a guarantee of truth. The guarantee of truth is a consequence of the necessary truth of the proposition believed. Since my goal is not to offer an analysis of the relevant concept, I will not attempt to resolve this problem. For my more limited purposes, it is sufficient that we can identify those cases in which the definition is satisfied but the justification in question does not provide a guarantee of truth and take care not to use such cases in the subsequent discussion.

it does not follow that

(SP) S's belief that p is strongly p-infallibly justified by source A.

For example, suppose that S is a competent mathematician whose belief that p is justified on the basis of following a valid deductive proof from true premises S is justified in believing. Furthermore, suppose that one of S's colleagues whom S has no reason to distrust presents a pseudoproof that not-p from *different* true premises S is equally justified in believing. S scrutinizes the pseudoproof and believes that it is sound. Since the proof that p and the pseudoproof that not-p are equally compelling for S, the pseudoproof defeats S's original justification. Hence, S's justified belief that p is defeasible and (SP) is false.

A modification of the above case shows that (SC) does not entail

(WP) S's belief that p is weakly p-infallibly justified by source A.

Assume that S is an average mathematics student and the proof is part of a homework assignment. Suppose that S's instructor reviews the proof and, mistakenly, informs S that it contains an error. Here the instructor's testimony that there is an error in the proof provides an experientially justified defeater for S's justified belief that p. Hence, (WP) is false.

I have argued that (SC) does not entail either (SP) or (WP). Since (SC) entails

(WC) S's belief that p is weakly c-infallibly justified by source A,

it follows that (WC) does not entail either (SP) or (WP). Neither strong nor weak c-infallibility entails either weak or strong p-infallibility.

Addressing the entailment from p-infallibility to c-infallibility is more complicated since the modal notion embedded in "defeasible" is opaque. Saul Kripke and others have stressed that the expression "p is knowable a priori" is indeterminate unless it is specified *by whom* p is knowable.[2] If, for example, we countenance omniscient spiritual beings, then perhaps all truths are knowable a priori. If we consider highly advanced alien mathematicians, then perhaps mathematical truths beyond human comprehension are knowable a priori. Since our concern is with *human* knowledge, such possibilities are of little interest.

A related point, which has not been recognized, is that unless features of the cognizer's epistemic setting are specified, a similar indeterminacy arises. For example, if we consider only human cognizers but countenance settings in which there are cognitive superscientists who significantly enhance basic human cognitive equipment and capacities, the range of what is knowable a priori by humans is considerably expanded. Furthermore, if we allow radical changes in the nature of the objects of human knowledge, the prob-

2. See Kripke, *Naming and Necessity*, 34–35, and Anderson, "Toward a Logic of A Priori Knowledge," 1–3.

lem again resurfaces. For example, if we countenance worlds whose structure is so simple and transparent that its fundamental laws are immediately evident, then perhaps some of those laws are known a priori. In such worlds, the experiences necessary to acquire the requisite concepts may be sufficient to justify belief in those laws. Once again, such possibilities are of little epistemic interest. Our concern is with what can be known by beings *like us*, inhabiting a world *like ours*, and having epistemic resources *similar to ours* for gathering information about that world. Hence, in determining whether *p* is knowable a priori, we don't consider all the possibilities. We fix certain features of the actual world such as the basic cognitive capacities of cognizers, the cognitive relationships among cognizers like expertise and division of cognitive labor, and the cognitive accessibility of the objects of knowledge.

There is a similar indeterminacy in (SP) and (WP). "Defeasible," like "knowable," involves a modal notion. Unless it is specified *for whom* a justified belief is defeasible and *in what circumstances*, the expression is indeterminate. For example, if we countenance omniscient beings, then none of their justified beliefs are defeasible. If we countenance disembodied spirits, then perhaps none of their justified beliefs are defeasible by experiential evidence. On the other hand, if we consider only human cognizers but countenance worlds inhabited by omniscient beings who publicly monitor their cognitive activities, then perhaps all human justified beliefs are defeasible. Once again, however, our concern is with human cognizers and human settings. We want to know if our justified beliefs can be defeated in settings like ours, inhabited by beings like us, having epistemic resources similar to ours. Hence, in determining whether S's justified belief that *p* is defeasible, not all possible worlds are relevant. Irrelevant worlds include those in which there are radical changes in the cognitive capacities of the inhabitants, the means for acquiring knowledge, or the accessibility of information.[3]

Although these remarks do not provide a fully determinate content for (SP) or (WP), they put us in a better position to assess the consequences of p-infallibility. The view that (SP) and (WP) entail (SC) draws its support from a very wide reading of the modal notion embedded in "defeasible." It is plausible to maintain that, unless S's justification guarantees the truth of *p*,

---

3. Kitcher, *The Nature of Mathematical Knowledge*, 26, makes a similar point about the modal notion embedded in his account of a priori warrant:

> We are not just envisaging any logically possible world. We imagine a world in which X has similar mental powers to those he has in the actual world. By hypothesis, X's experience is different. Yet the capacities for thinking, reasoning, and acquiring knowledge which X possesses as a member of *Homo sapiens* are to remain unaffected: we want to say that X, *with the kinds of cognitive capacities distinctive of humans*, could have undergone processes of the appropriate type, even if his experiences had been different.

there are worlds in which there is additional evidence such that, when it is added to S's original evidence for believing that p, S's total evidence no longer justifies the belief that p. However, if the scope of possible worlds is limited to those in which our cognitive situation is not radically altered, then such worlds may not be relevant in evaluating the truth of (SP) or (WP).

Suppose that

(SP) S's belief that p is strongly p-infallibly justified by source A.

Providing an uncontroversial example of such a belief is challenging. The most promising example is one's belief that one exists. It is difficult to envisage defeating evidence for this belief since one's having any defeating evidence for the belief entails that it is true and the entailment is as evident as any. Unfortunately, for our purposes, one's belief that one exists is also strongly c-infallibly justified. It is not logically possible that one have a false justified belief that one exists.

Consider, however, a closely related belief. Suppose that one believes on the basis of memory that one existed a moment ago. One's justified belief that one existed a moment ago does not entail that one did exist a moment ago. It is logically possible that one just came into existence along with memories of the past. Hence, the belief that one existed a moment ago is not strongly c-fallibly justified. This belief, however, is strongly p-infallibly justified. No belief justified by memory to the effect that one did *not* exist a moment ago could defeat one's original justification since such a belief would be less justified than one's original belief. Moreover, since any potential defeater based on testimony would be justified in part by memory, it could not defeat one's justification for believing that one existed a moment ago without defeating its own justification. Finally, any belief calling into question the reliability of memory would also be self-defeating. Such a belief would be justified either by one's own recollection of past failures of memory or the testimony of others about such failures. Consequently, it could not defeat one's justification for believing that one existed a moment ago without defeating its own justification. Since one's belief that one existed a moment ago is strongly p-infallibly justified but is not strongly c-infallibly justified, (SP) does not entail

(SC) S's belief that p is strongly c-infallibly justified by source A.

Furthermore, since (SP) entails

(WP) S's belief that p is weakly p-infallibly justified by source A,

(WP) does not entail (SC).

Does this example also show that (SP) does not entail

(WC) S's belief that p is weakly c-infallibly justified by source A?

The matter is complex since it raises a basic question about epistemic justification. If one's belief that one existed a moment ago is not weakly c-infallibly justified by memory, then it is justified by memory and false. But if one's belief that one existed a moment ago is false, then virtually all of one's beliefs based on memory are false. If virtually all are false, how can any be justified? Here we run up against the question of whether epistemic justification requires a connection with truth. For those who deny a truth connection, a variant of the previous example shows that (SP) does not entail (WC). We simply consider a world in which one's belief that one existed a moment ago is false. Such a belief is strongly p-infallibly justified but *not* weakly c-infallibly justified. Those who endorse a truth connection will reject the claim that one's false belief that one existed a moment ago is justified since if that belief is false, beliefs based on memory lack the connection with truth requisite for such justification. Is another example available that is more congenial to the latter camp?

Suppose that we inhabit a Cartesian world under the control of an omnipotent but not-so-evil demon who brings it about that each of us has a narrowly specified class of false memory beliefs that are indistinguishable from other memory beliefs. The class is small enough that it does not alter the justificatory status of memory beliefs. Furthermore, suppose that the demon also ensures that, for each cognizer and each memory belief in the specified class, no evidence is available that either conflicts with the belief or calls its justification into question. In such a world, for any cognizer S and any justified belief that p in the specified class, S's justified belief that p is strongly p-infallibly justified. Yet, since S's belief that p is false, it is not weakly c-infallibly justified. Hence, (SP) does not entail (WC).

This example is fanciful since our world is not Cartesian. Can we provide an actual example of a belief that is both strongly p-infallibly justified and not weakly c-infallibly justified? Reflection on the fanciful example indicates that this is not possible. The key feature of the example is that inhabitants of the Cartesian world have cognitive blind spots. They have a source of justified beliefs that produces some false beliefs but, because of the activity of the not-so-evil demon, they cannot acquire any further information, accurate or inaccurate, that suggests the falsehood of those beliefs or calls their justification into question. If there are actual examples of such beliefs, then humans have cognitive blind spots that are due to the inherent limitations of their cognitive resources rather than to the activity of a demon. If humans have a source of justified beliefs that produces some false beliefs whose falsehood is not humanly detectable, then we cannot provide examples of such false beliefs since, by hypothesis, their falsehood is not humanly detectable. Hence, if we grant that justification is connected with truth, then actual examples of beliefs that are strongly p-infallibly justified but not weakly c-infallibly justified are not available. Nevertheless, even if we restrict ourselves to non-Cartesian worlds, (SP) does not entail (WC) since the possibility that humans have cognitive blind spots is not merely logical. Cognitive blind spots are not ruled out by our current theories of human cognition. Since (SP) entails (WP), (WP) does not entail (WC).

Let us briefly take stock. I began by showing that neither strong nor weak c-infallibility entails either weak or strong p-infallibility. Addressing the entailment from p-infallibility to c-infallibility required discussion of two further issues: (1) the modality embedded in "defeasible" and (2) whether epistemic justification is truth-conducive. Subsequent to the discussion of these issues, I showed that neither strong nor weak p-infallibility entails either weak or strong c-infallibility. Hence, we can conclude that neither strong nor weak c-infallibility entails, or is entailed by, either strong or weak p-infallibility.

3.3   Three Senses of Fallible A Priori Justification

A number of recent writers have proposed accounts of a priori justification that reject the requirement of infallibility. Not surprisingly, different authors have stressed different senses of fallibility. For example, Laurence BonJour maintains that a priori justification involves an intuitive apprehension of necessity. He stresses, however, that he sees "no reason to regard such apprehensions as being in any useful sense infallible or certain; on the contrary, it is quite clear that mistakes can and do occur."[4] Here the relevant sense of infallibility is c-infallibility. BonJour is acknowledging both the possibility of *false* beliefs that are justified a priori and their actual occurrence. I shall introduce two corresponding senses of c-fallibility: S's belief that p is *strongly* c-fallibly justified by source A if and only if S's belief that p is justified by source A and p is false; S's belief that p is *weakly* c-fallibly justified by source A if and only if S's belief that p is justified by source A and it is possible that S's belief that p is justified by source A and p is false.

Donna Summerfield claims that "my characterization of a priori justification enables us to see . . . how we might have a priori knowledge that is defeasible."[5] Clearly, the concern here is to reject p-infallibility. There are two senses of p-fallibility: S's belief that p is *strongly* p-fallibly justified by source A if and only if S's belief that p is justified by source A and defeasible by some experiential evidence; S's belief that p is *weakly* p-fallibly justified by source A if and only if S's belief that p is justified by source A and defeasible by some evidence.

John Pollock maintains that a priori justification is grounded in logical intuitions, and he draws an analogy between such justification and perceptual justification:

> Our logical intuitions can profitably be compared with our faculty of sight. Logical intuitions do not provide us with conclusive reasons for a priori judgments, any more than our sight provides us with conclu-

---

4. BonJour, *The Structure of Empirical Knowledge*, 208.
5. Summerfield, "Modest A Priori Knowledge," 40.

sive reasons for judging the colors of things. . . . We can perfectly well recognize a logical intuition to be incorrect, just as we can recognize that something is not the color it looks to us. This is done by relying upon other logical intuitions and using them to prove the falsity of what we thought we intuited to be true.[6]

Pollock maintains that logical intuitions are *both* c-fallible and p-fallible. Prima facie reasons are defeasible; conclusive reasons are not. But Pollock also maintains that some intuitions can prove the falsehood of others. Hence, they are also c-fallible.

I have argued that neither weak nor strong c-infallibility entails, or is entailed by, either weak or strong p-infallibility. Hence, it follows that neither weak nor strong c-fallibility entails, or is entailed by, either weak or strong p-fallibility. Yet, as the passage from Pollock indicates, they are frequently associated. Are there additional principles that mediate some connection between these two senses of fallibility?

Pollock's analogy between sight and intuition provides an interesting suggestion. One point of the analogy is to draw attention to an important characteristic of sight: it is a *self-correcting* source of justified beliefs, that is, one that can correct its errors. Consider an elementary case of visual self-correction. I notice a sheet of paper on my desk, look at it, and form the belief that it is square. However, upon subsequent examination, one of its sides appears longer than another, and as a result I come to believe that the sheet is rectangular. If we add the further assumption that the sheet is rectangular, then we have a case of visual self-correction.

Some, but not all, of the changes we make among our visual beliefs are self-correcting. Although some of the changes move in the direction from false to true, others move in the opposite direction. On some occasions when I look again at a sheet of paper that I believe is square and, on that basis, come to believe that it is rectangular, the sheet *is* square. Visual belief revision sometimes results in error. Hence, sight is not only a self-correcting but also a self-revising source of justified beliefs, that is, one that can revise both its true and false deliverances. Let us say that A is a *self-revising* source of justified beliefs if and only if for every belief that p which A justifies for S, A can also justify for S the belief that not-p.[7] Self-revision involves a unique type of defeater for S's justified belief that p. S's justified belief that p is defeated by a belief that not-p which is justified by the *same* source as S's belief that p. Let us say that S's belief that p is *self-revised* just in case if S's belief that p is justified by source A then S's belief that not-p is also justified by source A.

6. Pollock, *Knowledge and Justification*, 320.
7. Self-revision comes in degrees. A weaker form can be defined as follows: for *some* belief that p which A justifies for S, A can also justify for S the belief that not-p. Other versions, both stronger and weaker, are possible.

Self-revision mediates some important connections from p-fallibility to c-fallibility. Suppose that

(1) S's belief that p is weakly p-fallibly justified by source A.

The conjunction of (1) and

(2) S's belief that p is self-revised

entails

(3) A justifies S's belief that p and A justifies S's belief that not-p.

If S's belief that p is false, then it follows that it is strongly c-fallibly justified by source A. If S's belief that not-p is false, then it is strongly c-fallibly justified by source A. Hence, (3) entails

(4) Either S's belief that p is strongly c-fallibly justified by source A or S's belief that not-p is strongly c-fallibly justified by source A.

However, (3) does not entail

(5) S's belief that p is strongly c-fallibly justified by source A

since it does not entail that p is false. Moreover, (3) does not entail

(6) S's belief that p is weakly c-fallibly justified by source A

since it does not entail that there is a world in which A justifies S's belief that p and p is false.

The situation, however, is puzzling. Consider (3) again. If p is false, then (3) entails (5) and, a fortiori, (6). If p is true, however, (3) entails

(5*) S's belief that not-p is strongly c-fallibly justified by source A

and, a fortiori,

(6*) S's belief that not-p is weakly c-fallibly justified by source A.

Suppose that p is true. Is it plausible to maintain that source A both weakly and strongly c-fallibly justifies the belief that not-p but does not weakly c-fallibly justify the belief that p? Consider, again, our earlier example. Let "p" be "The sheet of paper is square." Suppose that S's false belief that not-p is justified on the basis of the fact that one side of the sheet appears longer to S than another. If it is possible that two sides of equal length appear unequal to S, what would rule out the possibility that two sides of unequal length appear equal to S? But, if it is possible that two sides of unequal length appear equal to S, then it is also possible that S believes that p on that basis and p is false. Hence, if we grant the *Source Fallibility Principle*,

(SF) Source A is weakly c-fallible with respect to S's belief that p if and only if it is weakly c-fallible with respect to S's belief that not-p,

(3) entails (6). It follows from (3) that source A justifies either S's false belief that p or S's false belief that not-p. If the former, S's belief that p is strongly and, a fortiori, weakly c-fallibly justified by source A. If the latter, S's belief that not-p is strongly and, a fortiori, weakly c-fallibly justified by source A. If S's belief that not-p is weakly c-fallibly justified by source A, it follows, by (SF), that S's belief that p is also weakly c-fallibly justified by source A. Hence, the conjunction of weak p-fallibility, self-revision, and (SF) entails weak c-fallibility. Since

(7) S's belief that p is strongly p-fallibly justified by source A

entails

(1) S's belief that p is weakly p-fallibly justified by source A,

the conjunction of strong p-fallibility, self-revision, and (SF) also entails weak c-fallibility.

The conjunction of

(1) S's belief that p is weakly p-fallibly justified by source A,

self-revision, and (SF), does not entail

(5) S's belief that p is strongly c-fallibly justified by source A

since (3) does not entail that p is false. Therefore, neither strong nor weak p-fallibility, in conjunction with self-revision and (SF), entails strong c-fallibility.

Self-revision also mediates some important connections from c-fallibility to p-fallibility. Suppose that

(6) S's belief that p is weakly c-fallibly justified by source A.

The conjunction of (6) and

(2) S's belief that p is self-revised

entails

(3) A justifies S's belief that p and A justifies S's belief that not-p.

Since S's justified belief that not-p is a defeater for S's justified belief that p, it follows that

(1) S's belief that p is weakly p-fallibly justified by source A.

If we add to (6) and (2) the additional premise

(8) A is an experiential source,

it follows that

(7) S's belief that p is strongly p-fallibly justified by source A.

Hence, since strong c-fallibility entails weak c-fallibility, self-revision mediates a connection from both strong and weak c-fallibility to both weak and strong p-fallibility.

Let me briefly summarize. Both strong and weak c-fallibility, in conjunction with self-revision, entail weak p-fallibility. Both strong and weak c-fallibility, in conjunction with self-revision by an experiential source, entail strong p-fallibility. In the opposite direction, the conjunction of weak p-fallibility, self-revision, and source fallibility entails weak c-fallibility but not strong c-fallibility. Since strong p-fallibility entails weak p-fallibility, the conjunction of strong p-fallibility, self-revision, and source fallibility also entails weak c-fallibility but not strong c-fallibility.

There are premises involving defeaters that mediate connections between c-fallibility and p-fallibility analogous to those mediated by self-revision. To bring out these connections, let us distinguish between two types of defeaters for S's A-justified (i.e., justified by source A) belief that p: (a) S's justified belief that not-p is an *overriding* defeater for S's A-justified belief that p, and (b) S's justified belief that S's A-justification is inadequate or defective is an *undermining* defeater for S's A-justified belief that p.

Overriding defeaters for S's justified belief that p can typically be justified by more than a single source. For example, my belief that my grade book is in my office, which is justified by my recollection that I brought it to the office yesterday morning, can be defeated either by my subsequent recollection that I brought it home last night or by my failure to locate it in my office today. Overriding defeaters justified by the same source as the belief whose justification they override provide a connection from weak p-fallibility to weak c-fallibility. Suppose that

(1) S's belief that p is weakly p-fallibly justified by source A.

The conjunction of (1) and

(9) S's A-justified belief that p is defeated by an A-justified overriding defeater

entails

(3) A justifies S's belief that p and A justifies S's belief that not-p.

The conjunction of (3) and (SF) entails

(6) S's belief that p is weakly c-fallibly justified by source A

but not

(5) S's belief that p is strongly c-fallibly justified by source A

since (3) does not entail that p is false. Since strong p-fallibility entails weak p-fallibility, both strong and weak p-fallibility, in conjunction with overriding defeaters justified by the same source and (SF), entail weak, but not strong, c-fallibility.

The conjunction of

(6) S's belief that p is weakly c-fallibly justified by source A

and

> (9) S's A-justified belief that p is defeated by an A-justified overriding defeater

entails

> (1) S's belief that p is weakly p-fallibly justified by source A.

Since strong c-fallibility entails weak c-fallibility, the conjunction of strong c-fallibility and (9) also entails weak p-fallibility.

The conjunction of (6), (9), and

> (8) A is an experiential source

entails

> (7) S's belief that p is strongly p-fallibly justified by source A.

Since strong c-fallibility entails weak c-fallibility, the conjunction of strong c-fallibility, (8), and (9) also entails strong p-fallibility.

Undermining defeaters provide an analogous connection from weak p-fallibility to weak c-fallibility. Undermining defeaters for S's A-justified belief that p fall into two primary categories: (a) S's justified belief that many of S's relevantly similar A-justified beliefs are false and (b) S's justified belief that S's cognitive state or environment includes some feature that sufficiently decreases the likelihood that S's A-justified belief that p is true. Undermining defeaters that fall into the first category, like overriding defeaters, can typically be justified by more than a single source. For example, my belief that I frequently misidentify certain colors can be justified either by my subsequently looking at those colors more carefully or by a companion who informs me that I frequently make such mistakes. In the former case, the defeater is justified by the same source as the belief whose justification it defeats. Undermining defeaters that fall into the second category can also be justified by the same source as the belief whose justification they defeat. For example, suppose that I notice that I frequently make mistakes when visually identifying objects at dusk, and I do so by looking at the same objects in better lighting conditions. Here vision justifies my belief that a particular type of lighting condition impairs my ability to visually identify objects. Once again, the undermining defeater is justified by the same source as the belief whose justification it defeats. Let us say that S's justified belief that p is defeated by an A-justified undermining defeater d if and only if S's justified belief that d defeats S's justified belief that p and S's justification for the belief that d is based on S's being A-justified in believing of some beliefs a, b, c, . . . , justified by the same source as p, that not-a, not-b, not-c. . . .

Suppose that

> (1) S's belief that p is weakly p-fallibly justified by source A.

The conjunction of (1) and

(10) S's A-justified belief that p is defeated by an A-justified undermining defeater

entails

(11) There is some belief that q such that A justifies S's belief that q and A justifies S's belief that not-q.

The conjunction of (11) and (SF) entails

(6) S's belief that p is weakly c-fallibly justified by source A

but not

(5) S's belief that p is strongly c-fallibly justified by source A

since (11) does not entail that p is false. Since strong p-fallibility entails weak p-fallibility, both strong and weak p-fallibility, in conjunction with undermining defeaters justified by the same source and (SF), entail weak, but not strong, c-fallibility.

The conjunction of

(6) S's belief that p is weakly c-fallibly justified by source A

and

(10) S's A-justified belief that p is defeated by an A-justified undermining defeater

entails

(1) S's belief that p is weakly p-fallibly justified by source A.

Since strong c-fallibility entails weak c-fallibility, the conjunction of strong c-fallibility and (10) also entails weak p-fallibility.

The conjunction of (6), (10), and

(8) A is an experiential source

entails

(7) S's belief that p is strongly p-fallibly justified by source A.

Since strong c-fallibility entails weak c-fallibility, the conjunction of strong c-fallibility, (8), and (10) also entails strong p-fallibility.

Our investigation of the relationship between c-fallibility and p-fallibility yields both negative and positive results. On the negative side, neither version of c-fallibility entails, or is entailed by, either version of p-fallibility. On the positive side, there are additional principles that do mediate a connection between them. First, both versions of c-fallibility, in conjunction with self-revision, entail weak p-fallibility. Second, both versions of c-fallibility, in conjunction with self-revision by an experiential source, entail strong p-fallibility. Conversely, both versions of p-fallibility, in conjunction with self-revision and source fallibility, entail weak c-fallibility. Finally, defeaters justified by the same source as the belief whose justification they defeat mediate connections from both versions of c-fallibility to both versions of p-fallibility and from both versions of p-fallibility to weak c-fallibility analogous to those mediated by self-revision.

3.4   P-fallibility and A Priori Justification

One motivation for articulating the logical relations among the different senses of fallibility is to avoid committing the errors of some proponents of fallibilist conceptions of a priori justification. I begin by looking at the relationship between weak and strong p-infallibility:

> (SP) S's justified belief that p is not defeasible by any evidence

entails

> (WP) S's justified belief that p is not defeasible by any experiential evidence.

On the face of it, (WP) does not entail (SP).

Aron Edidin, however, argues to the contrary and concludes that (SP) and (WP) are equivalent. His ultimate goal is to reject both weak and strong p-infallibility as conditions on a priori justification. If (SP) and (WP) are indeed equivalent, the task is greatly simplified because, as I argued in chapter 1, (SP) is not a very plausible condition on a priori justification, and given the equivalence, (WP) falls with (SP). Unfortunately, as I shall now argue, the quick route to rejecting weak p-infallibility is unsuccessful. Edidin fails to show that (WP) entails (SP).

Edidin's strategy is to argue that

> (S) S's justified belief that p is defeasible by nonexperiential evidence

entails

> (W) S's justified belief that p is defeasible by experiential evidence.

If (S) entails (W), then not-(W) entails not-(S). Therefore, if S's justified belief that p is not defeasible by experiential evidence, then it follows that it is not defeasible by any evidence. The argument proceeds as follows:

> But suppose that I justifiedly believe p, and my justification for this belief is corrigible [defeasible] by non-empirical evidence. . . . Now suppose that someone who is familiar with my justification for p claims to have evidence which undermines that justification, but does not tell me what that evidence is. . . . If my estimate of her reliability is sufficiently high (and we may suppose that my experience with her war-

rants an estimate as high as is necessary), her claim will provide me with evidence that removes the warrant conferred on p by my initial justification for p.[8]

Edidin's central claim is that if nonexperiential defeating evidence for S's justified belief that p is possible, then *testimonial* defeating evidence for that belief is also possible—namely, the testimony of a reliable authority who claims to possess the relevant nonexperiential defeating evidence.

Edidin's argument is based on a single example, which is not developed in sufficient detail to support his conclusion. To establish that S's non-experientially justified belief that p is defeated by S's experientially justified belief that q, three key pieces of information are necessary: (1) the degree to which the nonexperiential evidence in question justifies S's belief that p, (2) the degree to which a belief that q must be justified in order to defeat a justified belief that p, and (3) the degree to which testimony justifies S's belief that q. Since Edidin's example lacks this information, it fails to establish that (S) entails (W). In support of this contention, I will offer a proposition (P), consistent with (S), such that the conjunction of (P) and (S) entails not-(W).

Suppose that S believes some proposition on the basis of following a proof. Let us assume that (A1): S's belief that the third step of the proof is valid is justified by a nonexperiential source, call it intuition, to the degree of certainty, which is the highest degree of epistemic justification. Let us also assume that (A2): S's justified belief that q defeats S's justified belief that p if and only if the degree of justification S has for q is at least as great as the degree of justification S has for p. Suppose that the third step of the proof contains a subtle flaw, which S uncovers at a later time, and that S's belief that the third step is not valid is also justified to the degree of certainty by intuition. Hence, it follows that, prior to the discovery of the flaw, S's belief that p is non-experientially justified and defeasible by nonexperiential evidence.

Let us now suppose that Edidin's testifier is also justified in believing to the degree of certainty that the third step of S's proof that p is not valid. Moreover, let us suppose that the testifier claims to have evidence that the third step of S's proof is not valid and that S has strong inductive justification that the testifier is reliable. Finally, let us assume that (A3): transmission of justification via a fallible source results in a diminishment of justification. Although S has very strong evidence that the testifier is reliable, testimony is not an infallible source of justification. Hence, although the testifier's belief that the third step in S's proof is not valid is certain, S's belief that the third step is not valid is *not* justified to the degree of certainty by testimony. Since S's belief that the third step is valid is justified to the degree of certainty by intuition and S's belief that the third step is not valid is justified to a degree less than certainty by testimony, S's justified belief that the third step is valid is not defeated by the testimonial evidence. Let (P) be the conjunction of

8. Edidin, "*A Priori* Knowledge for Fallibilists," 190.

(A1), (A2), and (A3). (P) is consistent with (S), and the conjunction of (P) and (S) entails not-(W). Hence, (S) does not entail (W).

Edidin goes on to defend the stronger claim that (S) entails

(W*) S's justified belief that p is defeasible by *nontestimonial* experiential evidence.

In support of this contention, Edidin offers a second argument in which the reliable testifier is replaced by an oracular infant who reliably predicts that defeating evidence is forthcoming. The argument proceeds as follows. Suppose that I frequently discuss matters related to p in the presence of the infant. On a number of occasions, when someone offers a justification for some claim, the infant exclaims, "Not necessarily!" Furthermore, suppose that these exclamations are usually followed by the discovery of defeating evidence for that justification. Finally, suppose that when I present my justification for some belief that p, the infant exclaims, "Not necessarily!" According to Edidin, "Since my justification for p was corrigible, it didn't warrant my absolute trust, and we may suppose that my experience with the child warrants a greater degree of trust in her interjection than my erstwhile justification warranted for p. In this case, I will no longer be justified in believing p."[9] Edidin's claim is that if nonexperiential defeating evidence for S's justified belief that p is possible, then *inductive* defeating evidence for that belief is also possible—namely, an inductively justified belief that defeating evidence for the belief in question is forthcoming.

The argument is open to the same objection that I raised against Edidin's initial argument. Once again, there is another proposition (P*), consistent with (S), such that the conjunction of (P*) and (S) entails not-(W*). Hence, (S) does not entail (W*). To construct (P*), I introduce a modification of the scenario I presented against his first argument. Let us suppose, as in the original scenario, that S's belief that the third step of the proof is valid is justified by intuition to the degree of certainty, that S later discovers that the third step contains a subtle flaw, and that S's later belief that the third step is not valid is also justified to the degree of certainty by intuition. Hence, it follows that, prior to the discovery of the flaw, S's belief that p is nonexperientially justified and defeasible by nonexperiential evidence.

Let us now suppose, and here I deviate from the original scenario, that S has strong inductive evidence that defeating evidence for S's intuitive justification that the third step of the proof is valid is forthcoming. Moreover, let us assume that (A4): if S's belief that p is based on inductive evidence, then S's belief that p is not justified to the degree of certainty. Since S's belief that the defeating evidence is forthcoming is *not* justified to the degree of certainty by induction and S's belief that the third step of the proof is valid is justified to the degree of certainty, the former does not defeat the latter.

9. Ibid., 192.

Let (P*) be the conjunction of (A1), (A2), and (A4). Since (P*) is consistent with (S) and the conjunction of (P*) and (S) entails not-(W*), (S) does not entail (W*).

I have argued that Edidin's examples fail to show that (S) entails either (W) or (W*). It follows that he has not established that (WP) entails (SP). Hence, his case against the weak p-fallibility condition on a priori justification fails.

3.5   Two Inconsistent Accounts

Proponents of fallible a priori justification typically deny that such justification is either strongly c-infallible or weakly p-infallible. Some, however, fail to fully appreciate the consequences of denying that a priori justification is strongly c-infallible. As a consequence, they propose conditions on a priori justification that are incompatible with the claim that such justification is weakly c-fallible. In this section, I argue that both Bob Hale and Donna Summerfield offer accounts of a priori justification that are incompatible with their endorsements of weak c-fallibility.

Both present their accounts in the context of rejecting Philip Kitcher's infallibilist conception of a priori justification:

> a is an a priori warrant for X's belief that p if and only if a is a process such that, given any life e, sufficient for X for p,
>
>   (a) some process of the same type could produce in X a belief that p
>   (b) if a process of the same type were to produce in X a belief that p, then it would warrant X in believing that p
>   (c) if a process of the same type were to produce in X a belief that p, then p.[10]

Condition (b) is a version of weak p-infallibility since it entails that if X's belief that p is justified a priori, then X's justification is not defeated in any experiential setting sufficient for X to believe that p. Condition (c), on the other hand, is a version of strong c-infallibility.

Bob Hale rejects both (b) and (c). He argues that (c) conflates the requirements of a priori *justification* with those of a priori *knowledge*: "But why assume, in the first place, that *a priori* warrants *must* produce true beliefs? . . . Obviously, for X to know *a priori* that p, it must be true that p. . . . It clearly does not follow that the satisfaction of this condition, in the case of knowledge *a priori*, must be ensured by the fact that X has *a priori* grounds to believe that p."[11] Hale's rejection of (c) commits him to the possibility of *false* beliefs that are justified a priori.

---

10. Kitcher, *The Nature of Mathematical Knowledge*, 24.
11. Hale, *Abstract Objects*, 129.

Hale observes, however, that Kitcher's primary arguments against the existence of a priori knowledge are based on the contention that alleged a priori processes fail to satisfy condition (b) of his analysis. Suppose that S knows a theorem of mathematics on the basis of following a proof from premises that S knows a priori. Kitcher contends that S's knowledge is not a priori because S's belief is justified by the process of following a proof and that process does not satisfy condition (b). If some eminent mathematicians were to testify that the theorem is false or that the proof is flawed, S's justification for the belief would be defeated by experience. Hence, according to Kitcher, beliefs based on the process of following a proof are not justified a priori.

Hale regards this consequence as implausible and rejects Kitcher's condition (b). His goal is to provide an alternative to (b) in which beliefs justified by the process of following a proof from premises known a priori are justified a priori despite the potential for defeating experiential evidence. He begins by distinguishing between *genuine* defeaters, those that actually show that S's grounds for believing that p are inadequate, and *apparent* defeaters, those that only appear to do so:

> In one sense, a man's grounds for his belief that p are undermined by the citation of new evidence in the light of which, pending a more thorough investigation, it would be unreasonable for him to continue to repose in those grounds the degree of confidence with which he formerly entertained them. But his grounds may, quite differently, be undermined by adducing further considerations which actually show either that they are not in fact grounds for his belief that p at all, or that they are not as good as he supposed them to be, and are, perhaps, insufficient to warrant his belief.[12]

Armed with this distinction, he proposes to replace (b) with the weaker condition:

> (H) If a is an a priori process and produces in X a belief that p, then there are no possible experiential settings in which a produces in X the belief that p and X's grounds are undermined by *genuine* defeaters.

If we now again consider Kitcher's example of knowing a theorem on the basis of following a proof from premises known a priori, Hale contends that

---

12. Ibid., 137. Hale's formulation of the distinction is not felicitous. The problem is that defeaters that *actually* show that one's grounds are not in fact good grounds for one's belief also make it *unreasonable* for one to continue to repose in them the degree of confidence with which one originally entertained them. Hence, if we take Hale at his word, any defeaters that fall into his second category also fall into the first. I assume, however, that his intention is to provide two mutually exclusive categories of defeaters since he later maintains that a priori knowledge is incompatible with the possibility of defeaters falling into the second category but compatible with the possibility of defeaters falling into the first.

(H) is satisfied "if following the proof against kindly background experience is to yield knowledge, the proof must be good, and if consideration of the envisaged unkind experiential background is to be relevant, we must suppose the same proof to be followed. Consequently, nothing in the unkind setting could show that the proof is flawed."[13] The crux of Hale's argument is that if S knows that p on the basis of following a proof from premises known a priori, then experientially justified genuine defeaters for S's justification are not possible.

Hale's argument, however, conflates the requirements of *knowledge* with those of *justification*. The argument involves two claims: (1) if the process of following a proof yields *knowledge* of its conclusion, then the proof must be sound, and (2) all experientially justified undermining defeaters for beliefs justified by the process of following a sound proof must be *apparent*. But, in order to show that a belief based on the process of following a proof satisfies (H), Hale must establish that

(1*) If the process of following a proof yields *justification* of its conclusion, then the proof must be sound.

For if the process of following a flawed proof yields justification of its conclusion and S believes that p on the basis of following such a proof, then there are genuine experiential defeaters for S's justified belief that p. The testimony of eminent mathematicians that p is false or that the proof is flawed provide examples. However, (1*) is true only if a priori justification is strongly c-infallible. If a priori justification need not provide a guarantee of truth, then there is no basis for denying that the process of following a flawed proof provides a priori justification of its conclusion. Since Hale denies that a priori justification is strongly c-infallible, he must also reject (1*). Hence, his contention that a priori justification is not strongly c-infallible is incompatible with the claim that beliefs based on the process of following a proof satisfy (H).

Hale's goal is to replace Kitcher's condition (b) on a priori justification with a weaker condition that does not have the consequence that beliefs justified by the process of following a proof are not a priori because of the possibility of experiential defeating evidence. The condition Hale proposes accomplishes this goal, however, only if genuine experiential defeaters for beliefs justified by the process of following a proof are not possible. Genuine experiential defeaters for beliefs justified by the process of following a proof are not possible only if only sound proofs justify their conclusions a priori. The view that only sound proofs justify their conclusions a priori is incompatible with the view that a priori justification is weakly c-fallible. Since Hale is committed to the view that a priori justification is weakly c-fallible, he fails to provide a condition on a priori justification that avoids

13. Ibid.

the consequence that beliefs justified by the process of following a proof are not justified a priori. The source of the problem is his failure to appreciate fully the implications of weak c-fallibility.

Donna Summerfield's account of a priori justification suffers from a similar defect. Following Hale, she rejects Kitcher's condition (c) and argues that a priori justification is weakly c-fallible: "It seems reasonable to say that a capable and careful mathematician may be warranted on the basis of following a proof in believing a theorem, even though the proof may contain an extremely subtle flaw that she has not (or not yet) detected."[14] Summerfield also rejects Kitcher's condition (b), maintaining that, in order for S's belief that p to be justified a priori, S's justification for the belief that p must not depend *positively* on experience but may depend *negatively* on experience.[15] Putting this point in our terminology, she maintains that S's justification for the belief that p must be nonexperientially justified but need not be indefeasible by experience. In addition, she offers an alternative to Kitcher's (b):

(S) A modest apriorist may insist that if a is an a priori warrant, then, if a process of the same type as a were to occur in a counterfactual situation in which there are defeating experiences or defeating empirical beliefs, it would provide the same degree (quantity) of support for the belief even though the status of the belief would be different (i.e., it would fail to be knowledge or to be fully justified).[16]

This proposal is based on the distinction between (1) the degree of support for a belief that p and (2) the status of the belief that p. Summerfield's central claim is that if S's belief that p, which is fully justified in the actual world, is evaluated in a counterfactual situation, the status of the belief can change while its degree of justification remains the same. Since Kitcher requires that an a priori justified belief retain its *status* as fully justified, whereas Summerfield requires only that it retain its *degree* of justification, her requirement is weaker.

Consider an example that illustrates this point.[17] Suppose that a mathematician, Claudia, believes that p on the basis of producing a proof, but in some counterfactual situation other mathematicians perversely convince her that her capacity to produce sound proofs is deficient. Summerfield maintains that Claudia's belief that p is fully justified and known in the actual world but neither fully justified nor known in the counterfactual situation.

14. Summerfield, "Modest A Priori Knowledge," 46. In a note to this passage, Summerfield indicates that she uses the term "theorem" in a broad sense that allows for *false* theorems.
15. Ibid., 42.
16. Ibid., 47.
17. The example is Summerfield's; see ibid., 50.

Since full justification and knowledge pertain to the status of a belief, Claudia's belief does not satisfy Kitcher's condition (b). She alleges, however, that the process of following a proof provides the same degree of support in both the actual world and the counterfactual situation. Hence, (S) is satisfied.

Summerfield's overall position is difficult to assess since it is not fully articulated. In particular, she does not indicate how she determines the degree to which a belief is justified in a counterfactual situation. My goal is to argue that Summerfield's claim that the degree of support that the process of following a proof provides for a belief that p across relevant counterfactual situations does not change is incompatible with the position that a priori justification is weakly c-fallible.

Consider a variation on the Claudia example. Suppose that Claudia believes that p on the basis of producing a proof that p, but in the counterfactual situation her colleagues perversely convince her that not-p by providing a convincing pseudoproof for that conclusion. In this situation, there is some plausibility to the claim that although Claudia's belief that p is no longer fully justified, the process of constructing a proof provides the same degree of support in the counterfactual situation as in the actual world. In this situation, the pseudoproof that not-p provides support for the belief that not-p and her belief that p is no longer fully justified because she now has at least as much support for the belief that not-p as for the belief that p. Overriding defeaters for the belief that p provide support for the belief that not-p.

Undermining defeaters for the belief that p, however, do not provide support for the belief that not-p. They call into question the adequacy of the grounds that are alleged to support the belief that p. They provide evidence that those grounds are defective and, consequently, do not support the belief that p. Hence, in the original Claudia case, her belief that p is no longer fully justified because her colleagues have provided evidence that the proofs she produces are not sound. To maintain, as Summerfield does, that the process of following the proof continues to support Claudia's belief is to fail to recognize the distinctive manner in which undermining defeaters remove full justification.

One might respond to my contention by introducing a distinction between the support S's grounds *actually* provide for the belief that p (the *objective* sense of support) and the support S *takes* those grounds to provide for the belief that p (the *subjective* sense of support). One could then maintain that, in the objective sense, Claudia's belief is supported to the same degree in both situations since the proof is sound. The two situations differ in how Claudia takes those grounds. She takes them to be adequate in the actual, but not in the counterfactual, situation.

This response fails because it cannot accommodate cases that involve *genuine* defeaters. Suppose that Leo is a mathematician whose belief that p is fully justified by the process of following a subtly flawed proof. Since the process fully justifies Leo's belief that p in the actual world, it also provides a certain degree of support for that belief in the actual world. If we now consider a counterfactual situation in which Leo believes that p on the basis of the same subtly flawed proof and the testimony of his eminent colleagues convinces him that the proof is flawed, Leo's belief that p is no longer fully justified. Furthermore, in the counterfactual situation, Leo's belief is not supported in either the objective or subjective sense. The flawed proof does not actually support its conclusion, and Leo no longer takes it to support its conclusion. Yet, by hypothesis, the proof does provide a certain degree of support for its conclusion in the actual world. Therefore, neither sense of support underwrites Summerfield's contention that the process of following a proof provides the same degree of support for the belief that p across counterfactual situations.

Summerfield's failure to recognize that weak c-fallible sources of justification do not satisfy (S) is due to the fact that she considers only cases in which the defeaters in the counterfactual situations are *apparent*. There is some plausibility in maintaining that if S's belief that p is justified on the basis of following a sound proof and the testimony of eminent mathematicians justifies S's false belief that the proof is flawed, then in the objective sense the proof continues to support S's belief that p despite the fact that the belief is no longer fully justified. This point is analogous to Hale's point. But Summerfield, like Hale, fails to recognize that weak c-fallibility introduces the possibility of *genuine* defeaters. As a consequence, her account of a priori justification is at odds with the requirements of weak c-fallibility.

3.6 Conclusion

The contemporary discussion of a priori justification has given special prominence to the concepts of fallibility and infallibility. These concepts, however, have not been clearly articulated, and as a consequence some recent claims about fallible a priori justification are erroneous. My first goal is to advance the discussion by exploring the logical terrain surrounding these concepts in more detail. I distinguish between two senses of infallibility. The first, c-infallibility, entails some connection between justification and truth. The second, p-infallibility, entails some connection between justification and defeasibility. I argue that c-infallibility and p-infallibility are logically independent of each other. I also distinguish between two corresponding senses of fallibility—c-fallibility and p-fallibility—and articulate some interesting relations between them that are mediated by the concept of self-revision and the concept of a defeater justified by the same source as the belief whose justification it defeats.

My second goal is to evaluate three arguments against Kitcher's weak p-infallibility condition on a priori justification. Edidin attempts to dismiss the condition on the grounds that it entails strong p-infallibility, which he rejects on independent grounds. I argue, however, that weak p-infallibility does not entail strong p-infallibility. Both Hale and Summerfield offer alternatives to Kitcher's condition, which, I argue, are incompatible with their contention that a priori justification is weakly c-fallible. These negative results bolster the positive results of the first two chapters. On the one hand, the sustained argument offered in chapter 2 against the weak p-infallibility condition proves to be necessary, given the failure of Edidin's strategy. On the other hand, since (AP2) rejects outright the weak p-infallibility condition, (AP2) is compatible with the view that a priori justification is weakly c-fallible. Hence (AP2) coherently combines both p-fallibility and c-fallibility.

PART II

IS THERE A PRIORI KNOWLEDGE?

4

The Supporting Arguments

4.1 Introduction

The focus of part I is the concept of a priori knowledge. My primary conclusion is that a priori knowledge is knowledge whose justification is nonexperiential. This result provides the theoretical basis for part II, which addresses the existence of a priori knowledge, by identifying the fundamental issue that divides proponents and opponents of the a priori. Part II consists of three chapters. Chapter 4 addresses arguments that support the existence of a priori knowledge. Chapter 5 scrutinizes the opposing arguments. My goal is to show that none of the arguments, which are themselves largely a priori in character, provides a compelling case for or against the a priori. In chapter 6, I offer an alternative strategy for addressing the existence of a priori knowledge, which involves providing empirical supporting evidence for the claim that there are nonexperiential sources of justification.

Chapter 4 surveys the leading arguments in support of the existence of a priori knowledge. There are three approaches to arguing for the a priori. The first is to offer an analysis of the concept of a priori knowledge and to argue that some knowledge satisfies the conditions in the analysis. The second is to identify criteria of the a priori and to show that some knowledge satisfies the criteria. The third is to argue that radical empiricist theories of knowledge are deficient in some respect and that the only remedy for the deficiency is to embrace the a priori.[1]

---

1. I use "radical empiricism" to refer to the view that *denies* the existence of a priori knowledge, and "apriorism" to refer to the view that *affirms* the existence of such knowledge. Similarly, I use "radical empiricist" to refer to a person or theory

In section 4.2, I examine two conceptual arguments. Hilary Putnam and Hartry Field offer analyses of the a priori and contend that some logical principles are justified a priori. Sections 4.3, 4.4, and 4.5 examine three criterial arguments. The first, following Kant, maintains that necessity is a criterion of the a priori. The second, advanced by A. J. Ayer and Carl Hempel, invokes irrefutability by experience. The third, offered by Bertrand Russell, appeals to certainty. In sections 4.6, 4.7, and 4.8, I address four deficiency arguments presented by Laurence BonJour. My primary contention is that none of these arguments provides a compelling case for the existence of a priori knowledge.

4.2   Conceptual Arguments

Hilary Putnam and Hartry Field adopt the first strategy: both endorse a concept of a priori justification that involves an indefeasibility condition. I argued in chapter 2 that a priori justification does not involve either a strong or a weak indefeasibility condition. Therefore, satisfying such a condition is not necessary for a priori justification. Nevertheless, if their proposed conditions are sufficient for such justification, they can be utilized in defense of the existence of the a priori. Hence, two questions must be addressed. Does either conception provide conditions sufficient for a priori justification? Do any beliefs satisfy the proposed conditions? My primary concern is with the first question.

Putnam maintains that an a priori statement is one "we would never be *rational* to give up."[2] He argues that the minimal principle of contradiction (MPC)—not every statement is both true and false—is rationally unrevisable. His argument is directed against his own earlier contention that no statements are rationally unrevisable.[3] According to his earlier view, traditional proponents of the a priori confused the property of being a priori with the related but different property of being *contextually* a priori. The source of the confusion is a failure to recognize two types of grounds for rational revision. *Direct* grounds for rationally revising some belief that p consist of some observation whose content justifies the belief that not-p. *Theoretical* grounds consist of a set of observations that is better explained by a theory that does not contain the statement that p than by any theory that does contain the statement that p. A statement is contextually a priori just in case it is rationally unrevisable on direct grounds but rationally revisable on theoretical grounds. A statement is a priori just in case it is rationally unrevisable

---

endorsing radical empiricism, and "apriorist" to refer to a person or theory endorsing apriorism.

2. Putnam, "There Is at Least One A Priori Truth," 98.

3. See, for example, Putnam, "The Analytic and the Synthetic."

on any grounds. Traditional proponents of the a priori identified statements that are not rationally revisable on direct grounds and maintained that they are not rationally revisable on any grounds. Putnam, however, argues that the purported a priori statements are rationally revisable on theoretical grounds.

The crux of his present argument is that there are no possible theoretical grounds for rationally revising MPC. How can we rule out the possibility that some future physical theory, perhaps one that we cannot now conceive, might imply the denial of MPC but nevertheless be accepted because it explains a diverse range of phenomena, yields surprising predictions that are subsequently verified, and enhances our understanding of the world? We can do so, according to Putnam, because we know at present that such a theory will have to consist of every statement and its negation. But a theory that excludes nothing is no theory at all. Hence, there are no circumstances under which it would be rational to accept it.

Putnam's proposal is unclear in two important respects. First, he is not explicit on the question of whether a priori justified belief in logical principles, such as MPC, requires supporting evidence and, if so, the nature of that evidence. There are at least three possible readings of his proposed condition on a priori justification:

(A) p is rationally unrevisable and S believes that p.
(B) p is rationally unrevisable and S is justified in believing that p.
(C) p is rationally unrevisable and S is justified in believing
     that p is rationally unrevisable.

Condition (A) is not sufficient for a priori justification; it is compatible with S's having *no* justification for the belief that p. According to (A), anyone who believes that MPC for whatever reason, however whimsical, would thereby be a priori justified in believing that MPC (assuming that MPC is indeed rationally unrevisable). But, as I argued in chapter 2, a priori justification for the belief that p requires nonexperiential justification for that belief.

Condition (B) is also insufficient for a priori justification since it is compatible with S's having *experiential* justification for the belief that p. For example, suppose that Hilary looks at his hand, notes the number of fingers, and on that basis comes to believe that the statement "My hand has five fingers" is true and that the statement is not false. Hilary is justified, on a posteriori grounds, in believing that some statement is not both true and false.

Putnam, however, rejects this contention on the following grounds:

It might turn out that there are not five fingers on my hand. For example, my hand may have been amputated and what I'm looking at may be a plastic substitute. .... But even if it turned out that I don't have a hand, or that my hand has only four fingers, or seven fingers, or whatever, discovering that I was wrong about the observation report would not at all shake my faith in my belief that that observation report is not both true and false.[4]

This argument is not germane. Suppose, for example, that Hilary believes on the basis of looking at his hand that the statement "My hand has five fingers" is true, but when he looks again he discovers that his hand has only four fingers. The subsequent observation that his hand has only four fingers justifies him in believing that the statement "My hand has five fingers" is false and that the statement is not true. Hence, his faith in the belief that the original observation report is not both true and false should remain unshaken since the subsequent observation also justifies that belief. Putnam's point here may be that his recognition that no epistemically possible situation would shake his faith that MPC is true justifies his belief that MPC is true. This reading of his argument leads to (C).

Condition (C) is not sufficient for S's belief that p to be justified a priori since (C) is compatible with S's having *experiential* justification for believing that p is rationally unrevisable. For example, a student may believe that MPC is rationally unrevisable solely on the testimony of a philosophy instructor. But if the student's justification for believing that MPC is true is based on the justified belief that MPC is rationally unrevisable, then if the latter belief is justified a posteriori, the former is also justified a posteriori. Moreover, even if S believes that MPC is rationally unrevisable on the basis of determining the consequences of denying MPC and finding some of those consequences unacceptable, it still does not follow that S's belief that MPC is rationally unrevisable is justified a priori. There are two related problems. First, in determining the consequences of denying MPC one must employ *other* principles of logic. But, in order to be justified a priori in believing that MPC is rationally unrevisable, one must be justified a priori in believing the logical principles one utilizes in deriving the consequences of denying MPC. Putnam, however, cannot appeal to (C) to establish that the logical principles used to derive the consequences of denying MPC are themselves a priori. Such an appeal invites a regress since one must consider the consequences of denying those principles, which will require further principles of logic. Moreover, in order to be justified a priori in believing that MPC is rationally unrevisable, one must be justified a priori in believing a theory that excludes nothing is not a genuine theory. Putnam, however, does not address whether such nonlogical principles are justified a priori.

The second respect in which Putnam's account is unclear is that he does not explicitly distinguish between two types of rational unrevisability: (1) rational unrevisability in light of experiential evidence and (2) rational unrevisability in light of any evidence. He presents his argument in the context of rejecting Quine's contention that all statements are revisable. Although Quine is not explicit on this point, his argument strongly suggests

---

4. Putnam, "There Is at Least One A Priori Truth," 106.

that the view he wishes to defend is that all statements are revisable in light of experiential evidence. Moreover, Putnam's supporting argument for his claim indicates that his goal is to show that MPC is not revisable on the basis of being embedded in a broader theory that provides a better explanation for some range of observations. Yet, when Putnam explicitly states his position, he maintains without any qualification that an a priori statement is one that is rationally unrevisable. Hence, it is not clear whether his position is that MPC is rationally unrevisable or that it is rationally unrevisable on the basis of experiential evidence. Although the point is moot in this context since the stronger condition entails the weaker and I have argued that the stronger is not sufficient for a priori justification, it becomes relevant in assessing the truth of Putnam's claim. For example, Marcus Giaquinto offers a description of possible developments in logic and semantics that he claims would underwrite a rejection of MPC.[5] Although Giaquinto is not explicit on this matter, the investigations he has in mind do not appear to be empirical in character. If this is correct, then although he has presented a scenario that, if cogent, would show that MPC is rationally revisable, it would not show that MPC is rationally revisable in light of experiential evidence.

Hartry Field's goal is more ambitious. He maintains that *all* the principles of classical logic are strongly a priori: "A principle is *weakly a priori* if it can be known or justifiably believed on a basis other than empirical evidence for it; *strongly a priori* if in addition it is empirically indefeasible, that is, if there is no possibility of undercutting our apparent knowledge of it or justified belief in it by empirical evidence."[6] He later qualifies his characterization of the strongly a priori by distinguishing between two types of defeating evidence for a claim: "One is for evidence to be amassed that outweighs the non-empirical basis we had for making the claim; the other is for evidence to be amassed showing that we did not after all have the non-empirical basis we

---

5. Giaquinto, "Non-Analytic Conceptual Knowledge," 252–253, alleges that

we might come to accept the familiar claims that truth is relative to a language or language fragment and that no language fragment can contain its own truth-predicate; we may in addition come to hold that truth is a matter of degree and that there are no maximal degrees of truth and falsehood (having the order-type of an open interval of reals, say). Coming to regard these propositions as having a high degree of truth in some relevant fragment of English, we may also take it that, for any given language fragment L, the sentence of the form "every L-statement is L-true to some degree and L-false to some degree" has a high degree of M-truth, where M is a semantic metalanguage for L. In this situation we should reject the saying that not every statement is both true and false, on the grounds that it fails to be properly specific, there being no reference to a language fragment; and even if the context supplies the missing reference to a language fragment L, we might reject the claim as incompatible with the theory that any instance of the schema "every L-statement is L-true to some degree and L-false to some degree" has a high degree of truth in the relevant metalanguage.

6. Field, "The A Prioricity of Logic," 359.

thought we had for making the claim."[7] Strong a priori justification is incompatible with only the former type of empirical defeating evidence. It is incompatible with empirically justified overriding defeaters but not incompatible with empirically justified undermining defeaters.[8]

Field's defense takes place in the context of a *nonfactualist* view of epistemic justification in general and a priori justification in particular: "It is a matter of policy rather than fact whether logic should be treated as a priori, and the question is only whether it is a good policy."[9] Within this context, there are two salient themes in Field's defense of the view that classical logic is a priori. The first is the role of logic in our evidential systems. The second is the lack of alternatives to the principles of classical logic.

The first emerges in Field's discussion of our actual evidential system. Suppose that Putnam's so-called quantum logic is developed in more detail and that in the near future it is adopted as our best response to quantum anomalies. Would this establish that our *present* evidential system allows the distributive law to be empirically defeated? Field demurs on two grounds. First, if reflection on the quantum anomalies indicates that we have overlooked a conceptual possibility that we should have recognized independently of quantum mechanics, then the revision should not be considered empirically based.[10] Second, and more important, the principles of logic are an essential element of our evidential systems. As a consequence, any shift in the logical principles we endorse is also a shift in our evidential system. If adopting the principles of quantum logic involves adopting a new evidential system, then it is the *new*, rather than our *current*, evidential system that allows the distributive law to be empirically defeated. More generally, Field alleges that

> it is clear that by far the most natural ways to formalize systems of evidence involve building into the system all the central principles of the logic employed by a user of that system of evidence. . . . If we formulate our evidential systems in these ways, it obviously makes no sense to speak of the evidential system as licensing any sort of revision of those logical principles.[11]

---

7. Ibid., 362.

8. In the subsequent discussion of Field, my use of "defeasible," "rationally unrevisable," and their cognates will involve a tacit restriction to *overriding* defeaters.

9. Field, "The A Prioricity of Logic," 377.

10. There are at least two problems with this claim. First, it appears to assume that any conceptual possibility recognized on the basis of empirical considerations can be recognized independently of such considerations. Second, even if we grant that such possibilities can be recognized independently of experience, if they are in fact recognized on the basis of empirical considerations, our justification is empirical. Field offers no support for the claim that they should not be considered as empirically based.

11. Field, "The A Prioricity of Logic," 367–368.

If logical principles are essential components of an evidential system, their revision cannot be licensed by the system.

Suppose that we grant that our evidential systems do not license the revision of logical principles. We are now faced with the evaluative question of whether it is a good policy to adopt an evidential system that does not allow logical principles to be empirically defeated. The primary concern with such a policy is that it is open to the charge of dogmatism; it appears to insulate logical principles from potential disconfirming evidence. Field counters that dogmatism is a concern only if there is evidence to which our logical beliefs should be responsive: "If there is such possible evidence, it is certainly unclear what it is, or how we ought to respond to it. Without some idea as to what a better system of evidence would be, it makes little sense to criticize the one we have."[12] The reason that it is difficult to come up with better evidential systems is that they involve logical principles:

> There is no obvious alternative to an evidential system that adheres to *classical* logic strongly a priori. Many 'alternative logics' have been proposed, such as intuitionistic logic and quantum logic. But if we are to take these as proposals for an all-purpose logic, they are seriously underspecified: no directions have been given for how to use them in daily life.[13]

Hence, according to Field, the only available "all-purpose" logic is classical logic.

The lack of feasible alternatives to classical logic conjoined with nonfactualism yields the conclusion that classical logic is strongly a priori. According to nonfactualism, to determine whether it is good policy to employ an evidential system that treats classical logic as strongly a priori, we compare that evidential system to other currently available evidential systems: "It is a matter of seeing how well it does so *in comparison to other systems we might use instead* . . . a very large part of the reason for regarding classical logic as a priori seems to me to be the apparent lack of minimally decent feasible alternatives—either of the sort that take logic to be empirical, or of the sort that take *some other* logic as a priori."[14] Given that there are no currently available alternatives to an evidential system that treats classical logic as strongly a priori, it is good policy to adopt that system.

In evaluating Field's case, I propose to concede (or, at least, not dispute) his nonfactualism concerning epistemic claims. My primary goal is to show that Field's argument, if cogent, proves too much. If cogent, it establishes that the principles of classical logic are not justified by any evidence and that they are not defeasible in light of any evidence.

Field offers the following sufficient condition for a principle to be weakly a priori justified:

12. Ibid., 369.
13. Ibid., n. 10.
14. Ibid., 378.

(F) It can be justifiably believed on a basis other than empirical evidence for it.

(F) is ambiguous for it does not explicitly indicate whether justification requires a basis in evidence. If it does, then (F) is roughly equivalent to the concept of a priori justification endorsed in chapter 2. If it does not, (F) leaves open the possibility that a weakly a priori principle need not be based on any evidence. Field's view emerges more clearly in the context of his supporting argument for the evaluative claim that it is good policy to have an evidential system that licenses logic weakly a priori:

> In the case of logic, it is completely evident that any decent evidential system must license the use of some logic or other a priori—an evidential system that did not allow deductive reasoning until evidence favouring it was in would have nothing to recommend it, and it is hard to imagine what sort of evidence could ever be gathered by such a system that would allow deductive reasoning to begin when it was initially prohibited.[15]

This argument, if cogent, establishes the general conclusion that if an evidential system requires positive supporting evidence of any kind, empirical or otherwise, for the justification of the principles of deductive logic, then there would be nothing to recommend it. Hence, in Field's view, the basic principles of deductive logic are justified in the absence of *any* supporting evidence.

Let us grant that logical principles are justified in the absence of any positive, supporting evidence. Can this concession be parlayed into a defense of the claim that logical principles are justified a priori? No. To see why, we must first distinguish three distinct positions about the epistemic status of logical principles:

(L1) Logical principles are justified on the basis of *nonexperiential* evidence.

(L2) Logical principles are justified on the basis of *experiential* evidence.

(L3) Logical principles are justified but *not* on the basis of *any* evidence.

I argued in chapter 2 that S's belief that p is justified a priori only if S's belief that p is justified by nonexperiential evidence. It follows from this result that (L3) does not entail that logical principles are justified a priori. More generally, the argument of chapter 2 establishes that Field's so-called weakly a priori justification is not a priori justification at all. It is *too* weak.

The primary dispute between proponents and detractors of the a priori is over basic sources of evidence. Proponents maintain that some are nonexperiential; detractors deny this. Field's account raises a more general issue. Does justification require positive, supporting evidence or are some beliefs

---

15. Ibid., 365.

justified in the absence of any supporting evidence? This issue is independent of the issue of the existence of a priori justification. Although the view
that some beliefs are justified in the absence of any positive, supporting
evidence entails the falsehood of

(1) All beliefs are justified by experiential evidence,

it does not entail

(2) Some beliefs are justified by nonexperiential evidence.

Hence, the view that some beliefs are justified in the absence of any positive, supporting evidence is neutral with respect to the issue of the existence of a priori justification.

Field's argument in support of the conclusion that the principles of classical logic are not rationally revisable on the basis of empirical evidence also
establishes a more general conclusion. Field appeals to two features of such
principles in defending their strongly a priori status: (a) a formalization of
our evidential systems includes the central principles of the logic that we
employ, and (b) there are no current alternatives to our present evidential
system because there are no sufficiently articulated alternatives to classical
logic. The primary consequence of the first observation is that a shift in logic
is best viewed as a shift in our current evidential system. But, if a shift in
logic is best viewed as a shift in our current evidential system, then *any* shift
in logic, regardless of whether it is based on empirical or conceptual considerations, is best viewed as a shift in our current evidential system. If the
fact that a shift in logic is best viewed as a shift in our current evidential
system is sufficient to establish that our current evidential system does not
allow revision of central principles of classical logic on *empirical* grounds,
it is also sufficient to establish that our current evidential system does not
allow revision of central principles of classical logic on *conceptual* grounds.

The second observation yields a similar result. Let us grant Field's
nonfactualism concerning epistemic justification. The primary upshot of
nonfactualism is that the choice to adopt an evidential system is a compara-
tive matter: we compare that system to others we might adopt in its place.
Field's primary argument for the view that classical logic is strongly a priori
is that there are no feasible alternatives to classical logic and, hence, no alternative evidential systems to one that maintains that classical logic is strongly
a priori. But, once again, if the fact that there are no feasible alternatives to
classical logic is sufficient to establish that it is not defeasible by *empirical*
considerations, it is also sufficient to establish that it is not defeasible by
conceptual considerations. As Field notes, proposals about intuitionist logic,
which are based on conceptual considerations, are on a par with proposals
about quantum logic, which are based on empirical considerations. Both are
seriously underspecified. Hence, the upshot is that Field's arguments establish not only that classical logic is not revisable by *empirical* evidence but
also that classical logic is not revisable by *any* evidence. If we conjoin this

result with our previous result, Field's position commits him to the view that the principles of classical logic can neither be justified nor revised in light of any evidence.

Both Putnam and Field attempt to show that some principles of logic are a priori by offering an analysis of the concept of the a priori and arguing that the relevant logical principles satisfy the conditions in the proposed analysis. I distinguish three different interpretations of Putnam's proposed condition on the a priori and argue that none of them is sufficient for a priori justification. I also argue that Field's account leads to the consequence that logical principles are neither justifiable nor defeasible by any evidence. Although this view, if correct, would show that such principles are not empirically justified, it fails to show that they are justified a priori. So both attempts fall short of their goal.

4.3   Criterial Arguments: Necessity

Criterial arguments for the existence of a priori knowledge have a common structure. They identify some feature of propositions that we purportedly know and allege that we cannot know a posteriori propositions having that feature, from which it follows that knowledge of such propositions must be a priori. Criterial arguments differ from conceptual arguments since they do not claim that the feature alleged to be sufficient for a priori knowledge is included in the analysis of the concept of a priori knowledge.

Kant provides the best known and most influential criterial argument. He maintains that necessity is a *criterion* of the a priori: "If we have a proposition which in being thought is thought as *necessary*, it is an *a priori* judgment."[16] This claim is based on the observation, "Experience teaches us that a thing is so and so, but not that it cannot be otherwise."[17] Kant goes on to argue that "mathematical propositions, strictly so called, are always judgments *a priori*, not empirical; because they carry with them necessity, which cannot be derived from experience."[18] Hence, he concludes, knowledge of mathematical propositions is a priori.

Kant's argument, the *Argument from Necessity*, can be presented as follows:

(1) Mathematical propositions are necessary.
(2) One cannot know a necessary proposition on the basis of experience.
(3) Therefore, one cannot know mathematical propositions on the basis of experience.

16. Kant, *Critique of Pure Reason*, 43. Kant's claim is echoed by Russell, *The Problems of Philosophy*, chap. 7, and by Chisholm, *Theory of Knowledge*, 2nd ed., chap. 3.
17. Kant, *Critique of Pure Reason*, 43.
18. Ibid., 52.

The first premise is controversial. Some question the cogency of the concept of necessary truth. Others maintain that modal sentences do not express truths or falsehoods. For our purposes, I propose to grant that (1) expresses a truth in order to address the epistemic issues that it raises.

The phrase "know a necessary proposition" in (2) is ambiguous. Let me introduce the following distinctions:

(A) S knows the *general modal status* of p just in case S knows that p is a necessary proposition or S knows that p is a contingent proposition.

(B) S knows the *truth value* of p just in case S knows that p is true or S knows that p is false.

(C) S knows the *specific modal status* of p just in case S knows that p is necessarily true or S knows that p is necessarily false or S knows that p is contingently true or S knows that p is contingently false.

(A) and (B) are logically independent. One can know that p is a mathematical proposition and that all mathematical propositions are necessary but not know whether p is true or false. Goldbach's conjecture—every even number greater then two is the sum of two prime numbers—provides an example. Alternatively, one can know that some mathematical proposition is true but not know whether it is a necessary or contingent truth. (C), however, is not independent of (A) and (B). One cannot know the specific modal status of a proposition unless one knows both its general modal status and its truth value.

Utilizing these distinctions, we can now see that the Argument from Necessity breaks down into two distinct arguments. The first, the *Kantian Argument*, goes as follows:

(1) Mathematical propositions are necessary.

(2*) One cannot know the *general modal status* of a necessary proposition on the basis of experience.

(3*) Therefore, one cannot know the *truth value* of mathematical propositions on the basis of experience.

Kant argues in this fashion. He admits that experience can provide evidence that a thing is so and so, or, more perspicuously, that it is the case. What he denies is that experience can provide evidence that something *must* be the case, or, more perspicuously, that it is necessary. (2*) articulates this reading. Kant concludes, on this basis, that knowledge that 7 + 5 = 12 (not knowledge that "7 + 5 = 12" is necessary) is a priori.[19]

19. Katz, "What Mathematical Knowledge Could Be," 504–505, provides a more recent example of the Kantian argument. He maintains that the idea of basing knowledge of abstract objects on perceptual contact is "misguided": "They [abstract objects] couldn't be otherwise than they are." However, "perceptual contact cannot provide information about how something must be." The argument shows at most that perceptual contact cannot provide information about the general modal status of propositions about abstract objects. It does not preclude the possibility of perceptual knowledge of their truth value.

The Kantian Argument involves the following assumption:

(4) If the general modal status of p is knowable only a priori,
then the truth value of p is knowable only a priori.

However, (4) is false. Consider a contingent proposition such as that this cup is white. If one can know only a priori that a proposition is necessary, then one can know only a priori that a proposition is contingent. The evidence relevant to determining the latter is the same as that relevant to determining the former. For example, if I determine that "$2 + 2 = 4$" is necessary by trying to conceive of its falsehood and failing, I determine that "This cup is white" is contingent by trying to conceive of its falsehood and succeeding. But if my knowledge that "This cup is white" is contingent is a priori, it does not follow that my knowledge that this cup is white is a priori. On the contrary, it is a posteriori. Hence, (4) must be rejected.

Proponents of the argument might retreat at this point to a weaker version of (4):

(4*) If p is a necessary proposition and if the general modal
status of p is knowable only a priori, then the truth value of
p is knowable only a priori.

There are, however, plausible counterexamples to (4*). If Kripke is correct about the semantics of proper names, then true identity statements involving different proper names are necessary truths.[20] Knowledge that such propositions are necessary is based on thought experiments: the inability to conceive that some object is different from itself. But knowledge that they are true is based on experience: astronomical observations in the case of Hesperus and Phosphorus. Another familiar example arises when one comes to believe, and apparently know, mathematical propositions on the basis of the testimony of a teacher or the authority of a textbook.[21] Given the argument against the more general (4), the apparent counterexamples to (4*), and the lack of any supporting argument for (4*), (4*) cannot carry the burden of the Kantian argument.

The second version of the Argument from Necessity, the *Modal Argument*, proceeds as follows:

(1)   Mathematical propositions are necessary.
(2*) One cannot know the *general modal status* of a necessary
proposition on the basis of experience.
(3**) Therefore, one cannot know the *general modal status* of
mathematical propositions on the basis of experience.

The Modal Argument is less ambitious than the Kantian Argument and, as a consequence, is not open to the objection raised against the latter.

---

20. Kripke, "Identity and Necessity" and *Naming and Necessity*. Kripke's views are addressed in chapter 7.
21. Burge, "Content Preservation," disputes this claim.

The less ambitious character of the Modal Argument raises a significant issue about the scope of a priori knowledge. If the Modal Argument is the only argument that supports the existence of a priori knowledge, then such knowledge is limited to an esoteric branch of metaphysics that classifies propositions as either necessary or contingent. There is no a priori knowledge of the truth value of nonmodal propositions. Traditional proponents of the a priori, including Kant himself, believed that more was at stake in the controversy over the a priori than this bit of metaphysical knowledge. They believed that important domains of nonphilosophical knowledge are a priori. More specifically, returning to the case at hand, they maintained that mathematical knowledge is significantly different from scientific knowledge. The Modal Argument is too weak to establish that mathematical knowledge differs from scientific knowledge. If sound, it establishes that knowledge of the general modal status of both mathematical and scientific propositions is a priori and is compatible with the view that knowledge of the truth value of both is a posteriori.

Nevertheless, since it is incompatible with the more general thesis that all knowledge is a posteriori, the Modal Argument merits careful scrutiny. What can be said in support of (2*)? The standard move is to invoke the Kantian claim that experience can teach us only what is the case or its Leibnizian counterpart to the effect that experience can provide knowledge of only the actual world but not of other possible worlds.[22] If this claim is granted, then (2*) is plausible. But a good deal of our ordinary practical knowledge and the bulk of our scientific knowledge provide clear counterexamples to the claim. My knowledge that my pen will fall if I drop it does not provide me with information about what is the case because the antecedent is contrary to fact. It provides me with information about some possible worlds other than the actual world. Scientific laws are not mere descriptions of the actual world. They support counterfactual conditionals and, hence, provide information beyond what is true of the actual world. In the absence of further support for premise (2*), the Modal Argument should also be rejected.

4.4   Criterial Arguments: Irrefutability

In defending the existence of a priori knowledge, Kant draws attention to the alleged necessity of mathematical propositions. Proponents of logical empiricism, who were reacting against John Stuart Mill's contention that we know mathematical propositions, such as that $3 + 2 = 5$, on the basis of inductive generalization from observed cases, draw attention to a different

---

22. See, for example, Chisholm, *Theory of Knowledge*, 2nd ed., 37; and McGinn "*A Priori* and *A Posteriori* Knowledge," 204. Kitcher, "Apriority and Necessity," 100–101, also maintains that the plausibility of the Modal Argument depends on this claim. He rejects the argument for reasons different from mine.

feature of mathematical propositions: their alleged irrefutability by experience. Carl Hempel puts the point as follows:

> Consider now a simple "hypothesis" from arithmetic: $3 + 2 = 5$. If this is actually an empirical generalization of past experiences, then it must be possible to state what kind of evidence would oblige us to concede the hypothesis was not generally true after all. If any disconfirming evidence for the given proposition can be thought of, the following illustration might well be typical of it: We place some microbes on a slide, putting down first three of them and then another two. Afterwards we count all the microbes to test whether in this instance 3 and 2 actually added up to 5. Suppose now that we counted 6 microbes altogether. Would we consider this as an empirical disconfirmation of the given proposition, or at least as a proof that it does not apply to microbes? Clearly not; rather, we would assume we had made a mistake in counting or that one of the microbes had split in two between the first and the second count.[23]

Since Hempel maintains that we would not regard any experiential evidence as disconfirming a mathematical proposition, he concludes that such propositions are not confirmed by experience.

Hempel's argument, the *Irrefutability Argument*, can be stated as follows:

(1) No experiential evidence can disconfirm mathematical propositions.

(2) If experiential evidence cannot disconfirm mathematical propositions, then it cannot confirm such propositions.

(3) Therefore, experiential evidence cannot confirm mathematical propositions.

This argument is valid and the second premise is uncontroversial. Premise (1), however, is not obviously true. Moreover, Hempel's defense of (1) is not very strong. He considers only the weakest possible case of potential experiential disconfirming evidence.

To bring out this point more clearly, let us first note two familiar features of inductive practice: (a) our assessments of the degree to which a particular case confirms or disconfirms a generalization is a function of the total available evidence, and (b) apparent disconfirming cases of a generalization can always be explained away in a fashion that leaves the original hypothesis unaffected. Hempel's defense of (1) is weak in several respects. First, it does not take into account the number of apparent confirming instances of the proposition in question. Second, it involves only a single disconfirming instance of the proposition. Third, the hypotheses that are invoked to explain away the apparent disconfirming instance are not subjected to independent empirical test. In a situation in which there is a strong background

---

23. Hempel, "On the Nature of Mathematical Truth," 36. Ayer, *Language, Truth and Logic*, 75–76, offers a similar argument.

of supporting evidence for a generalization and an isolated disconfirming instance, it is reasonable to discount the disconfirming instance as apparent and to explain it away on whatever empirical grounds are most plausible.

The case against premise (1) can be considerably strengthened by revising Hempel's scenario as follows: (a) increase the number of disconfirming instances of the proposition so that it is large relative to the number of confirming instances; and (b) subject the hypotheses invoked to explain away the apparent disconfirming instances to independent tests that fail to support them. Let us now suppose that we have experienced a very large number of apparent disconfirming instances of the proposition that $3 + 2 = 5$ and, furthermore, that empirical investigations of the hypotheses invoked to explain away these disconfirming instances produce very little, if any, support for the hypotheses. Given these revisions, the proponent of the Irrefutability Argument can continue to endorse premise (1) only at the expense of either divorcing mathematics from its empirical applications or holding empirical beliefs that are at odds with the available evidence.

This point can be brought out more clearly by considering the following set of propositions:

(a) The mathematical proposition that $3 + 2 = 5$ is applicable to microbes.

(b) The empirical procedure of counting microbes provides *only apparent* disconfirming evidence for the proposition that $3 + 2 = 5$.

(c) The results of independent empirical investigation do not support the auxiliary hypotheses introduced to explain away the disconfirming evidence as only apparent.

Although (c) does not entail not-(b), it does provide strong grounds for rejecting (b). Clearly, the proponent of the Irrefutability Argument cannot simply assert (b), for to simply assert (b) without independent support is to beg the question against the radical empiricist. But (c) establishes that the independent reasons offered in support of (b) are unfounded. Hence, (b) must be rejected. The proponent of the Irrefutability Argument, however, cannot accept both (a) and not-(b). If the disconfirming evidence provided by the procedure of counting microbes is not merely apparent, then it is genuine. So only two alternatives remain: either (i) reject (a) and hold that mathematics is not applicable to microbes, or (ii) continue to hold (b) despite (c). Neither alternative is palatable since (i) effectively divorces mathematics from its empirical applications, and (ii) puts one in a position of holding a belief that is counter to one's available evidence. The most plausible alternative is to accept (a) and reject (b). But to reject (b) is to reject premise (1) of the Irrefutability Argument. Hence, the argument falls short of its mark.

One might attempt to defend Hempel at this point by maintaining that he has a stronger argument for (1) that has been overlooked, for the passage quoted above continues in the following manner:

But under no circumstances could the phenomenon just described invalidate the arithmetical proposition in question; for the latter asserts nothing whatever about the behavior of microbes; it merely states that any set consisting of 3 + 2 objects may also be said to consist of 5 objects. And this is so because the symbols "3 + 2" and "5" denote the same number: they are synonymous by virtue of the fact that the symbols "2," "3," "5," and "+" are *defined* (or tacitly understood) in such a way that the above identity holds as a consequence of the meaning attached to the concepts involved in it.[24]

This passage is difficult to interpret but the structure of the argument appears to be as follows:

(4) The identity "3 + 2 = 5" holds as a consequence of the meaning attached to the symbols involved in it.

(5) Therefore, "3 + 2 = 5" asserts nothing whatever about the results of counting microbes.

(6) Therefore, the results of counting microbes cannot invalidate the arithmetical proposition that 3 + 2 = 5.

(6) provides direct support for (1).

The proposed defense faces two problems. First, Hempel endorses

(a) The mathematical proposition that 3 + 2 = 5 is applicable to microbes.

Therefore, in order to maintain that the results of counting microbes cannot invalidate that 3 + 2 = 5, he must also endorse

(b) The empirical procedure of counting microbes provides *only apparent* disconfirming evidence for the proposition that 3 + 2 = 5.

Hence, the proposed defense leaves Hempel faced with the same dilemma posed earlier: either hold that mathematics is not applicable to microbes or continue to endorse (b) despite evidence to the contrary. Second, the proposed defense significantly alters the structure of Hempel's argument. The argument, as originally formulated, does not invoke the *semantic* thesis that mathematical propositions are analytic to support the *epistemic* thesis that mathematical propositions are knowable only a priori. But (4), which is the leading premise of the proposed defense, is a version of the *semantic* thesis that "3 + 2 = 5" is an analytic proposition. Hence, to invoke (4) in support of (1) is to offer a version of the *Analyticity Argument*:

(7) Mathematical propositions are analytic.

(8) Therefore, mathematical propositions are not knowable on the basis of experience.

Such arguments are addressed in chapter 8.

24. Hempel, "On the Nature of Mathematical Truth," 36.

4.5   Criterial Arguments: Certainty

The third criterial argument is also directed against the view that mathematical propositions are known on the basis of inductive generalization from observed cases. The leading premise of the argument is that some mathematical propositions, simple and obvious truths such as that 2 + 2 = 4, are known with certainty. The conclusions of inductive generalizations, however, are never known with certainty. Even in the case of the best confirmed inductive generalizations, one cannot be certain that a disconfirming instance is not forthcoming. Hence, mathematical propositions are not known on the basis of experience.

The *Argument from Certainty*, in its simplest form, can be stated as follows:

(1) Some mathematical propositions are known with certainty.
(2) No proposition known on the basis of induction is known with certainty.
(3) Therefore, some mathematical propositions are not known on the basis of induction.[25]

Assessing this argument is difficult since there are many different epistemological senses of certainty. To determine whether any satisfies premises (1) and (2), let us adopt Roderick Firth's framework, which holds that such senses fall into three classes: (a) truth-evaluating, (b) warrant-evaluating, and (c) testability-evaluating.[26]

The characteristic feature of truth-evaluating senses of certainty is that

(C*) p is certain for S

entails that p is true. The classic example of such a sense is provided by the notion of incorrigibility:

(A) p is certain for S just in case, necessarily, if S believes that p then p is true.

(A) is satisfied by familiar Cartesian propositions such as "I exist" and "I believe something," which is a welcome result since they are typically regarded as certain. However, (A) is also satisfied by *any* necessary truth. This leads to two unwelcome consequences. First, it entails that all mathematical knowledge is certain. But it is implausible to hold that if S knows some mathematical proposition that p on the basis of a complex proof or on the basis of the authority of a textbook, then p is certain for S. Second, it entails that premise (2) is false since if S knows some necessary truth that p on the

25. Russell, *The Problems of Philosophy*, chap. 7, offers a version of this argument. Kim endorses it in "The Role of Perception in A Priori Knowledge: Some Remarks." Kant, *Critique of Pure Reason*, 44, may have had this argument in mind when he claimed that strict universality is a criterion of the a priori.
26. Firth, "The Anatomy of Certainty."

basis of inductive evidence, p is certain for S. Hence, (A) is of no avail to proponents of the Argument from Certainty.

There is, however, a truth-evaluating sense of certainty, inspired by reliabilism, that is significantly applicable to necessary propositions. The reliability of a belief-forming process is a function of its tendency to produce true beliefs over a range of possible circumstances. Reliability comes in degrees. The maximal degree, *ultra-reliability*, can be defined as follows:

> (U) M is an ultra-reliable belief-forming process just in case, necessarily, for any belief that p, if M produces the belief that p, then p is true.

We can utilize (U) to introduce a second truth-evaluating sense of certainty:

> (B) p is certain for S just in case p is produced in S by an ultra-reliable belief-forming process.[27]

(B) is significantly applicable to necessary propositions. For example, assume that "2 + 2 = 4" is necessarily true and that S's belief that 2 + 2 = 4 is produced by a process P. It does not follow that S's belief is certain in sense (B). For S's belief to be certain, *all* beliefs produced by P must be true. Therefore, it is not a trivial consequence of the fact that p is necessarily true that p is certain in sense (B).

Despite its attractions, (B) has a significant shortcoming: in this sense of certainty, premise (1) is false. It is a common feature of mathematical practice that beliefs are rationally revised. Mathematical propositions accepted as true at one time are later rejected as false. One might maintain that such belief revision is incompatible with (1) only on the assumption that all mathematical belief-forming processes are ultra-reliable. If there are many mathematical belief-forming processes, only some of which are ultra-reliable, it remains possible that the false beliefs in question are not produced by these latter processes. This possibility, however, appears to be remote. The two most familiar examples of a priori belief-forming processes are constructing proofs and intuitive self-evidence. But there are plausible examples of revision of beliefs based on each. Everyone commits errors in constructing proofs and adjusts one's beliefs when the error is discovered. And there are many cases of principles once regarded as intuitively self-evident but which are now either rejected or in dispute. Familiar examples are the parallel postulate of Euclidean geometry and the principle that the whole is greater than any of its proper parts. One could insist, in the face of such examples, that the processes involved in producing the false beliefs are different from those producing the true beliefs. But, in the absence of some independent supporting evidence, the response is ad hoc.

---

27. This sense of certainty is suggested by Kitcher, *The Nature of Mathematical Knowledge*, chap. 1.

The defining characteristic of warrant-evaluating senses of certainty is that (C*) entails (i) p has a specifiable degree of warrant for S, and (ii) that degree of warrant is identified by reference to some standard that is logically independent of the warrant that S has for p. This sense of certainty admits of a broad degree of variation. To have a particular example for scrutiny, let us consider the definition offered by R. M. Chisholm:

(C) h is *certain* for S = Df h is beyond reasonable doubt for S,
      and there is no i such that accepting i is more reasonable for
      S than accepting h.[28]

(C) poses a dilemma for the proponent of the Argument from Certainty. Let h be the proposition that $2 + 2 = 4$ and assume that h is beyond reasonable doubt for S. Let i be the proposition that S would express by the sentence "I exist." Is accepting that $2 + 2 = 4$ as reasonable as accepting that one exists? Chisholm's position is difficult to assess since "more reasonable than" is one of his primitive expressions. The axioms he offers for this expression are formal and provide limited information about how to assess particular cases. It is plausible to maintain that accepting the proposition that one exists is more reasonable than accepting any mathematical proposition, for if one considers the two propositions, one is immediately aware that, in order to accept any mathematical proposition, one must exist. If it is more reasonable to accept that one exists than to accept any mathematical proposition, then premise (1) of the argument is false. On the other hand, if accepting $2 + 2 = 4$ is as reasonable as accepting that one exists, premise (2) of the argument is false. If "$2 + 2 = 4$" is beyond reasonable doubt for S and S accepts that $2 + 2 = 4$ on the basis of induction, then $2 + 2 = 4$ is certain for S. Consequently, (C) does not advance the case for the Argument from Certainty.

Finally, let us look at testability-evaluating senses of certainty. The characteristic feature of these senses is that (C*) entails something about the possibility of confirming or disconfirming p that is not entailed by a statement to the effect that p has a specifiable degree of warrant for S. Firth offers the following example:

(D) p is certain for S at t if and only if there is no imaginable
      event such that if S were justified at t in believing that it
      will occur after t, not-p would therefore become warranted
      for S at t.[29]

In sense (D), the Argument from Certainty collapses into the Irrefutability Argument. The burden of the argument rests on the claim that although there are imaginable future events that would justify S in believing that the conclusion of any inductive generalization is false, there are no such events that

28. Chisholm, *Theory of Knowledge*, 2nd ed., 10.
29. Firth, "The Anatomy of Certainty," 214, maintains that this sense is employed by Malcolm in "Knowledge and Belief."

would justify S in believing that some simple mathematical propositions are false. But, if the argument of section 4.4 is correct, then this claim is false. Hence, mathematical propositions do not satisfy (D).

We have not yet identified a sense of certainty that satisfies both premises of the Argument from Certainty. What, then, is the source of the initial intuitive plausibility of this argument? It comes, I believe, from a consideration of the nature of mathematical proof. Consider the Goldbach conjecture. Suppose that we initially verify the conjecture on the basis of examining a sampling of even numbers. Encouraged by these confirming instances, we then program a computer to examine a large number of even numbers, say 10^{10}. Finally, on the basis of the fact that the computer does not uncover any disconfirming instances, we infer that the conjecture is true. Despite our reasonable assurance at this point, we are not absolutely certain that the conjecture is true. We recognize that, for all we know, there remains the possibility of a disconfirming instance. On the other hand, if someone were to construct a general proof of the conjecture, this uncertainty would be removed. We can define this sense of certainty as follows:

(E) p is certain for S just in case (i) there is a set of propositions q such that S knows each member of q, (ii) S knows that q entails p, and (iii) S's belief that p is based on (i) and (ii).

Can (E) be utilized to advance the case for the Argument from Certainty? It appears doubtful. Since (E) is applicable only to mathematical propositions known on the basis of a proof, it does not underwrite premise (1) of the argument, which claims that simple and obvious mathematical propositions, such as that 2 + 2 = 4, are known with certainty. Furthermore, from the fact that p satisfies (E), it does *not* follow that p is known a priori, for if q contains any members that are known a posteriori, then S's knowledge that p is also a posteriori. Therefore, (E) is of little consequence unless it is supplemented by another sense of certainty applicable to the premises of mathematical proofs. My prior results indicate that such a sense is not available.

The criterial arguments in support of the existence of a priori knowledge fail. The Argument from Necessity breaks down into two arguments: the Kantian Argument and the Modal Argument. I argue that the former is invalid and that the latter is unsound. In the case of the Irrefutability Argument, I reject its leading premise, which maintains that empirical evidence cannot disconfirm mathematical propositions. Finally, I articulate five senses of certainty and argue that none satisfies both premises of the Argument from Certainty.

4.6   Deficiency Arguments

Deficiency arguments draw attention to alleged shortcomings of radical empiricist theories and claim that theories embracing the a priori avoid those shortcomings. Laurence BonJour's recent defense of the a priori consists of four arguments that purport to establish that radical empiricism leads to a number of undesirable consequences that are circumvented by the moderate rationalist epistemology he endorses. The first is general and directed toward all forms of radical empiricism. The other three have more specific targets: two are directed against coherentist versions, and one against externalist versions, of radical empiricism.

Deficiency arguments provide a basis for preferring theories that embrace the a priori over their radical empiricist counterparts only if the former theories avoid the undesirable consequences alleged to plague the latter. My goal is to argue that moderate rationalism is open to each of BonJour's four deficiency arguments and that, as a consequence, none provides a basis for preferring moderate rationalism over radical empiricism. The general argument is discussed in this section. The arguments against coherentist radical empiricism are addressed in section 4.7. Foundationalist versions of radical empiricism, both internalist and externalist, are explored in section 4.8.

BonJour's first argument charges that radical empiricism leads to skepticism. The supporting argument, called the *Skeptical Argument*, is straightforward. Assume that some beliefs are directly justified solely by experience. Such beliefs are "particular rather than general in their content and are confined to situations observable at specific and fairly narrowly delineated places and times."[30] Either some beliefs whose content goes beyond direct experience are justified or skepticism is true. The justification of beliefs whose content goes beyond direct experience requires inference from the directly justified beliefs. But inference involves principles that are justified a priori: "For if the conclusions of the inferences genuinely go beyond the content of direct experience, then it is impossible that those inferences could be entirely justified by appeal to that same experience."[31] Hence, either radical empiricism is false or skepticism is true.

The Skeptical Argument, however, proves too much. The very same argument can be marshaled against moderate rationalism. Assume that some beliefs are directly justified by rational insight. Either some beliefs whose content goes beyond direct rational insight are justified or skepticism is true. The justification of beliefs whose content goes beyond direct rational insight requires principles of inference that are justified a posteriori: For if the conclusions of the inferences genuinely go beyond the content of direct rational insight, then it is impossible that those inferences could be entirely justified by appeal to that same insight. Hence, either moderate rationalism is false or skepticism is true.

No moderate rationalist would take this argument seriously. The obvious reply is that a belief directly justified by some rational insight R, in conjunction with a belief in a general principle directly justified by some other rational insight R^*, can indirectly justify a belief whose content goes

---

30. BonJour, *In Defense of Pure Reason*, 4.
31. Ibid.

beyond that of the directly justified beliefs. The same response, however, is open to radical empiricists. They can maintain that a belief directly justified by some experience *E*, in conjunction with a belief in a general principle directly justified by some other experience *E**, can indirectly justify a belief whose content goes beyond that of the directly justified beliefs. Hence, for the Skeptical Argument to succeed, BonJour must show that experience cannot directly justify principles of inference.

Although he is not explicit on this point, the underlying argument appears to turn on three claims. The first is a thesis about the nature of experience: it is limited to *particular* objects in close spatiotemporal proximity. The second is an epistemic thesis: no experience can directly justify a belief whose content goes beyond that of the experience. The third is a thesis about principles of inference: they are *general* in character. Putting these claims together yields the following argument, called the *Generality Argument*:

(1) Experience is limited to *particular* objects.
(2) No experience can directly justify a belief whose content goes beyond that of the experience.
(3) Principles of inference are *general*.
(4) Therefore, experience cannot directly justify principles of inference.

The question we must now address is whether moderate rationalism is also vulnerable to the Generality Argument.

Premise (2) of the argument appears to be a consequence of a more general epistemic principle:

(2*) No cognitive state can directly justify a belief whose content goes beyond that of the state.

Premise (3) is also general. Indirect a priori justification, as well as indirect empirical justification, requires *general* principles of inference. Hence, if rational insight is limited to particular objects, the Generality Argument also establishes that rational insight cannot directly justify principles of inference.

Moderate rationalists claim that experience and thought differ in a fundamental respect: although we can experience only particular objects, we can apprehend the properties of objects.[32] Hence, they can avoid the skeptical consequences of the Generality Argument only if they can sustain the claim that we apprehend abstract entities such as properties. To sustain this claim, moderate rationalists must offer a nonmetaphorical characterization of this alleged cognitive capacity. Characterizations in terms of expressions

32. BonJour, ibid., 162, articulates the view as follows: "A person apprehends or grasps, for example, the properties redness and greenness, and supposedly 'sees' on the basis of this apprehension that they cannot be jointly instantiated. Such a picture clearly seems to presuppose that as a result of this apprehension or grasping, the properties of redness and greenness are themselves before the mind in a way that allows their natures and mutual incompatibility to be apparent."

such as "apprehend" and "insight" suggest an analogy to perception. Perception, however, requires causal contact with the object perceived, and properties cannot stand in causal relations. Moderate rationalists allege that the perceptual metaphor is misleading. But, in the absence of a nonmetaphorical characterization, they are not in a position to state, let alone defend, the claim that we apprehend general features of objects.

BonJour maintains that the apprehension of properties necessary for a priori justification is the same as that involved in thought in general. His goal is to explain the apprehension of properties in terms of a more general theory of how a thought can be about, or have as its content, some particular property. If the more general theory is to successfully underwrite the contention that the apprehension of properties does not involve a quasi-perceptual relation to those properties, it must explain, without appeal to such relations, how a thought can have as its content some particular property. BonJour proposes that a thought has as its content some particular property in virtue of its *intrinsic* character: "In order for the intrinsic character of the thought to specify precisely *that* particular property to the exclusion of anything else, the property in question must *itself* somehow be metaphysically involved in that character."[33]

Yet, a thought about, for example, the property triangularity cannot literally instantiate that property since the thought is not itself triangular. BonJour refines the proposal by maintaining that such a thought instantiates a complex universal that involves triangularity as a constituent: "The key claim of such a view would be that it is a necessary, quasi-logical fact that a thought instantiating a complex universal involving the universal triangularity in the appropriate way . . . is about triangular *things*."[34] The refinement is suggestive but incomplete in a crucial respect. The complex universal of which triangularity is a constituent cannot be a conjunctive universal since that would have the consequence that a thought instantiating the complex universal is triangular. BonJour, however, does not offer an alternative account of the structure of such complex universals. The refined proposal also faces a second, more serious problem. It provides an account of how a thought can have as its content *particular* triangular *things*, rather than an account of how a thought can have as its content the *property* triangularity. Hence, it does not provide the basis of a nonrelational account of the apprehension of properties.

Let us take stock. Moderate rationalism can avoid the skeptical consequences of the Generality Argument only if it can sustain the claim that we can apprehend properties. Moderate rationalism can sustain this claim only if it can provide a nonmetaphorical account of the apprehension of properties that does not involve some kind of quasi-perceptual relation to those

33. Ibid., 182.
34. Ibid., 184 (emphasis mine).

properties. BonJour proposes to explain the apprehension of properties in terms of an account of how a thought can have as its content some particular *property*, such as triangularity, but he provides only the bare outline of an account of how a thought can have as its content *particular* triangular *objects*. Since he does not provide an account of how a thought can have as its content some property, he fails to provide any account, let alone a nonrelational account, of the apprehension of properties. Hence, BonJour's moderate rationalism does not avoid the skeptical consequences of the Generality Argument.

Moderate rationalists are faced with a dilemma. Either (a) they can concede that the apprehension of *particular objects* instantiating properties, rather than the apprehension of the *properties themselves*, directly justifies general principles, or (b) they can insist that only the apprehension of the *properties themselves* directly justifies general principles. If they opt for (a), then they must reject (2*). If they reject (2*), then, in the absence of some further argument, their endorsement of premise (2) of the Generality Argument is ad hoc. Moderate rationalists cannot, without further argument, concede that the apprehension of particular objects instantiating properties, rather than the apprehension of the properties themselves, can directly justify general principles but deny that the experience of particular objects instantiating properties can directly justify general principles. If moderate rationalists opt for (b), they must acknowledge that although BonJour has taken an important first step toward providing an account of the apprehension of properties, the account is incomplete.[35] Since moderate rationalism has not offered a nonmetaphorical account of the apprehension of properties, it cannot underwrite the key claim that the content of thought is not limited to particular objects and, as a consequence, is also open to the Generality Argument. Therefore, moderate rationalism fares no better than radical empiricism with respect to the Generality Argument.

4.7   Coherentist Radical Empiricism

BonJour's second two arguments are directed toward W. V. Quine's version of radical empiricism. Quine rejects foundationalism in favor of coherentism. BonJour alleges that coherentist radical empiricism is open to two serious objections.[36] In this section, I argue that moderate rationalism is also vulnerable to both objections.

---

35. BonJour, ibid., 185, appears to embrace this horn of the dilemma: "It is clear that the distinction between thinking about an instance of a property and thinking about the property itself, between thinking about a triangular thing and thinking about triangularity, would have to be somehow accounted for."

36. BonJour offers a third argument against the naturalized version of coherentist radical empiricism. I don't consider this argument since, as he acknowledges, coherentist radical empiricism and naturalism are independent positions.

The first maintains that in order for a person to be justified in believing that p, the person must be in possession of a reason for thinking that p is likely to be true. According to coherentist radical empiricism, a system of beliefs that satisfies standards such as simplicity, scope, fecundity, explanatory adequacy, and conservatism is justified. But, asks BonJour, "What reason can be offered for thinking that a system of beliefs which is simpler, more conservative, explanatorily more adequate, etc., is thereby more likely to be true, that following such standards is at least somewhat conducive to finding the truth?"[37] Coherentist radical empiricists are faced with a dilemma. They must offer either an a priori argument or an empirical argument in support of the truth conduciveness of the standards. The former is incompatible with radical empiricism. The latter is question begging since it must ultimately appeal to some of the standards it is attempting to justify.

The first objection turns on the claim that being epistemically justified in believing that p requires having a reason for thinking that p is likely to be true. The expression "having a reason to think that p is likely to be true" is ambiguous. Let us distinguish between two senses:

(B) S has a *basic* reason R to believe that p if and only if S has R and R makes it likely that p is true.

(M) S has a *meta*reason R to believe that p if and only if S has R and S has reason to believe that R makes it likely that p is true.

Let Φ be the set of conditions that, according to coherentist radical empiricism, constitutes coherence. Assume that belonging to a system of beliefs satisfying Φ makes it likely that p is true. If S cognitively grasps the fact that p belongs to such a system, then S has a *basic* reason to believe that p. BonJour's charge is that coherentist radical empiricists cannot offer an argument to show that such reasons are truth conducive. Hence, the problem pertains to having a *meta*reason to believe that p.

Does moderate rationalism fare any better on this score? Assume that having an apparent rational insight that p makes it likely that p is true. Hence, if S has an apparent rational insight that p, then S has a *basic* reason to believe that p. Moderate rationalists are now faced with the question, What reason can be offered for thinking that a belief based on apparent rational insight is thereby more likely to be true? An a priori argument is circular since it is based on rational insight, and an empirical argument undercuts the a priori status of justification based on rational insight.[38]

BonJour recognizes the problem. His response is to argue that a priori justification does *not* require a metareason. The requirement is question begging because moderate rationalism maintains that apparent rational in-

37. BonJour, *In Defense of Pure Reason*, 91.
38. BonJour's contention that an empirical argument undercuts the a priori status of justification based on rational insight is addressed in section 6.4.

sight is an excellent reason, in its own right, for accepting a belief: "[It] amounts simply and obviously to a refusal to take rational insight seriously as a basis for justification: a refusal for which the present objection can offer no further rationale, and which is thus question-begging."[39] Therefore, a priori justified belief that *p* only requires having a basic reason for that belief.

Coherentist radical empiricists, however, can offer a similar response. According to coherentist radical empiricism, *p*'s belonging to a system satisfying Φ is a basic reason to believe that *p*. BonJour does not dispute this claim. Instead, he moves directly to a demand for a metareason. But such a demand presupposes that belonging to a system of beliefs satisfying Φ is not an excellent reason, in its own right, for accepting a belief, which begs the question against coherentist radical empiricism.[40] Hence, coherentist radical empiricism fares no worse than moderate rationalism with respect to the demand for metareasons.[41]

BonJour's second objection to coherentist radical empiricism is that its standards for belief revision do not impose any constraints on epistemic justification: "After all, any such standard, since it cannot on Quinean grounds be justified or shown to be epistemically relevant independently of considerations of adjustment to experience, is itself merely one more strand (or node?) in the web, and thus equally open to revision."[42] Hence, whenever those standards appear to dictate that some belief should be revised, such revision can be avoided by revising the standards themselves. The response that such revision is not reasonable or justified cannot be sustained: "To appeal to the very standards themselves, for example, to the principle of conservatism in order to defend the reluctance to revise the principle of conservatism, is obviously circular; while any further standard, even a meta-standard having to do with the revision of first-level standards, will itself be equally open to revision."[43] Therefore, coherentist radical empiricists lack a rationale for not revising the principles of coherence in the face of recalcitrant experience as opposed to giving up some other belief in the system.

BonJour's objection rests on two principles:

(P1) Beliefs justified by experience are revisable.
(P2) The standards for revising beliefs justified by experience are themselves justified by experience.

39. BonJour, *In Defense of Pure Reason*, 145.
40. BonJour, ibid., 43, n. 9, maintains that a priori and empirical knowledge are sufficiently different that what holds for one need not hold for the other. But he is not explicit about the relevant differences.
41. BonJour, ibid., 148, n. 12, concludes that apparent rational insight is so fundamental that it does not admit of independent justification but contends that coherence does not have this status since it "depends essentially on principles, such as the principle of non-contradiction and others, that must be justified in some other way." The latter claim is clearly question-begging since it simply denies that the principles that define coherence do not admit of independent justification.
42. Ibid., 92.
43. Ibid.

From these two principles it follows that

(P3) The standards for revising beliefs justified by experience are themselves revisable.

But moderate rationalism endorses analogues of these two principles:

(P1*) Beliefs justified by apparent rational insight are revisable.
(P2*) The standards for revising beliefs justified by apparent rational insight are themselves justified by apparent rational insight.

Hence, moderate rationalism is committed to

(P3*) The standards for revising beliefs justified by apparent rational insight are themselves revisable.

The remainder of BonJour's argument applies with equal force to moderate rationalism and coherentist radical empiricism. Any attempt to block revision of the standards for belief revision either appeals to the standards themselves, which is circular, or invokes some further standard, which is itself revisable. Hence, once again, moderate rationalism fares no better than radical empiricism.

An examination of BonJour's account confirms this conclusion. He offers two procedures for a priori belief revision: (1) reflection on the state or process that led to the belief in question, and (2) coherence among a priori justified beliefs.[44] Consider the second. Let Φ = the principles that underlie coherence. Assume that S has an a priori justified belief that p, an a priori justified belief that q, an a priori justified belief that Φ, and an a priori justified belief that $\sim\Phi(p, q)$. In the face of such incoherence, S can retain both the belief that p and the belief that q by revising the principles that underlie coherence. BonJour blocks this move by maintaining this:

> The *prima facie a priori* justification of the fundamental premises or principles that underlie the conception of coherence in question must be stronger than that of the other claims whose justification is being assessed, so that there is *a priori* justification for thinking that in a case of incoherence, it is some among those other claims, rather than the fundamental premises or principles of coherence themselves, that are mistaken.[45]

If S's a priori justification for the belief that Φ is greater than S's justification for either the belief that p or the belief that q, then the expedient of rejecting Φ is blocked.

Can this strategy be sustained? Consider S's belief that

(5) My justification for the belief that Φ is greater than my justification for either the belief that p or the belief that q.

44. Ibid., 116–118.
45. Ibid., 118.

This belief is itself justified a priori and subject to revision. Hence, S can preserve both the belief that p and the belief that q by revising (5). The moderate rationalist will surely respond that such a revision is unjustified or unreasonable. But the response cannot be defended. To claim that S's justification for the belief that (5) is greater than S's justification for either the belief that p or the belief that q is circular. It appeals to a belief about the strength of a priori justification to defend the reluctance to revise a belief about the strength of a priori justification. If one introduces some further standard concerned with the revision of justified beliefs about one's degree of a priori justification, that standard itself is open to revision. The only remaining option is to maintain that beliefs about the degree of one's a priori justification are so fundamental that they cannot be independently justified.

Moderate rationalists can constrain a priori belief revision by claiming that a priori justification comes in degrees and that beliefs about the degree of one's a priori justification are not subject to independent justification. But, surely, the same strategy is open to coherentist radical empiricists. They can also maintain that not all beliefs within a coherent system are justified to the same degree and that beliefs about the degree of one's empirical justification are not subject to independent justification. Hence, unconstrained belief revision is no more a problem for coherentist radical empiricism than for moderate rationalism.

4.8   Foundationalist Radical Empiricism

We have arrived at the conclusion that coherentist radical empiricism fares no worse than moderate rationalism with respect to BonJour's criticisms. What are the prospects for a foundationalist version of radical empiricism? The only argument against foundationalist radical empiricism is the Generality Argument. If foundationalist radical empiricism cannot offer an account of the justification of general principles, as BonJour alleges, then it is committed to a version of skepticism: the *only* justified beliefs are those directly justified by experience. The Generality Argument, however, involves an important internalist constraint on epistemic justification: S is justified in believing that p only if S has some reason to believe that p is likely to be true. The basic claim of the Generality Argument is that experience alone cannot provide a reason for believing that a general principle is likely to be true. There are two options for the foundationalist radical empiricist: the first is to endorse internalism and address the Generality Argument; the second is to reject internalism in favor of externalism.

Internalist foundationalist radical empiricism is open to the Generality Argument. But, as I argued in section 4.6, moderate rationalism is also open to the argument. Hence, moderate rationalists are faced with a dilemma: either accept or reject (2*). If (2*) is accepted, then internalist foundationalism is not a viable option for *either* moderate rationalism or radical empiricism. Both varieties of internalist foundationalism lead to skepticism. If (2*) is rejected, however, internalist foundationalism is a viable option for *both* moderate rationalism and radical empiricism.

Moderate rationalists who reject (2*) maintain that some apprehensions of particular objects instantiating properties directly justify general beliefs. A fully articulated moderate rationalist theory of this sort will include a basic epistemic principle stating conditions under which such apprehensions directly justify general principles. This option, however, is also open to radical empiricists. They can maintain that some experiences of particular objects instantiating properties directly justify general principles. A fully articulated radical empiricist theory of this sort will include a basic epistemic principle stating conditions under which such experiences directly justify general principles. Moderate rationalists may balk at such a principle. But, unless they can offer some reason for preferring their epistemic principle over that of the radical empiricist, the claim is ad hoc. Although BonJour does not explicitly address the question of criteria for the acceptability of epistemic principles, he suggests, in the context of his discussion of coherentist radical empiricism, that one such criterion is truth conduciveness. But, since he also concedes that moderate rationalists cannot provide a reason to believe that apparent rational insight is truth conducive, they are not in a position to maintain that this criterion provides a basis for preferring moderate rationalism over radical empiricism. Hence, internalist foundationalist radical empiricism is no more problematic than moderate rationalism.

BonJour briefly considers the possibility that radical empiricists might reject internalism in favor of externalism. More specifically, the radical empiricist might deny the claim that S's justified belief that p requires having a reason to believe that p is likely to be true. As we saw in section 4.7, the expression "having a reason for thinking that p is likely to be true" is ambiguous. Hence, we must distinguish between two versions of internalism. According to *basic* internalism,

(BI) S's belief that p is justified only if S has a *basic* reason to believe that p.

According to *meta*internalism,

(MI) S's belief that p is justified only if S has a *meta*reason to believe that p.

Analogously, there are two versions of externalism. Basic externalism denies that basic reasons are necessary for justification; metaexternalism denies that metareasons are necessary.

BonJour offers only one argument against externalism: "Whatever account externalists may offer for concepts like knowledge or justification, there is still a plain and undeniable sense in which if externalism is the final story, we have no reason to think that any of our beliefs are true; and this result obviously amounts by itself to a very strong and intuitively implausible version of skepticism."[46] Although he is not explicit in this context about what is required to avoid skepticism, he maintains elsewhere, "The fundamental skeptical move is to challenge the adequacy of our reasons for accepting our beliefs. . . ."[47] Clearly, (BI) is not sufficient to meet this challenge. Although (BI) requires that one possess some reason R in order to be justified in believing that p, it does not require that one have a reason for thinking that R is truth conducive. But, to address the charge that R is not an adequate reason to believe that p, one must offer some reason to believe that R is truth conducive. On the other hand, (MI) does address the skeptical challenge. Since (MI) requires, for being justified in believing that p, that one possess both some reason R for believing that p and some reason for believing that R is truth conducive, one who satisfies these conditions is in a position to offer some reason for thinking that one's reasons are adequate. As we saw in section 4.7, however, BonJour acknowledges that moderate rationalism cannot meet the demand for metareasons. Hence, (MI), which addresses the skeptic's challenge, is not an option for moderate rationalists, and (BI), which is an option for moderate rationalists, does not address the skeptic's challenge. Since the only version of internalism available to moderate rationalism cannot meet the skeptical challenge, moderate rationalism fares no better than externalism with respect to skepticism. Therefore, we conclude that neither internalist nor externalist foundationalist radical empiricism is worse off than moderate rationalism.

The deficiency arguments offered by BonJour fall short of their goal. Even if he is correct in maintaining that radical empiricism leads to undesirable consequences such as skepticism and unconstrained belief revision, we have shown that moderate rationalism leads to the very same consequences. Hence, the deficiency arguments do not provide support for moderate rationalism since they fail to show that it offers any advantages over radical empiricism.

4.9   Conclusion

There are three categories of arguments in support of the a priori: conceptual, criterial and deficiency. I consider two conceptual arguments. Putnam claims that an a priori statement is one that is rationally unrevisable. I offer three readings of his proposed condition and argue that none provides a plausible sufficient condition for being justified a priori. Field argues that the principles of classical logic are strongly a priori. My examination of his supporting arguments reveals that if they are adequate to establish that such principles cannot be either justified or revised by empirical evidence, they

46. Ibid., 96.
47. Ibid., 87.

are also adequate to establish that such principles cannot be either justified or revised by any evidence.

I examine three criterial arguments. The Argument from Necessity breaks down into two arguments. The first purports to establish that knowledge of the truth value of necessary propositions must be a priori, and the second purports to establish that knowledge of the general modal status of necessary propositions must be a priori. In each case, I identify a key presupposition of the argument and show that it is false. The Irrefutability Argument purports to establish that experience cannot confirm mathematical propositions since it cannot disconfirm such propositions. Here I argue that the example of empirical disconfirming evidence that proponents of the argument reject is the weakest possible, and I offer a stronger example that can be dismissed only at the cost of either divorcing mathematical propositions from their applications or holding empirical beliefs at odds with the available evidence. In the case of the Argument from Certainty, I articulate five different senses of certainty and argue that there is no single sense in which both premises of the argument are true.

Finally, I consider four versions of the deficiency argument. One is directed at all forms of radical empiricism, two are directed against coherentist versions of radical empiricism, and the fourth is directed against externalist versions of radical empiricism. I argue, in each case, that moderate rationalism fares no better than radical empiricism in avoiding the problematic consequences. Hence, even if the arguments succeed in exposing deficiencies of radical empiricism, they provide no basis for favoring moderate rationalism over radical empiricism.

5

The Opposing Arguments

5.1 Introduction

In this chapter I address the leading arguments against the existence of a priori knowledge. The opposing arguments fall into three broad categories. Those in the first category offer an analysis of the concept of a priori knowledge and allege that no cases of knowledge satisfy the conditions in the analysis. Those in the second category offer radical empiricist accounts of knowledge of propositions alleged to be knowable only a priori. Arguments in the third category maintain that a priori knowledge is incompatible with plausible constraints on an adequate theory of knowledge.

In section 5.2, I examine the views of Hilary Putnam and Philip Kitcher, who maintain that the concept of the a priori entails rational unrevisability. I distinguish between two versions of the unrevisability condition—unrevisability in light of any evidence and unrevisability in light of any experiential evidence—and argue that neither is entailed by the concept of the a priori. In section 5.3, I address two radical empiricist accounts of knowledge of propositions traditionally alleged to be knowable only a priori: the inductivist version associated with John Stuart Mill and the holistic version associated with W. V. Quine. The inductivist strategy fails since it overlooks the possibility of epistemic overdetermination. The holistic version either collapses into one of the rejected conceptual arguments or rests on an unsubstantiated claim about the relationship between the a priori and the analytic. The leading incompatibility arguments maintain that a priori knowledge is incompatible with epistemic naturalism. In section 5.4, I articulate two versions of epistemic naturalism: philosophical and scientific. In section 5.5, I argue that the most promising version of philosophical naturalism is compatible with a priori knowledge. My investigation, however, uncovers some potential obstacles that any plausible defense of the a priori must address. In section 5.6, I reject scientific naturalist arguments on the grounds that they essentially involve extrascientific premises, which proponents of such arguments purport to reject.

5.2   Conceptual Arguments

Hilary Putnam and Philip Kitcher provide clear examples of conceptual arguments. Both hold that the concept of a priori justification includes an unrevisability condition. According to Putnam, an a priori statement is one "we would never be *rational* to give up."[1] Kitcher maintains that for a process to justify beliefs a priori, it must be able to "warrant those beliefs against the background of a suitably recalcitrant experience."[2] They go on to argue that beliefs traditionally alleged to be justified a priori fail to meet the requisite unrevisability condition. I argued in chapter 2 that the concept of a priori justification does not include an unrevisability condition. An a priori justified belief is one that is justified by a nonexperiential source. There remains, however, the possibility that although the concept of a priori justification does not include an unrevisability condition, it entails such a condition.

Let us call the general thesis that a priori justification entails rational unrevisability the *Unrevisability Thesis* (UT), and let us distinguish between a strong and weak version of it:

>   (SUT)   Necessarily, if S's belief that p is justified a priori, then S's belief that p is rationally unrevisable in light of *any* evidence.
>   (WUT)   Necessarily, if S's belief that p is justified a priori, then S's belief that p is rationally unrevisable in light of any *experiential* evidence.

My goal is to argue that both (SUT) and (WUT) should be rejected.

I begin by considering an example that draws out more explicitly the consequences of (SUT). Suppose that Mary is a college student who has had some training in logic. As a result, she is able to discriminate reliably between valid and invalid elementary inferences on the basis of reflective thought. Today Mary wonders whether "$p \supset q$" entails "$\sim p \supset \sim q$." She reflects on the statements in question and on the basis of this reflection concludes that the former does indeed entail the latter. After she assents to this conclusion, a counterexample occurs to her. The occurrence of the counterexample results in her rejecting her former conclusion and coming to believe that "$p \supset q$" entails "$\sim q \supset \sim p$." The salient features of the example are (1) Mary's

---

1. Putnam, "There Is at Least One A Priori Truth," 98. For a lucid summary of his case against the a priori, see "'Two Dogmas' Revisited."
2. Kitcher, *The Nature of Mathematical Knowledge*, 88.

initial belief is based on a non-experiential process that is reliable but not infallible, (2) a process of the *same type* leads Mary to conclude that the initial belief is mistaken and to arrive at the correct conclusion, and (3) Mary's conclusions as stated in (2) are justified beliefs. Now for some more controversial claims: (4) Mary's original belief that "$p \supset q$" entails "$\sim p \supset \sim q$" is also *justified*, and (5) Mary's original belief is justified *a priori* despite the subsequent revision.[3]

What can be said in favor of (4) and (5)? Mary's original belief appears to be similar in all relevant respects to the following case. Mary sees a sheet of paper on the table and on that basis forms the belief that it is square. A second, closer visual examination reveals that two of the sides are slightly longer than the other two. On this basis, Mary rejects her former belief about the shape of the paper and comes to believe that it is rectangular. Since the circumstances under which Mary perceived the page were normal and Mary is a reliable discriminator of shapes, her initial belief is justified. The fact that our discriminatory powers sometimes fail us does not entail that beliefs based on shape perception are not justified. Furthermore, if such beliefs are typically justified, we don't single out particular cases as unjustified merely in virtue of the fact that they are false. Some other relevant difference must be cited, such as that the perceiver was impaired or the environment was gerrymandered. Hence, the routine failure of Mary's otherwise reliable shape-discriminating ability does not entail that her belief that the paper is square is unjustified despite the fact that it is false. Similarly, the routine failure of Mary's otherwise reliable ability to discriminate valid inferences does not entail that her belief that "$p \supset q$" entails "$\sim p \supset \sim q$" is unjustified despite the fact that it is false.

The only remaining question is whether Mary's original belief is justified a priori or a posteriori. A proponent of (SUT) must maintain that the belief is justified a posteriori merely in virtue of the fact that it was revised. This point can be brought out more clearly by introducing the notion of a *self-correcting process*:

> (SCP)   A process Φ is self-correcting for S just in case, for any
> false belief that p, produced in S by Φ, Φ can also justify
> for S the belief that not-p.[4]

---

3. I have attempted to construct this counterexample and the others that follow in a manner that is neutral with respect to competing theories of epistemic justification and, in particular, the controversy between internalists and externalists. The example highlights two features of Mary's belief: it is based on reflection, and it is reliably produced. The process of reflection yields an internally accessible cognitive state of the sort favored by internalist accounts of noninferential a priori justification. The reliability of the process provides a condition of the sort favored by externalist accounts of such justification. Jeshion, "On the Obvious," disputes the counterexample.

4. Self-correction comes in degrees. A weaker form can be defined as follows: for *some* false belief that p produced in S by Φ, Φ can also justify for S the belief that not-p. Other versions, both stronger and weaker, are possible.

(SUT) entails

> (1) If a process Φ is self-correcting and justifies for S some false belief that p, then Φ does not justify a priori S's belief that p.

(1) is implausible. It is insensitive to the central question of whether the justificatory process in question is experiential or nonexperiential. Hence, to endorse (1) is to divorce the notion of a priori justification from the notion of independence from experiential evidence. It is more plausible to reject (1) on the grounds that Mary's original belief, as well as the belief that led her to revise the original belief, is based on nonexperiential evidence. Since experiential evidence plays no role either in the original justification or in the subsequent revision of Mary's belief, if it is justified, it is justified a priori. Once we reject (1), (SUT) must also be rejected.

Our rejection of (SUT) has been based on a single case. This case may appear questionable since it involves the controversial claim that there can be a priori justified false beliefs. To reinforce our conclusion, let us consider a second example, which does not involve this claim. Suppose Carl believes that p entails q on the basis of a valid proof P_1. Since the proof is the result of a process of reflective thought, Carl's belief is justified nonexperientially. But now let us suppose that (a) there exists a pseudoproof, P_2, from p to not-q; and (b) if this pseudoproof were brought to Carl's attention, he would not be able to detect any flaws in it or to discount it in any other fashion. Given that the pseudoproof never comes to Carl's attention, his belief remains justified despite the fact that were it to be brought to his attention his justification would be defeated. (SUT) entails that Carl's belief is not justified a priori despite the fact that (i) it is justified; (ii) it is based on nonexperiential evidence; and (iii) the potential defeating evidence, if it were to become available to Carl, would also be based on a process of reflective thought. Given that (SUT) entails that Carl's belief is *not* justified a priori despite the fact that experiential evidence plays no role in either the original justification for Carl's belief or its possible subsequent defeat, it is evident that (SUT) divorces the notion of a priori justification from the notion of nonexperiential justification. Instead, (SUT) bases its claim that Carl's belief is not justified a priori solely on the following consideration:

> (2) The justification conferred on Carl's belief by the process of reflective thought is defeasible.

But (2) is not a sufficient reason for maintaining that Carl's belief is not justified a priori. It fails to take into account whether the justification of the potential defeaters for Carl's justified belief is experiential or nonexperiential. Hence, (SUT) must be rejected.[5]

---

5. Pollock, *Knowledge and Justification*, chap. 10, and Steiner, *Mathematical Knowledge*, chap. 4, acknowledge that beliefs based on intuition are defeasible but maintain that they are justified a priori. Hence, (SUT) rules out *by stipulation* a feature that some proponents of the a priori attempt to build into their accounts.

(SUT) is implausible because it overlooks the fact that revision can take place on the basis of a priori considerations. Hence, one cannot argue that the justification conferred on a belief by a process is not a priori simply on the basis of the fact that the process is self-correcting or that the justification it provides is defeasible. A similar observation is germane to evaluating the claim of Hilary Putnam that the presence of quasi-empirical methods in mathematics shows that mathematics is not a priori. By "quasi-empirical" methods, Putnam has in mind "methods that are analogous to the methods of the physical sciences except that the singular statements which are 'generalized by induction', used to test 'theories', etc., are themselves the product of proof or calculation rather than being 'observation reports' in the usual sense."[6]

Among the numerous examples of the use of quasi-empirical methods in mathematics that Putnam discusses, Zermelo's introduction of the axiom of choice is the most striking. Zermelo is explicit in maintaining that his justification for this move is intuitive self-evidence and necessity for science.[7] By necessity for science, Zermelo has in mind the indispensability of the axiom for proving certain theorems. So, in effect, the justification is akin to the use of the hypotheticodeductive method in scientific reasoning. What are the implications of Zermelo's justification for the issue of the alleged apriority of mathematics?

Suppose that T is a mathematical theory and that $\{p_1, \ldots, p_n\}$ is a set of statements belonging to T each of whose members is accepted on the basis of nonexperiential evidence. Suppose that we now introduce p_{n+1}, which is neither self-evident nor formally derivable from T. But from p_{n+1}, we can derive $\{p_1, \ldots, p_n\}$ and, in addition, some other principles that are neither self-evident nor provable from T but prove fruitful in furthering research in this area of mathematics. Putnam regards two features of the example as salient: (1) no formal proof exists for p_{n+1}, and (2) theoretical considerations might lead to a rejection of p_{n+1}. Putnam stresses (1) because he assumes that if there exists a formal proof of p_{n+1}, then p_{n+1} is rationally unrevisable. But this assumption overlooks the possibility of misleading evidence. As we saw in the earlier example, the fact that Carl's belief that p was based on a valid formal proof did not preclude the rational revisability of that belief. Once we recognize that formal proof does not preclude revisability, (2) does not appear to introduce any novel considerations about the apriority of mathematics. The set of statements $\{p_1, \ldots, p_n\}$ is justified nonexperientially. When one confirms p_{n+1}, one derives formally the members of the set $\{p_1, \ldots, p_n\}$. Additional confirmation comes from the fact that other statements, $\{p_{n+2}, \ldots, p_{n+i}\}$, are derivable from p_{n+1} taken in conjunction with T, which

6. Putnam, "What Is Mathematical Truth?" 62.
7. Zermelo, "A New Proof of the Possibility of a Well Ordering," 187, and quoted in Putnam, "What Is Mathematical Truth?" 66.

are both fruitful and not derivable from T alone. Hence, the only mode of justification involved is formal proof. No novel form of justification has been introduced at this point. What about the circumstances that would lead to a rejection of p_{n+1}? Given the fruitfulness of p_{n+1} there seem to be only two circumstances in which it would be rejected: (a) if it is shown that although T is consistent, $(T \& p_{n+1})$ is inconsistent, or (b) $(T \& p_{n+1})$ but not T alone entails some p_i and not-p_i is independently well supported. But, in either case, the only mode of justification involved is formal proof. Consequently, the use of hypotheticodeductive reasoning in mathematics has no tendency to show that mathematical knowledge is not a priori.[8] It would do so only if (a) the method of proof itself is not a priori; or (b) the members of the set $\{p_1, \ldots, p_n\}$, which form the confirmation base for p_{n+1}, are justified experientially.

(WUT) avoids the primary problem with (SUT). It distinguishes between revisions based on experiential evidence as opposed to revisions based on nonexperiential evidence and maintains that only the former are incompatible with a priori justification. Nevertheless, (WUT) is also open to objection.

We again begin by considering an example. Suppose that Pat is a working logician who regularly and consistently arrives at interesting results. Pat, however, is bothered by the fact that although he is a *reliable* producer of interesting proofs, he is not an *infallible* producer of such proofs. As it turns out, he has a colleague, May, who has done pioneering work in the neurophysiological basis of cognitive processes. As a radical means to self-improvement, Pat asks May to conduct a study of his efforts at constructing proofs in order to see if she can uncover some, hopefully reversible neurophysiological cause for his infrequent erroneous proofs. The investigation reveals that (1) a particular interference pattern is present in Pat's brain when and only when he constructs an erroneous proof, and (2) whenever Pat constructs a proof under the influence of this pattern and the pattern is subsequently eradicated by neurophysiological intervention, he is able to see the flaw in the original proof and go on to correct it. Finally, an accepted neurophysiological theory supports the hypothesis that such a pattern should cause cognitive lapses. Now suppose that Pat believes that p entails q on the basis of constructing a proof, which he carefully scrutinizes and finds acceptable. Despite his careful scrutiny, the proof is flawed. He later discovers in a subsequent meeting with May that (1) she had been monitoring his brain activity at the time the proof was constructed with a remote sensor, (2) the sensor indicated that the interference pattern was present, and

8. This argument can be extended to the cases of inductive justification offered by Polya, *Induction and Analogy in Mathematics*, such as Euler's discovery that the sum of the series $1/n^2$ is $\pi^2/6$. Since the statements that confirm the inductive generalization are known nonexperientially, there is no reason to suppose that the generalization is not known a priori. The epistemological significance of inductive procedures in mathematics is discussed by Putnam, "What Is Mathematical Truth?" and Steiner, *Mathematical Knowledge*, chap. 3.

(3) standard tests indicated that all of the equipment was functioning properly. Pat is still unable to uncover the flaw in his proof but nevertheless concludes, on the basis of May's empirical findings, that his proof is flawed, and he withholds the belief that p entails q.

The salient features of the example are (1) Pat's initial belief that p entails q is based on a process of reflective thought that is reliable but not infallible, (2) Pat's initial belief that p entails q is justified by the nonexperiential process of reflective thought, and (3) the justification that the process of reflective thought confers on his belief is subsequently defeated by the empirical evidence indicating that the interference pattern is present. (1) is uncontroversial. (2) is more controversial since it assumes that false beliefs can be justified a priori. This assumption was defended earlier in the discussion of the Mary example. I propose to grant (3) for purposes of assessing (WUT). Consider now the following claim: (4) Pat's initial belief that p entails q is justified a priori despite the later revision in light of experiential evidence. (4) appears to be a straightforward consequence of (2). Since Pat's belief is justified by a nonexperiential process, it is justified a priori. A proponent of (WUT) can resist this conclusion only by insisting that since experiential evidence defeated the justification conferred on the belief by the nonexperiential process, the belief is justified, at least in part, by experiential evidence.

The proposed defense of (WUT) invokes the following relationship, called the *Symmetry Thesis*, between justifying and defeating evidence:

> (ST) If evidence of kind A can defeat the justification conferred on S's belief that p by evidence of kind B, then S's belief that p is justified by evidence of kind A.

However, (ST) is not very plausible. Consider, for example, introspective knowledge of one's bodily sensations such as pains and itches. Some maintain that introspective knowledge is indubitable. There are no possible grounds for doubting the truth of an introspective belief about one's bodily sensations. This claim has been challenged by the so-called EEG argument.[9] The basic idea is that although introspection presently provides our only evidence for the presence of bodily sensations, it is possible that neurophysiology will evolve to the point where electroencephalograph readings also provide such evidence. Furthermore, in suitably chosen circumstances, the EEG readings may override our introspective evidence in support of a belief about the presence of a bodily sensation. Our purpose here is not to evaluate the argument. Suppose we grant

> (N) Neurophysiological evidence can defeat the justification conferred on a belief about one's bodily sensations by introspection.

---

9. See for example, Armstrong, "Is Introspective Knowledge Incorrigible?"

Clearly, it does not follow that my present justified belief that I have a mild headache is based, even in part, on neurophysiological evidence. Consequently, (ST) must be rejected.

One might offer an alternative strategy for linking defeating evidence with justificatory evidence. Suppose that S's belief that p is justified by some nonexperiential evidence and that the justification conferred on S's belief by that evidence can be defeated by some experiential evidence. It follows that the nonexperiential evidence can justify S's belief that p only in the *absence* of the potential defeating evidence. Hence, for S to be justified in believing that p, S must be justified in believing that the defeating evidence is absent. But such justification can come only from experience. This line of argument presupposes a thesis analogous to (ST):

> (ST*) If evidence E_1 can defeat the justification conferred on S's belief that p by E_2, then E_2 does not justify S's belief that p unless S is justified in believing that not-E_1.

However, (ST*) runs up against a problem similar to that faced by (ST). Suppose that we grant that (N) is true. It does not follow that my present introspective belief that I have a mild headache is justified only if I have some justified beliefs about my present neurophysiological state. Consequently, (ST*) must also be rejected.

One might attempt to rehabilitate (ST) or (ST*) by narrowing the scope of relevant defeaters. For example, Kitcher divides empirical defeaters into three categories: direct, theoretical, and social.[10] A direct defeater for a justified belief that p is an experience whose content justifies the belief that not-p. A theoretical defeater for a justified belief that p is a sequence of experiences that is explained more simply by a theory that does not contain the statement that p than by any theory that does contain the statement that p. A social defeater for a justified belief that p is the testimony of an apparent authority to the effect either that not-p or that one's alleged justification for believing that p is in some way defective. The example I used in arguing against (ST) is a theoretical defeater. Hence, we might restrict (ST), for example, to either direct or social defeaters.

Restricting (ST) to social defeaters clearly fails since testimonial defeaters can defeat justification conferred on a belief by any source. Hence, from the fact that one's justification for a particular belief is defeated by testimony, it does not follow that the belief is justified by testimony. One might attempt to argue that testimony does not generate justification but merely preserves justification generated from other sources.[11] Hence, testimonial defeaters are not justified by testimony but by some other source. But, unless it can be shown that testimonial defeaters justified by one source cannot defeat the

---

10. Kitcher, *The Nature of Mathematical Knowledge*, 55.
11. See Burge, "Content Preservation."

justification conferred on a belief by a different source, this move will not suffice to resurrect (ST). Restricting (ST) to direct defeaters fares no better. For example, as I argued in chapter 2, beliefs justified by memory can be defeated by beliefs justified by perception and vice versa. This fact also casts doubt on the strategy of rehabilitating the restricted version of (ST) by arguing that testimony merely preserves justification. If, for example, a belief justified by perception can be defeated by a belief justified by memory, then the former can also be defeated by a testimonial belief justified by memory.

The arguments offered against (ST) indicate that optimism about uncovering some plausible version of the thesis is rooted in a failure to appreciate a pervasive feature of epistemic justification: *overdetermination*. Most, if not all, of our beliefs can be justified by more than one source. As a consequence, defeaters for those beliefs can also be generated from more than one source. Therefore, any strategy for defending a version of (ST) will have to be coupled with an argument to the effect that the beliefs in question can be justified only by a single source. But it is difficult to see how that can be accomplished in this context without begging the question. To do so, one must identify a class of propositions, say, mathematical propositions, and argue (1) that they are defeasible by a particular type of empirical evidence and (2) that only such evidence can justify propositions in that class. The latter claim, however, begs the question, for the principle is being employed as a premise in an argument whose conclusion is that the propositions in the designated class are not justified a priori.

Our case against (WUT) has been based on a single example. One might balk at this example since, like the Mary example, it involves the claim that there can be a priori justification for a false belief. But this feature can easily be eliminated, as in the Carl example, by introducing misleading evidence. Let us suppose that Pat's proof that *p* entails *q* is in fact correct but that May's sensor has malfunctioned, erroneously indicating the presence of the interference pattern. The standard tests, however, fail to detect the malfunction. Finally, let us suppose that were Pat to become aware that (a) the sensor had indicated the presence of the interference pattern and (b) the standard tests indicated that the sensor was functioning correctly, he would conclude that his proof that *p* entails *q* is erroneous. Nevertheless, since May never reveals her observations to Pat, his belief remains justified. (WUT) entails that Pat's belief is not justified a priori despite the fact that (i) it is justified; and (ii) it is based on a process of reflective thought. Clearly, to substantiate the claim that Pat's belief is justified by experiential evidence, the proponent of (WUT) must again appeal to (ST). Since (WUT) cannot be defended without appeal to (ST), it should be rejected.

The most prevalent conceptual arguments against the a priori are based on the claim that the concept of a priori justification entails rational unrevisability. In this section, I distinguish between a strong and a weak version of the unrevisability thesis and maintain that both should be rejected. The argument proceeds at two levels: identifying and rejecting a principle presupposed by each version of the thesis and offering counter-examples to each version. We now turn to the second category of arguments: those that offer radical empiricist accounts of the justification of beliefs traditionally alleged to be justified a priori.

5.3   Radical Empiricist Accounts

One common strategy of arguing against the existence of a priori knowledge is to consider the most prominent examples of propositions alleged to be knowable only a priori and to argue that such propositions are known empirically. Let us focus on mathematical knowledge since it has received the most attention. Radical empiricist accounts of mathematical knowledge can be divided into two broad categories: inductive and holistic. The leading idea of inductive theories is that *epistemically basic* mathematical propositions are directly justified by observation and inductive generalization. Nonbasic mathematical propositions are indirectly justified by virtue of their logical and explanatory relationships to the basic mathematical propositions. Holistic theories deny that some mathematical propositions are directly justified by observation and inductive generalization. All mathematical propositions are part of a larger explanatory theory, which includes scientific and methodological principles. Only entire theories, rather than individual propositions, are confirmed or disconfirmed by experience.

John Stuart Mill is the most prominent proponent of inductivism. In the case of mathematics, his primary concern is with the first principles, the axioms and definitions, of arithmetic and geometry. His view, succinctly stated, is that these principles are justified inductively on the basis of observation. The view faces formidable obstacles. For example, definitions do not appear to require empirical justification. Moreover, the properties connoted by some mathematical terms do not appear to be exemplified by the objects of experience. Mill maintains, however, that definitions of mathematical terms assert the existence of objects that exemplify the properties connoted by the terms in the definitions and that mathematical definitions are only approximately true of the objects of experience.[12]

Very few find Mill's account to be plausible. My goal here is not to defend it.[13] Instead, I propose to grant its cogency in order to determine whether it can be parlayed into an argument against the a priori. If Mill is correct, it follows that all epistemically basic mathematical propositions are justified by experience. Moreover, all other mathematical propositions justified on the basis of the basic propositions are also justified by experience. Nevertheless, the success of the account does not establish that there is no a priori

---

12. Mill, *A System of Logic*, bk. II, chaps. V and VI.
13. I offer a defense of inductivism in "Necessity, Certainty, and the A Priori."

knowledge of these mathematical propositions. To draw such a conclusion is to overlook the possibility of *epistemic overdetermination*: the possibility that mathematical propositions are (or can be) justified both experientially and nonexperientially.

Mill is aware of this gap in his argument and appeals to a version of the principle of simplicity:

> Where then is the necessity for assuming that our recognition of these truths has a different origin from the rest of our knowledge, when its existence is perfectly accounted for by supposing its origin to be the same? when the causes which produce belief in all other instances, exist in this instance, and in a degree of strength as much superior to what exists in other cases, as the intensity of the belief itself is superior?[14]

Mill maintains that there is no need to hypothesize that there is a priori knowledge to account for our knowledge of mathematics. But the appeal to simplicity is misguided. The goal of an epistemological theory is not to offer the *simplest* account of our knowledge of some target set of propositions. The goal is to offer an *accurate* account of our knowledge: one that provides a complete picture of our cognitive resources for the domain of truths in question. It is an open question whether, given our cognitive resources, we have more than a single source of justification for beliefs within a given domain. The assumption that for any given domain of human knowledge there is only a single source of justification is without foundation. The principle of simplicity rules out overdetermination of justification. Hence, Mill's radical empiricism, even if cogent, cannot be parlayed into an argument against the a priori in the absence of an argument against epistemic overdetermination.

Philip Kitcher, in a probing and sympathetic reconstruction, offers an alternative approach to defending Mill's radical empiricism. His primary focus is Frege's well-known objection to Mill's claim that arithmetical definitions, such as "2 = 1 + 1," depend on the observation of some associated matter of fact. Frege points out that a proof of an arithmetical statement involving large numbers, such as "23,671 + 49,823 = 73,494," requires a definition for each of the numbers involved.[15] But it is implausible to maintain that we have observed the matters of fact alleged to be associated with such definitions. Kitcher offers the following response: "Mill would allow that certain sentences of our language are true in virtue of the connotations of the expressions they contain, and that we can defend our assertion of these sentences by citing our understanding of the language. However, he would deny that assertion of sentences on this basis constitutes a priori knowledge of the propositions they express."[16]

14. Ibid., 41.
15. Frege, *The Foundations of Arithmetic*, 9e.
16. Kitcher, "Arithmetic for the Millian," 219.

This response allows Mill to maintain that our justification for believing mathematical definitions such as "73,494 = 73,493 + 1" derives from our understanding of language rather than from experience. But, if such justification is not based on experience, isn't it a priori? No, according to Kitcher:

> Our defense is adequate only so long as our right to use our language is not called into question. In particular, if experience gives us evidence that certain concepts are not well-adapted to the description of reality our assertion of sentences involving those concepts is *no longer justified*, even if the truth of those sentences stems from the connotations of the terms they contain.[17]

Although definitions are justified nonexperientially, Kitcher maintains that for Mill they are not justified a priori since such nonexperiential justification is defeasible by subsequent experience.

Kitcher's reconstruction deviates from the traditional understanding of Mill's position in a significant respect. On the traditional view, Mill holds that mathematical first principles are justified by induction from observed cases. Kitcher, however, attributes to Mill the view that mathematical definitions are justified nonexperientially but are defeasible by experience. Can this reading of Mill be parlayed into an argument against a priori knowledge of such definitions? Kitcher's reading is not open to the overdetermination argument that I present against the more traditional reading. He does not argue that definitions are justified by experience and overlook the possibility that they may also be justified nonexperientially. Instead, he concedes that they are justified nonexperientially but maintains that, nevertheless, they are justified a posteriori. Hence, Kitcher's reading can be parlayed into an argument against the a priori only if the concept of a priori justification entails indefeasibility by experience. But, as I argued in section 5.2, that assumption is false. So, once again, even if we concede the cogency of Mill's radical empiricism, construed nontraditionally, it cannot be parlayed into an argument against the a priori.

Holistic radical empiricism faces a related difficulty. The classic presentation of the position is provided by W. V. Quine.[18] There are (at least) two readings of the argument in "Two Dogmas." The traditional reading is that Quine is providing a unitary argument against the cogency of the analytic/synthetic distinction, which proceeds by examining a variety of alternative proposals for marking the distinction. The second, following Hilary Putnam, is that he is providing two distinct arguments: an (unsuccessful) argument in the first four sections, targeting the analytic/synthetic distinction, and a (successful) argument in the concluding two sections, targeting the existence of a priori knowledge.[19]

---

17. Ibid. (emphasis mine).
18. Quine, "Two Dogmas of Empiricism."
19. Putnam, "'Two Dogmas' Revisited."

On Putnam's reading, when Quine argues that no statement is immune to revision, he is targeting a priori knowledge. The target of the attack is the view that there are some statements confirmed no matter what. Putnam's claim is that the concept of a statement confirmed no matter what is not a concept of analyticity but a concept of apriority. Quine was misled into thinking that it was a concept of analyticity because of positivist assumptions about meaning. Hence, according to Putnam, if Quine's argument is sound, it establishes that there is no a priori knowledge.

My goal here is not to adjudicate between the two readings of Quine's argument but to assess the epistemic implications of both. Let me begin with Putnam's reading of the argument and concede that Quine has successfully established that no statement is immune to revision. Can Quine's conclusion be parlayed into an argument against the existence of a priori knowledge, as Putnam alleges? Clearly, that conclusion, taken by itself, is not sufficient to do so. The additional premise that a priori justification entails rational unrevisability is also necessary. But, despite Putnam's claim to the contrary, the additional premise is false.

Let me now turn to the more traditional reading of Quine's argument and, once again, concede that Quine has successfully shown that the analytic/synthetic distinction is not cogent. Does this result provide the radical empiricist with the resources necessary to argue that there is no a priori knowledge? Once again, this premise alone does not suffice. I argued in chapter 1 that the analysis of the concept of a priori justification does not include the concept of analyticity. Hence, there is no immediate or obvious connection between the two concepts. The possibility remains that there is some more mediate connection. But, if there is such a connection, some supporting argument must be offered to show this. Whether such an argument is forthcoming is discussed in chapter 8. Hence, once again, we arrive at the conclusion that in order to move from the premise that there is no cogent analytic/synthetic distinction to the conclusion that there is no a priori knowledge, an additional questionable and unsubstantiated premise is necessary.

In this section, I examine three strategies for arguing that propositions traditionally alleged to be knowable a priori are known empirically, and show that none straightforwardly entails that the propositions in question are not knowable (or known) a priori. The first strategy is *direct*. It consists in arguing that mathematical propositions are justified on the basis of experience and inductive generalization. This result does not entail that mathematical propositions are not knowable (or known) a priori in the absence of an argument against epistemic overdetermination within the domain of mathematics. The remaining two are *indirect*. The second maintains that mathematical beliefs are revisable in light of experiential evidence. This result cannot be parlayed into an argument against a priori knowledge in the absence of an argument that establishes that such knowledge is incompatible with revision in light of experience. The final strategy is to deny the cogency of the analytic/synthetic distinction. This result achieves its goal only if conjoined with an argument that establishes that the concept of a priori knowledge either involves or entails the concept of analyticity. I now turn to arguments based on the requirements of knowledge or justification.

5.4   Incompatibility Arguments

Paul Benacerraf provides the classic example of an argument that falls into the third category.[20] He maintains that our best theory of truth provides truth conditions for mathematical statements that refer to abstract entities, and our best account of knowledge requires a causal relation between knowers and the entities referred to by the truth conditions of the statements that they know. Given that abstract entities cannot stand in causal relations, there is a tension between our best account of mathematical truth and our best account of mathematical knowledge.[21] Since it is widely held that most, if not all, a priori knowledge is of necessary truths and that the truth conditions for such statements refer to abstract entities, Benacerraf's argument raises a more general question about the possibility of a priori knowledge.

Some dismiss the argument on the grounds that its epistemic premise, which endorses a causal condition on knowledge, rests on the generally rejected causal theory of knowledge.[22] Benacerraf's argument, however, has proved to be more resilient than the causal theory of knowledge. Proponents of the argument maintain that the causal condition endorsed by the epistemic premise of the argument draws its support from the requirements of a naturalized epistemology rather than from the causal theory of knowledge.[23]

Assessing the claim that epistemic naturalism underwrites Benacerraf's causal condition on knowledge is complicated since there are many competing versions of the view. At the risk of oversimplifying, let us identify two general varieties. The movement takes its name from W. V. Quine's well-known article, in which he rejects the traditional epistemological project of providing an a priori, philosophical justification of scientific knowledge and offers in its place a vision of epistemology as a branch of science:

20. Benacerraf, "Mathematical Truth."
21. Kim, "The Role of Perception in A Priori Knowledge," and Maddy, "Perception and Mathematical Intuition," maintain that abstract entities can stand in causal relations.
22. See Goldman, "Discrimination and Perceptual Knowledge," and Klein, "Knowledge, Causality, and Defeasibility," for some telling criticisms.
23. Hart, "Review of Mark Steiner," 125–126, argues that "it is a crime against the intellect to try to mask the problem of naturalizing the epistemology of mathematics with philosophical razzle-dazzle. Superficial worries about the intellectual hygiene of causal theories of knowledge are irrelevant to and misleading from this problem, for the problem is not so much about causality as about the very possibility of natural knowledge of abstract objects."

Epistemology, or something like it, simply falls into place as a chapter of psychology and hence of natural science. It studies a natural phenomenon, viz., a physical human subject. This human subject is accorded a certain experimentally controlled input—certain patterns of irradiation in assorted frequencies, for instance—and in the fullness of time the subject delivers as output a description of the three-dimensional external world and its history. The relation between the meager input and the torrential output is a relation that we are prompted to study for somewhat the same reasons that always prompted epistemology; namely, in order to see how evidence relates to theory, and in what ways one's theory of nature transcends any available evidence.[24]

The project of naturalized epistemology is to provide a scientific account of how human subjects arrive at their scientific beliefs. The study of the relation between "meager input and torrential output," although motivated by the desire to see "how evidence relates to theory," replaces the traditional epistemological enterprise of articulating and supporting principles of justification with the scientific project of uncovering nomological connections.

Quine's brand of naturalism, *scientific* naturalism, espouses replacing traditional philosophical projects with scientific projects. It requires that philosophy become a chapter of psychology or some other appropriate science and that philosophical questions be subsumed by questions that arise from within the particular area of science that replaces or incorporates philosophy. There is, however, as Jaegwon Kim reminds us, another brand of epistemic naturalism within contemporary epistemology: "A salient characteristic of the naturalistic approach has already emerged, which we can put as follows: justification is to be characterized in terms of *causal* or *nomological* connections involving beliefs as *psychological states* or *processes*, and not in terms of the *logical* properties or relations pertaining to the *contents* of these beliefs."[25] This brand of naturalism, *philosophical* naturalism, is less radical than scientific naturalism. Rather than advocating the replacement of philosophical projects with scientific projects, philosophical naturalism advocates placing naturalistic constraints on traditional philosophical projects. In the case of conceptual analysis, for example, it requires that the analysans of a concept include only naturalistically respectable concepts.

We can now distinguish between two different naturalistic approaches to providing support for Benacerraf's epistemic premise. The philosophical approach maintains that an adequate naturalized analysis of knowledge or justification involves or entails a causal condition incompatible with knowledge of abstract entities. The scientific approach maintains that our best scientific theory underwrites such a condition. An epistemic naturalist who wishes to exploit either approach must offer two types of supporting argu-

24. Quine, "Epistemology Naturalized," 82–83.
25. Kim, "What Is 'Naturalized Epistemology'?" 48.

ment: a *metaepistemological* argument and a *substantive epistemological* argument. Philosophical naturalists must offer a metaepistemological argument in favor of adopting naturalistic constraints on traditional philosophical projects. For example, they might argue, in the case of conceptual analysis, that naturalistically respectable concepts are better understood than those philosophers have traditionally favored. They must also offer a substantive epistemological argument in support of the particular naturalized analysis they endorse. For example, they might argue that the causal theory of knowledge more plausibly handles Gettier-type cases than any other available analysis. Analogously, scientific naturalists must offer a metaepistemological argument in favor of absorbing traditional epistemology into some scientific discipline, such as psychology, as opposed to continuing to pursue it as a separate discipline. They might, for example, argue that the lack of progress in solving traditional epistemological problems provides evidence that the enterprise is bankrupt. They must also offer a substantive epistemological argument in support of their particular naturalistic commitments. For example, they might argue that certain causal constraints on the acquisition of mathematical knowledge are supported from within the branch of science that is replacing traditional epistemology.

My focus will be on the question of whether there is either a substantive philosophical naturalist argument or a substantive scientific naturalist argument that supports a causal condition incompatible with knowledge of abstract entities. More specifically, I will address two questions. Have philosophical naturalists offered an adequate analysis of the concept of knowledge or justification that involves or entails a causal condition incompatible with knowledge of abstract entities? Have scientific naturalists offered compelling evidence, from within psychology or some other branch of science, that such a causal condition is part of our best scientific account of scientific knowledge?

My focus on the substantive arguments is supported by two considerations. First, if philosophical naturalists cannot offer a naturalized analysis of knowledge or justification involving a causal condition incompatible with knowledge of abstract entities, then the metaepistemological controversy over adopting naturalistic constraints on philosophical projects is moot for our purposes. Similarly, if scientific naturalists cannot offer evidence from within science that supports such a causal condition, then the metaepistemological controversy between traditional and naturalized epistemologists is moot for our purposes. Second, if philosophical naturalists offer a naturalized analysis of the concept of knowledge or justification involving a causal constraint incompatible with knowledge of abstract entities, the analysis must be evaluated on its own merits. If it is superior to its competitors, the analysis will stand on its merits apart from any more general commitment to philosophical naturalism. Similarly, if scientific naturalists offer scientific evidence supporting such a condition, the evidence must be evaluated on its own merit. If the evidence is compelling, the condition will stand on that evidence apart from any more general commitment to scientific naturalism.

5.5   Philosophical Naturalism

I begin with the question of whether philosophical naturalism underwrites a causal condition on knowledge or justification that is incompatible with knowledge of abstract entities. Two aspects of the question must be distinguished. Does an adequate naturalized analysis of the concept of knowledge or justification involve or entail some causal condition? Is that condition incompatible with knowledge of abstract entities? A negative answer to either question is sufficient to rebuff the philosophical naturalist. Mark Steiner offers a negative response to the second question. He endorses the causal theory of knowledge but argues that the causal condition, correctly understood, is compatible with knowledge of abstract entities.[26] Penelope Maddy offers a negative response to the first. She rejects the causal theory and argues that its most promising naturalized descendent, reliabilism, imposes no causal constraints on knowledge or justification.[27] My goal is to show that neither response fully circumvents Benacerraf's problem. With respect to the first response, I argue that Steiner's version of the causal condition is too weak to play any role in a theory of knowledge or justification. With respect to the second, I distinguish two forms of reliabilism: reliable indicator theories and process reliabilism. I argue that the former involve a condition incompatible with knowledge of abstract entities and that the latter is vulnerable to potential defeaters generated by causal considerations.

The classic formulation of the causal theory of knowledge is from Alvin Goldman:

> (G1) *S knows that p* if and only if *the fact p is causally connected in an "appropriate" way with S's believing p.*[28]

Steiner balks at this formulation on the grounds that facts are abstract entities and thus cannot stand in causal relations. He argues, however, that the causal theorist can remedy this shortcoming by talking about causal *explanations* rather than causal *relations*. Thus, (G1) might be reformulated as follows:

> (S) One cannot know that a sentence *S* is true, unless *S* must be used in a causal explanation of one's knowing (or believing) that *S* is true.[29]

---

26. Steiner, "Platonism and the Causal Theory of Knowledge" and *Mathematical Knowledge*, chap. 4.

27. Maddy, "Mathematical Epistemology."

28. Goldman, "A Causal Theory of Knowing," 82.

29. Steiner, "Platonism and the Causal Theory of Knowledge," 60.

Steiner goes on to argue that although (S) provides the most plausible version of the causal theory it is not incompatible with knowledge of abstract entities.

The argument proceeds as follows:

(1) Suppose that we believe the axioms of analysis or of number theory.
(2) There exists a theory that causally explains our belief.
(3) This theory, like all others, contains the axioms of number theory and of analysis.
(4) In order to provide an explanation a sentence must be true.
(5) The only known interpretation to guarantee the truth of these axioms is Tarski's.
(6) Therefore, any causal explanation of our belief in the axioms contains the axioms.

Steiner's leading idea is that the causal condition can be formulated in two different ways, either in terms of causal *relations* or in terms of causal *explanations*. Sentences whose truth conditions refer to abstract entities, however, can figure in causal explanations even if abstract entities cannot stand in causal relations. Thus, if the correct formulation of the causal condition on knowledge is in terms of causal explanations, the causal inertness of abstract entities is not incompatible with that condition.

Steiner's position is difficult to evaluate since (S) provides a necessary but not sufficient condition for knowledge. Nevertheless, there is good reason to doubt its adequacy. The point of introducing a causal condition into the analysis of knowledge is either (1) to distinguish between justified and unjustified beliefs or (2) to distinguish between knowledge and justified true belief. (S) is too liberal to accomplish either of these objectives, for *any* belief in an axiom of analysis or of number theory, however fortuitously acquired, will satisfy this condition. This is a direct consequence of Steiner's claim that any causal explanation of a belief in the axioms contains the axioms.

Suppose, for example, that Jill is driven by a compulsion to trick people into believing false propositions by deceptive means. She happens to overhear someone at a party claim that T is *not* an axiom of number theory. Jill knows very little mathematics but, nevertheless, forms the belief that T is not an axiom of number theory solely on the basis of overhearing the remark. She then proceeds to trick Jack into believing that she is a mathematics professor in order to convince him that T is an axiom of number theory. She succeeds, but it turns out that T is in fact an axiom of number theory. So Jack's belief is true, and T figures as part of the causal explanation of his belief that T is an axiom of number theory. But Jack's belief that T is not justified.

The first response fails. Steiner does not reconcile the causal theory of knowledge with knowledge of abstract entities. The causal condition he proposes, in terms of causal explanation, is too weak to be of epistemic interest. Any epistemically interesting causal condition on knowledge will be in terms of causal relations. The second response rejects the causal theory in favor of reliabilism and maintains that reliabilism does not impose any causal conditions on justification or knowledge. We now turn to the requirements of reliabilism, first considering reliable indicator theories and then turning to process reliabilism.

Reliable indicator theories are typically modeled on the operation of measuring instruments such as thermometers or barometers. D. M. Armstrong, for example, introduces his account in the following manner: "Suppose, on a certain occasion, a thermometer is reliably registering 'T⁰'. There must be some property of the instrument and/or its circumstances such that, if anything has this property, and registers 'T⁰', it must be the case, as a matter of natural law, that the temperature *is* T⁰."[30] Applying this characterization to the case of knowledge, we get

A's non-inferential belief that c is a J is a case of non-inferential *knowledge* if, and only if:
   (i) Jc
   (ii) $(\exists H)$ [Ha & there is a law-like connection in nature $(x)(y)\{$if Hx, then (if BxJy, then Jy)$\}$],[31]

where *H* is a predicate variable ranging over conditions and/or circumstances of cognizers, x ranges over beings capable of cognition, and y ranges over particulars that can figure in "beliefs concerning things at particular times and places."[32]

To articulate Armstrong's account of mathematical knowledge, we must first address the *semantic* issue of how mathematical propositions are to be analyzed. Armstrong contends that the proposition that $2 + 3 = 5$ can be analyzed as the conjunction of two *general* propositions:

   (1) For all x and y, *if* x is a set having two and only two members, and y is a wholly distinct set having three and only three members, *then* the union of x and y has only five members.
   (2) For all z, *if* z is a set having five and only five members, *then* there exist wholly distinct subsets of z, v, and w, such that v has two members and w has three members.

Hence, to believe that $2 + 3 = 5$ is to believe the conjunction of (1) and (2).

But what is it to believe a general proposition? Armstrong proposes to analyze belief in a general proposition as a disposition to create and/or causally sustain certain further beliefs about particular matters of fact given certain other beliefs about particular matters of fact. More formally, we have

---

30. Armstrong, *Belief, Truth and Knowledge*, 167.
31. Ibid., 170.
32. Ibid., 5.

A believes that (x)(if Fx, then Gx) if, and only if:
A is so *disposed* that, for all x, if A believes that Fx, then this belief-
state will both create (if necessary) and weakly causally sustain within
A's mind the belief that Gx is true.[33]

Consequently, to fully articulate Armstrong's treatment of belief in mathematical propositions, we need to know what sorts of particular beliefs are
dispositionally connected when one believes a general proposition such as
(1) or (2).

For the sake of simplicity, let us focus exclusively on (1). The beliefs about
particular matters of fact that are dispositionally connected by the belief that
(1) are illustrated by the following example: "An instance of an appropriate
antecedent belief might be the conjunctive belief that there are two and only
two apples in this bowl *and* that there are three and only three apples in
that other bowl. This belief might then create and sustain the belief that there
are five and only five apples in the two bowls taken together."[34] Hence, S's
belief that 2 + 3 = 5 is analyzed ultimately in terms of S's disposition to form
beliefs about *aggregates of physical objects* such as apples and causal connections among these beliefs.

An immediate problem arises: Armstrong's analysis of the mathematical
proposition that 2 + 3 = 5 treats number as a property of sets. Furthermore,
he explicitly endorses the view that number and other mathematical notions
such as primeness are properties of sets. However, when we turn to his account of the *belief* that 2 + 3 = 5 and, in particular, focus on the particular
beliefs in terms of which the general belief is analyzed, there is no mention
of sets of apples. Instead, there is only mention of the apples in the bowls.

This vacillation points to a fundamental and irresolvable tension in
Armstrong's account that parallels Benacerraf's problem. Armstrong explicitly maintains that only spatiotemporal particulars stand in lawlike connections to beliefs. Noninferential knowledge is limited to knowledge of
particular matters of fact. Hence, Armstrong's *epistemic* theory requires that
number be a property of *aggregates of spatiotemporal particulars* such as
apples. His *semantic* theory, however, requires that number be treated as a
property of *sets*. Armstrong attempts to finesse this problem by observing
that some sets have spatiotemporal particulars as their only members. Although the observation is correct, it is beside the point. It does not follow
from the fact that a set has only spatiotemporal particulars as members, that
the set itself is a spatiotemporal particular. This fundamental point undermines Armstrong's claim that some substitution instances for the variables
in mathematical propositions such as (1) and (2) yield propositions about
particular matters of fact. Aggregates of apples are *not* sets. But it is only
terms that designate sets that can serve as substitution instances of these

33. Ibid., 201.
34. Ibid., 101.

variables. Therefore, we can conclude that the semantic and epistemic requirements of Armstrong's account are irreconcilable.

Although I have focused exclusively on Armstrong's version of the reliable indicator theory, my results have more general application. Reliable indicator theories are examples of *local* reliability theories.[35] Such theories analyze S's knowledge (or justified belief) that p in terms of some relation between S's belief that p and the proposition that p or the entities referred to by its truth conditions. The challenge they face is to provide a relation that yields plausible results in cases where p's truth conditions make reference to abstract entities. If the account invokes a *causal relation* between S and the entities specified by the truth conditions of the proposition believed, then it faces the problem that abstract entities cannot stand in causal relations. If the account retains the causal condition but weakens it to require only that the proposition that p figure in a *causal explanation* of S's belief that p, then the account is too weak to be of any epistemic interest. If the account reverts to an analysis that does not overtly invoke causal notions but employs, instead, a *counterfactual conditional* such as "If p were not true then S would not believe that p," then it faces the problem of providing truth conditions for counterfactuals with impossible antecedents.[36] If the account appeals to *lawlike connections*, then, since such connections support counterfactual conditionals, the account is again faced with the problem of providing truth conditions for counterfactuals with impossible antecedents. Finally, if the account introduces a relation, such as *conditional probability*, that has no counterfactual implications, the resulting condition is too weak for either knowledge or justified belief.[37] Hence, our results provide strong evidence that no local reliability theory is compatible with knowledge of abstract entities.

Process reliabilism is not immediately open to the objections raised against reliable indicator theories; those objections depend on the assumption that S's knowledge (or justified belief) that p must consist in part on a relationship between S's belief that p and the unique proposition that p or the entities referred to by its truth conditions. Process reliabilism, however, is an example of a *global* reliability theory. Such theories analyze S's knowledge (or justified belief) that p in terms of the propensity of the process that produces the belief to produce true beliefs in a *range* of distinct propositions. Our primary concern is to determine whether process reliabilism underwrites any conditions that are incompatible with knowledge of abstract entities.

Penelope Maddy endorses a version of process reliabilism that, she maintains, is free of such conditions:

35. McGinn, "The Concept of Knowledge," and Goldman, *Epistemology and Cognition*, chap. 3, discuss the distinction between local and global reliability theories.

36. Nozick, *Philosophical Explanations*, chap. 3, offers such an analysis.

37. See, for example, Swain, "Justification and Reliable Belief." I argue in "Causality, Reliabilism, and Mathematical Knowledge" that Swain's condition is too weak.

(M1) S's belief that p is (non-inferentially) justified if it results immediately from a reliable process.[38]

Since (M1) does not require that S stand in some causal relation to the entities in virtue of which *p* is true, it does not rule out the possibility of S's having justified beliefs about abstract entities. Unfortunately, (M1) is an inadequate formulation of process reliabilism. For example, suppose that S's belief that *p* is produced by some reliable process *R* but S has other evidence that *p* is false or that *R* is unreliable. Under such circumstances, S's belief that *p* is *not* justified despite satisfying the antecedent of (M1).

Alvin Goldman is sensitive to this problem and offers a more sophisticated version of process reliabilism:

(G2) S's believing p at t is justified if and only if
  (a) S's believing p at t is permitted by a right system of J-rules, and
  (b) this permission is not undermined by S's cognitive state at t.[39]

According to (G2), any belief produced by a basic reliable psychological process satisfies (a). Such a belief is justified provided that S does not possess defeating evidence such as that the belief is false or that it is produced by an unreliable process. (G2) also appears to be compatible with the possibility of justified beliefs about abstract entities since neither (a) nor (b) involves any causal conditions. However, (G2) is open to objection.

Let us begin by considering Laurence BonJour's case that involves a belief formed by the process of clairvoyance:

Norman, under certain conditions which usually obtain, is a completely reliable clairvoyant with respect to certain kinds of subject matter. He possesses no evidence or reasons of any kind for or against the general possibility of such a cognitive power or for or against the thesis that he possesses it. One day Norman comes to believe that the President is in New York City, though he has no evidence either for or against this belief. In fact the belief is true and results from his clairvoyant power under circumstances in which it is completely reliable.[40]

BonJour argues that Goldman's (a) and (b) are both satisfied but Norman's belief is not justified. The belief is not justified because Norman has no reason to believe that he has clairvoyant power. Hence, if Norman's belief about the president is based on the belief that he is clairvoyant, it is unjustified since the belief on which it is based is unjustified. On the other hand, if his belief about the president is not based on the belief that he is clairvoyant, then Norman should reject it as an unfounded hunch.

---

38. Maddy, "Mathematical Epistemology," 48.
39. Goldman, *Epistemology and Cognition*, 63.
40. BonJour, *The Structure of Empirical Knowledge*, 41.

Goldman argues that the counterexample is only apparent:

> BonJour describes this case as one in which Norman possesses no evidence or reasons of any kind for or against the general possibility of clairvoyance, or for or against the thesis that he possesses it. But it is hard to envisage this description holding. Norman *ought* to reason along the following lines: 'If I had a clairvoyant power, I would surely find *some* evidence for this. I would find myself believing things in otherwise inexplicable ways, and when these things were checked by other reliable processes, they would usually check out positively. Since I lack any such signs, I apparently do not possess reliable clairvoyant processes.' Since Norman ought to reason this way, he is *ex ante* justified in believing that he does not possess reliable clairvoyant processes. This undermines his belief in N [that the president is in New York City].[41]

Hence, Goldman concludes that (b), correctly understood, is not satisfied by Norman's belief.

The leading idea of Goldman's response is that underminers for S's belief that *p* at *t* are not restricted to S's *actual* beliefs at *t*. We also need to take into account beliefs that would (or could) be justified by S's cognitive state at *t*. This idea is captured in the notion of *ex ante* justification:

> (EJ) S is justified *ex ante* at t in believing that p just in case S would (or could) be justified in believing p given his cognitive state at t.[42]

It is Norman's *ex ante* justified belief that he does not possess reliable clairvoyant processes that undermines his belief regarding the whereabouts of the president.

Goldman's response is not convincing. For Norman's belief that he does not have reliable clairvoyant processes to be justified *ex ante*, the premises from which he derives this conclusion must also be justified *ex ante*. Consider now the premise

> (P) If I had a clairvoyant power, I would surely find some evidence for this.

(P) is not justified *ex ante* for Norman unless his cognitive state contains some information about the conditions under which clairvoyance produces beliefs and the sorts of beliefs it produces. Unless Norman is justified *ex ante* in believing that

> (C) If I had a clairvoyant power, I would form beliefs of kind *K* under circumstances *C*,

he is not in a position to determine whether he would have evidence that he is clairvoyant if in fact he is. But there is no reason to suppose that (C) is

41. Goldman, *Epistemology and Cognition*, 112.
42. Ibid.

justified by Norman's cognitive state at t. Perhaps little information is available about clairvoyance, and even if it is available Norman may not possess it. Furthermore, even if we assume that Norman is justified *ex ante* in believing (C), it does not follow that he is justified *ex ante* in believing (P). For example, if circumstances C rarely obtain and, when they do, clairvoyance produces few beliefs, Norman would not be justified *ex ante* in believing (P). Hence, despite Goldman's claim to the contrary, (G2) remains vulnerable to BonJour's objection.

The source of (G2)'s vulnerability can be exposed by considering a different case.[43] Suppose that Maud belongs to an organization whose leaders believe, on flimsy grounds, that clairvoyance is a reliable source of knowledge. Furthermore, suppose that extensive empirical work has been done to investigate this phenomenon, the results have been negative, and this information is *present* in Maud's epistemic community. Others are aware of the information, which is widely reported by newspapers, magazines, books, and television. Moreover, Maud has *ready access* to this information. Others with whom she interacts have this information and would share it if asked. The newspapers and magazines that she sometimes reads report the information. Books and periodicals owned by the library that she frequently visits document the information. Television programs broadcast on channels that she views present the information. The leaders of the organization are aware of the negative evidence, the fact that it is widely publicized, and the fact that many of their followers have ready access to the information. As a consequence, they continually urge their followers to ignore information from outside sources on the subject. Maud adheres to their wishes and succeeds in forming very few beliefs about clairvoyance other than those promulgated within the organization. Now suppose that she is in fact clairvoyant, the process is reliable, and Maud forms the true belief that p via this process. Maud's belief is not justified since the evidence she has in support of the reliability of clairvoyance is flimsy and she chooses to ignore copious evidence to the contrary. Yet her belief satisfies both (a) and (b) in (G2). (b) is satisfied because Maud is not justified in believing that clairvoyance is not a reliable belief-forming process. Her belief system is too impoverished to justify that belief despite the fact that she has ready access to evidence that would support it.

(G2) is vulnerable to the case of Maud because it assumes that only evidence one possesses is relevant to the justification of one's beliefs. It does not take into account the social dimension of justification. Yet, as the case of Maud indicates, one cannot ignore readily available evidence, and such evidence, even if ignored, can be relevant to the justification of one's beliefs. Hence, any plausible account of undermining evidence must take into

---

43. This is a variation of a case presented by BonJour, *The Structure of Empirical Knowledge*, 40, and discussed by Goldman, *Epistemology and Cognition*, 111–112.

account evidence that one does not actually possess but which is present within one's epistemic community and to which one has ready access. Goldman's (b) must be replaced by

   (b*) This permission is not undermined by S's cognitive state at *t* or evidence present within S's epistemic community to which S has ready access at *t*.[44]

(b*) yields the correct result that Maud's justification is undermined by the readily accessible evidence present in her epistemic community about the unreliability of clairvoyance.

Norman's case is more delicate since his epistemic situation is not fully articulated by BonJour. There are two possibilities: either readily accessible evidence is present within his epistemic community that casts doubt on the general possibility of clairvoyance or its reliability, or no such evidence is present. If the former, then Norman's belief fails to satisfy (b*) and, hence, is unjustified. Indeed, *our* intuition that Norman's belief is not justified may be due to the tacit assumption that his epistemic setting is similar to ours, and as a consequence he has ready access to the same evidence that generates our doubts about the possibility of clairvoyance. If the latter, then it is hard to see on what basis it can be denied that Norman's belief is justified. One might maintain that Norman has no evidence that clairvoyant power is possible or that he possesses it. This contention is untenable on two grounds. First, it is at variance with our actual epistemic practices. We don't ordinarily require for the justification of our perceptual beliefs that we have evidence about the general possibility of reliable perceptual access to physical objects or the specific thesis that we possess it. Given that there is no evidence to the contrary, perceptual beliefs formed in normal circumstances are regarded as justified without further evidence. Why should clairvoyance be treated differently? Moreover, such a requirement, if generalized, leads to skepticism, for the evidence in question must derive from *some* cognitive power. But if evidence about the possibility or reliability of that power is necessary in order for its deliverances to be justified, justification cannot get off the ground.

What are the implications of replacing (b) by (b*) for the issue of knowledge of abstract entities? The primary consequence of (b*) is that information within S's epistemic community about both the possibility and the reliability of a belief-forming process is relevant to whether that process justifies the beliefs that it produces in S. Hence, the question we must address

---

44. Harman, *Thought*, chap. 9, and *Change in View*, chap. 5, forcefully draw attention to the importance of evidence one does not possess. Goldman, "What Is Justified Belief?" 20, acknowledges the relevance of available belief-forming processes in an earlier account of undermining evidence. That account, however, is too restrictive to handle the case of Maud since Goldman explicitly rules out gathering new evidence from the scope of available processes.

is whether the causal inertness of abstract entities provides any basis for questioning the possibility or reliability of the processes alleged to produce beliefs about such entities.

Let us first consider clairvoyance. Clairvoyants claim to have experiences of geographically distant events. Presumably, such experiences have a unique phenomenology that distinguishes them from, say, having a premonition that the event will occur. Such experiences give clairvoyants some basis for believing that they have epistemic access to geographically distant events. They also have access to contrary evidence of two sorts. First, there is controversy over the existence and reliability of the process. Other cognizers maintain that they do not have clairvoyant experiences. In addition, some also question the reliability of beliefs based on such experiences, maintaining that clairvoyants selectively focus on their successes and ignore their failures. In the face of evidence that others do not have such experiences, clairvoyants must believe that they have unique cognitive equipment, that the others have the same equipment but that it is malfunctioning, or that the others are less reliable reporters of the facts of their cognitive lives. There is little evidence to support any of the alternatives. Moreover, in the face of instances of clairvoyant error, clairvoyants can provide only anecdotal evidence to support the contention that the instances cited are anomalous and that the process is generally reliable.

Second, we have little information about the underlying neurophysiological mechanisms by which the process produces beliefs. Since we take for granted that all cognitive processes have a neurophysiological basis, the lack of supporting neurophysiological evidence reinforces the concern about the existence of the process. Moreover, the events reported in clairvoyant beliefs do not appear to play a role in producing those beliefs. The fact that these events do not play a role in producing beliefs about them indicates that clairvoyance produces beliefs in a manner different from those reliable cognitive processes that we do understand. Yet our ignorance about the neurophysiological mechanisms underlying clairvoyance precludes any alternative explanation. So the belief that clairvoyance is a reliable process introduces an explanatory gap, which reinforces the concern about the reliability of the process. Hence, even if S's belief that p is produced by a reliable process of clairvoyance, the presence of evidence that calls into question the possibility and reliability of clairvoyance suggests that (b*) is not satisfied and that S's belief is not justified.

Our observations about clairvoyance have clear parallels in the case of processes that are alleged to provide cognitive access to abstract entities. Proponents of the a priori maintain that they have cognitive access to abstract entities via a nonexperiential process, call it *intuition*, and that the process justifies beliefs about those entities. Associated with the process are cognitive states with a unique phenomenology that its proponents recognize. The experience of such phenomenologically distinct states provides them with some reason to believe that they have cognitive access to abstract entities. But there is also contrary evidence of two kinds. First, there is controversy over the existence and reliability of intuition. Some maintain that they do not have the cognitive states in question; others acknowledge having such states but deny that they provide cognitive access to abstract entities. Moreover, there are others who question the reliability of beliefs based on intuition, and there have been movements within the fields of mathematics and philosophy to dispel such appeals. In the face of evidence that others do not have such experiences, proponents of the a priori must believe that they have unique cognitive equipment, that the others have the same equipment but that it is malfunctioning, or that the others are less reliable reporters of the facts of their cognitive lives. There is little evidence to support any of the alternatives. In the face of alleged instances of intuitive error, proponents can provide only anecdotal evidence to support the contention that the instances cited are anomalous and that the process is generally reliable.

Second, these problems are reinforced by the fact that little is known about the neurophysiological mechanisms by which intuition produces beliefs. Since we take it for granted that all cognitive processes have a neurophysiological basis, the absence of supporting neurophysiological evidence heightens suspicions about the existence of the process. Moreover, the causal inertness of abstract entities ensures that they play no role in generating beliefs about them. Hence, if intuition is a reliable process, its reliability cannot be explained along the same lines as the reliability of our best understood cognitive processes. But, given that the underlying neurophysiological processes are unknown, we are not in a position to offer an alternative explanation. The belief that intuition is a reliable process introduces an explanatory gap, which reinforces the concerns about the reliability of the process.

The question before us is whether the causal inertness of abstract entities poses an obstacle to satisfaction of (b*) in (G2) by processes, such as intuition, that produce beliefs whose truth conditions refer to abstract entities. Beliefs produced by intuition satisfy (b*) only if there is no readily accessible evidence present within one's epistemic community that calls into question the possibility or reliability of intuition. The parallels between clairvoyance and intuition *suggest* that there is such evidence. Moreover, the causal inertness of abstract entities plays a role in that evidence since it introduces an obstacle to explaining the reliability of intuition. Reaching a final determination on the matter, however, requires a more detailed investigation of two issues: the scope and quality of the available evidence, and how strongly a potential defeater must be supported in order to defeat the justification conferred on a belief by virtue of its being reliably produced. This more detailed investigation goes beyond the scope of the present discussion.[45] My primary conclusion is that, within the framework of process

45. I will say more about it in chapter 6.

reliabilism, the causal inertness of abstract entities poses a threat to a priori justification. Although process reliabilism does not rule out the possibility that processes such as intuition justify beliefs whose truth conditions refer to abstract entities, the absence of an explanation of how those processes can reliably produce such beliefs generates potential defeaters for such justification.

Let us take stock. My primary concern is whether philosophical naturalism provides the resources to establish that a priori knowledge is incompatible with plausible constraints on an adequate theory of knowledge. My investigation yields two strategies for arguing against the a priori. The first is to endorse a naturalized concept of knowledge, such as the causal theory or the reliable indicator theory, that involves a causal constraint incompatible with knowledge of abstract entities. This strategy is not very promising since proponents of the a priori are in a position to offer a non-question-begging argument against the concepts in question. They can argue that there are compelling counterexamples to the analyses from the domain of empirical knowledge. Moreover, even in the absence of compelling counterexamples, they can reject the problematic concepts if they have available an alternative concept of knowledge that accommodates the same range of cases as the problematic concept but does not involve the causal constraint. In short, the first strategy can succeed only if the problematic naturalized analysis is clearly the best available analysis of the concept of knowledge. Neither the causal theory nor the reliable indicator theory enjoys such stature.

The second strategy is to endorse a naturalized concept of justification, such as process reliabilism, and argue that processes producing beliefs whose truth conditions refer to abstract entities do not satisfy the defeasibility condition articulated in (b*). Proponents of the a priori cannot meet this challenge by simply rejecting process reliabilism. Defeasibility conditions enjoy a certain degree of theory neutrality. There is general agreement among epistemologists that there are two important classes of defeaters for S's justified belief that p: overriding defeaters, which provide evidence that p is false, and undermining defeaters, which provide evidence that S's justification is defective. All theories of justification must accommodate both types of defeaters or cogently challenge the intuitions and arguments supporting them. Evidence against the possibility or reliability of a cognitive process is a familiar example of an undermining defeater. Faced with evidence that intuition is not possible or that it is unreliable, proponents of the a priori have two options. The first is to deny that such evidence defeats the justification conferred on beliefs by intuition. This option is not very promising, given widespread consensus to the contrary. The second is to argue that the evidence alleged to call into question the existence and reliability of intuition is insufficient to do so. This remains a viable option.

I conclude that there is no straightforward route from philosophical naturalism to the rejection of a priori knowledge. The primary threat is that the causal inertness of abstract entities exacerbates concerns about the existence and reliability of processes that are alleged to provide cognitive access to such entities by precluding any explanation of the reliability of such processes. Such concerns provide potential defeaters for beliefs justified by those processes. This threat, however, is more ominous than Benacerraf's original in one important respect: if the causal inertness of abstract entities generates defeaters for the processes that produce beliefs about them, the proponent of the a priori cannot circumvent the problem merely by rejecting philosophical naturalism. Intuitions about the conditions under which justification is defeated are not typically tied to particular theories of justification. Hence, the primary threat to the a priori that we have uncovered through our investigation of philosophical naturalism is not essentially tied to philosophical naturalism. It is a more general problem.

5.6   Scientific Naturalism

The final issue that we must address is whether scientific naturalism provides support for Benacerraf's concerns about knowledge of abstract entities. According to scientific naturalism, epistemology is to be replaced by the scientific study of scientific knowledge. Moreover, science, including the branch that replaces epistemology, is autonomous and not subject to philosophical demands from without. Hence, if scientific naturalism provides support for Benacerraf's epistemic concerns, that support must come from within some branch of science. The primary obstacle we face in determining whether there is such support is that few scientific naturalists present the relevant scientific results. Furthermore, when such support is presented, closer examination reveals that it arises from within philosophy rather than from within science.

Penelope Maddy provides the most articulate attempt to show that Benacerraf's epistemic concerns are underwritten by Quine's naturalized epistemology. She maintains that the causal inertness of abstract entities generates a problem concerning mathematical knowledge whose source is not some naturalized descendant of the causal theory, such as reliabilism:

> To the extent that these are intended as a priori philosophical theories of what knowledge or justification consists in, any broad sceptical conclusion based on them—e.g. that mathematics is not a science—errs against the tenets of epistemology naturalized. To the extent that reliabilism and the rest are proposals for naturalized accounts of what knowledge is, given the overwhelming evidence in favour of mathematical knowledge, they will not last long as parts of our best theory if they purport to rule it out.[46]

46. Maddy, *Realism in Mathematics*, 42–43.

The problem for the scientific naturalist is not conceptual but explanatory. When mathematicians, such as R. M. Solovay, form opinions on mathematical matters, they are usually correct. Hence,

> Even if reliabilism turns out not to be the correct analysis of knowledge and justification, indeed, even if knowledge and justification themselves turn out to be dispensable notions, there will remain the problem of explaining the undeniable fact of our expert's reliability. In particular, even from a completely naturalized perspective, the Platonist still owes us an explanation of how and why Solovay's beliefs about sets are reliable indicators of the truth about sets.[47]

The causal inertness of abstract entities, alleges Maddy, is a bar to explaining the reliability of Solovay's mathematical beliefs.

Three questions arise with respect to Maddy's claim that, from the perspective of scientific naturalism, some explanation of the reliability of Solovay's mathematical beliefs is necessary. First, does the demand for such an explanation arise from within science? Second, is there any basis, from within science, for believing that the causal inertness of abstract entities is a bar to providing such an explanation? Third, what are the scientific implications of failing to provide the explanation?

Maddy claims that some explanation of Solovay's reliability is necessary. But what is the source of the demand? From a completely naturalized perspective, science is an autonomous discipline that is not subject to philosophical demands from without. Hence, to show that the demand for an explanation of Solovay's reliability arises from within a completely naturalized perspective, Maddy must show that the demand arises from within science. The only evidence she offers is that two camps of naturalized realists agree that the reliability of experts requires explanation: "Both parties to the debate agree that Jobe's reliability needs explanation, and they agree on the sorts of facts that might provide one. When a person is reliable on some subject . . . that reliability needs an explanation."[48] But here we must distinguish between the views of philosophers who call themselves "naturalized" and the views of scientists engaged in the relevant scientific enterprise. Philosophers do not become scientists by adopting the label "naturalized." Moreover, their views do not qualify as scientific by virtue of the fact that they have adopted the label. Maddy's question about the reliability of Solovay's beliefs may very well arise from within science, but the evidence she cites does not support this contention.

Let us grant that the question of Solovay's reliability arises from within science. Is there any reason, from within science, for thinking that the causal inertness of mathematical entities poses an obstacle to providing a scientifically acceptable answer? "Obviously, what we are up against here is

47. Ibid., 43.
48. Ibid., 19.

another, less specific, version of the same vague conviction that makes the causal theory of knowledge so persuasive: in order to be dependable, the process by which I come to believe claims about xs must ultimately be responsive in some appropriate way to actual xs."[49] The alleged bar to explaining Solovay's reliability is a causal condition on reliable belief formation:

> (M2) The process by which S comes to have beliefs about xs is reliable (dependable) only if that process is appropriately responsive to xs.

If the alleged bar arises from within science, there must be evidence from within some relevant branch of science that supports (M2). Maddy offers three supporting considerations:

> (a) The mathematics/science analogy
> (b) The belief that all explanations are ultimately causal
> (c) A strong form of physicalism.

All three considerations appear to be philosophical in character. Moreover, Maddy does not attempt to dispel the appearance by offering some evidence that commitment to either (a), (b), or (c) arises from within science. She does, however, maintain that there is support for (a) from within mathematics.

According to the mathematics/science analogy, mathematics resembles natural science in two important respects:

> (a1) Some mathematical beliefs are basic and non-inferential.
> (a2) Basic mathematical beliefs are produced by a "perception-like" mechanism, which is most likely causal.[50]

The support Maddy offers for the analogy from within mathematics is that "mathematicians are not apt to think that the justification for their claims waits on the activities in the physics labs. Rather, mathematicians have a whole range of justificatory practices of their own, ranging from proofs and intuitive evidence, to plausibility arguments and defences in terms of consequences."[51]

Maddy's description of mathematical practice, if taken at face value, supports (a1); it supports a conception of mathematics as an autonomous discipline with its own justificatory procedures, some of which are non-inferential. The primary epistemic consequence of the description is that it undercuts Quine's holistic account of mathematical knowledge. Nothing in the description supports (a2). The only support that Maddy offers for (a2) is the opinion of one, albeit significant mathematician, Kurt Gödel. But from the fact that one mathematician endorses (a2), it does not follow that it is supported by *mathematical practice*. Mathematicians can have opinions

49. Ibid., 44.
50. Ibid., 45–46.
51. Ibid., 31.

about issues that don't arise from within mathematics, and not all issues about mathematics arise from within mathematics. Some arise from within traditional epistemology. What needs to be shown is that Gödel is addressing a question that arises from within the practice of mathematics and that his answer is generally accepted by mathematicians.

Finally, we must address the consequences of a failure to explain Solovay's reliability. First, if the question does not arise from within science, a failure to answer it is not likely to be of much scientific import. Second, in the context of discussing naturalized accounts of knowledge, Maddy observes that, given the overwhelming evidence in favor of mathematical knowledge, any account that entails mathematical skepticism would not last long as part of our best overall theory. This observation applies with equal force to her own position. Any principle, such as (M2), that entails that Solovay, and mathematicians generally, do not reliably form mathematical beliefs would not last long as part of our best overall theory.

Maddy is aware of the problem. In the context of a discussion of whether Benacerraf's epistemic concerns provide support for nominalism, she presents John Burgess's case that, from a naturalized perspective, they fail to do so:[52]

> Burgess considers the actual practices of scientists. Here we find well-confirmed affirmations of mathematical knowledge and no attributions of causal powers to mathematical entities. Thus, a causal requirement on knowledge of the sort enshrined in Benacerraf's first premiss simply doesn't turn up in the descriptive phase of epistemology naturalized.[53]

Maddy recognizes that this argument appears to undercut (M2), but she resists this conclusion:

> If Burgess is right, his arguments would undermine the effectiveness of Benacerraf-style worries as justifications for nominalism. However welcome this conclusion might be, it does nothing to take the compromise Platonist off the epistemological hook. By rejecting pure Quine/Putnamism, by embracing some version of Gödel's science/ mathematics parallelism, the compromise Platonist incurs the very real debt detailed in the last chapter: within the bounds of epistemology naturalized, she owes a descriptive and explanatory account of mathematical knowledge (or mathematical reliability) that does justice to the actual practice of mathematics, an account of both intuition and other peculiarly mathematical justifications.[54]

This response, however, fails to appreciate the force of Burgess's argument. His claim is that, within scientific practice, there are well-confirmed attributions of mathematical reliability and no attributions of causal powers to

---

52. Burgess, "Epistemology and Nominalism."
53. Maddy, *Realism in Mathematics*, 46.
54. Ibid., 48.

mathematical entities. Therefore, the causal condition enshrined in (a2) of the mathematics/science analogy does not appear within science. The upshot is that Maddy's compromise platonist is yet another philosopher placing constraints on scientific knowledge that do not arise from within science. In short, she is not a fully naturalized philosopher.

Hartry Field's view of Benacerraf's epistemic challenge is similar to Maddy's in two respects. First, he thinks that the challenge goes beyond the requirements of the causal theory of knowledge and its naturalized descendants. Second, the challenge, according to Field, is to explain how knowledge of mathematical entities is possible, not to explain how mathematical beliefs are justified: "The way to understand Benacerraf's challenge, I think, is not as a challenge to our ability to *justify* our mathematical beliefs, but as a challenge to our ability to *explain the reliability* of these beliefs."[55] This way of putting the challenge allows Field to concede that we may have some initial justification for our mathematical beliefs in terms of their initial plausibility or indispensability for scientific explanation, while insisting that there is a residual problem: "The challenge . . . is to provide an account of the mechanisms that explain how our beliefs about these remote entities can so well reflect the facts about them. The idea is that *if it appears in principle impossible to explain this*, then that tends to *undermine* the belief in mathematical entities, *despite* whatever reason we might have for believing in them."[56]

Can Maddy invoke Field's defense of Benacerraf's premise to bolster her case? Field does not claim to be offering a defense of Benacerraf's premise from the requirements of naturalized epistemology. Moreover, the defense he offers cannot be plausibly construed as arising from within science since he offers no evidence that the demand for an explanation of the reliability of our mathematical beliefs arises from within either mathematics or natural science. Furthermore, he provides no evidence that scientists view the abstractness of mathematical entities as posing a serious obstacle to providing such an explanation. Finally, he provides no reason to believe that scientists would view the failure to explain the reliability of our mathematical beliefs as evidence that we do not have mathematical knowledge. But, if the defense does not arise from the requirements of science, from where does it arise?

Field claims that Benacerraf's challenge is not about the justification of mathematical beliefs. He concedes that we have supporting reasons for such beliefs. The challenge is to explain the reliability of our mathematical beliefs. The challenge is significant, according to Field, because failure to answer it undermines our mathematical beliefs. If failure to answer the challenge undermines our mathematical beliefs despite our supporting reasons,

55. Field, *Realism, Mathematics and Modality*, 25.
56. Ibid., 26.

then presumably that failure undermines the justification that our supporting reasons confer on our mathematical beliefs. Hence, Field's argument
turns on a claim about the conditions under which justification is defeated.
But the project of articulating the conditions under which the justification
of a belief is defeated, like the project of articulating the conditions under
which a belief is known or justified, is one that falls squarely within the
province of traditional epistemology. Hence, Field's defense ultimately arises
from the requirements of the theory of knowledge.

I close with two observations about Field's defense of Benacerraf's
epistemic premise. First, it cannot be utilized by scientific naturalists, such
as Maddy, since it is supported by considerations from within the theory of
knowledge rather than by considerations from within science. Second, his
assessment of the challenge posed by the causal inertness of abstract entities
dovetails with the conclusion of section 5.5. There I argued that the causal
inertness of abstract entities plays a role in generating potential defeaters
for justified beliefs about them. Although Field makes the stronger claim
that the explanatory problem *undermines* whatever justification we have
for beliefs about abstract entities, he offers no supporting argument. In the
absence of an argument that articulates the degree of support our mathematical beliefs enjoy and the degree of support that the defeating evidence enjoys, the most we can conclude is that the explanatory problems generated
by the causal inertness of abstract entities *threaten* a priori justification.

In sections 5.4, 5.5, and 5.6 I investigate whether there are any plausible
constraints on an adequate theory of knowledge that are incompatible with
a priori knowledge. The primary challenge is from proponents of epistemic
naturalism who maintain that knowledge of statements whose truth conditions refer to abstract entities cannot be accommodated within a naturalized theory of knowledge. I distinguish between two forms of naturalism,
philosophical and scientific. The former places naturalistic constraints on
traditional philosophical projects, such as conceptual analysis, whereas the
latter advocates replacing those projects by a scientific account of scientific knowledge. With respect to philosophical naturalism, I argue that naturalized concepts of knowledge, such as the causal theory and the reliable
indicator theory, that involve conditions incompatible with knowledge of
abstract entities are inadequate. I also argue that, although process reliabilism
does not rule out the possibility of justified beliefs about abstract entities,
there is evidence that calls into question the possibility and reliability of
the processes that produce such beliefs. This evidence poses a threat to the
a priori since, if sufficient, it can defeat whatever justification such processes
confer on the beliefs that they produce. Moreover, such evidence has the
potential to constitute defeaters for a priori justification even if process
reliabilism is rejected. My evaluation of scientific naturalism is more straightforward. Scientific naturalists must provide evidence from within science
that indicates that knowledge of abstract entities is problematic. I argue that
the supporting evidence they offer is philosophical rather than scientific.

Hence, they have provided no reason to believe that scientific naturalism cannot accommodate the a priori.

5.7 Conclusion

Chapter 5 examines radical empiricist arguments against the existence of a priori knowledge. The arguments fall into three categories. Those in the first category are based on an analysis of the concept of a priori knowledge. They allege that a priori justification entails rational unrevisability. I distinguish between a strong and a weak version of the Unrevisability Thesis and argue that both are untenable. The arguments in the second category offer radical empiricist accounts of knowledge of propositions traditionally alleged to be knowable only a priori. The inductivist account falls short of its goal since it overlooks the possibility of epistemic overdetermination with respect to the class of propositions in question. The holistic approach either collapses into a version of the conceptual approach or depends on an unsubstantiated assumption about the relationship between the a priori and the analytic. Those in the third category maintain that epistemic naturalism is incompatible with a priori knowledge. My investigation of epistemic naturalism yields three primary conclusions. First, although there are naturalized concepts of knowledge, such as the causal theory of knowledge and the reliable indicator theory, that underwrite conditions on knowledge that are incompatible with knowledge of abstract entities, there are independent grounds for rejecting those concepts. Second, there are naturalized concepts of knowledge, such as process reliabilism, that are compatible with knowledge of abstract entities. My discussion of process reliabilism, however, reveals that the causal inertness of abstract entities introduces an obstacle to explaining the reliability of processes producing beliefs about such entities. This explanatory gap constitutes potential defeating evidence for beliefs justified by such processes that cannot be circumvented simply by rejecting process reliabilism. Evidence that calls into question the reliability of a process that is alleged to justify a belief is a generally accepted example of an undermining defeater for that belief's justification regardless of the particular account of justification that one endorses. Third, arguments based on scientific naturalism fail because they turn on philosophical premises for which there is no scientific support.

6

Toward a Resolution

6.1 Introduction

The first five chapters yielded two primary results, one regarding the *concept* of a priori justification and one regarding the *existence* of a priori justified beliefs. I argued that, within the traditional conceptual framework of the theory of knowledge, a coherent concept of a priori justification is available. A priori justification is nonexperiential justification. Traditional radical empiricists cannot coherently dispute the cogency of this concept. Their leading claim, which is that every justified belief is ultimately justified by experience, involves the concept of *experiential* justification.

One final issue remains to be resolved. Although traditional epistemologists, both apriorists and radical empiricists, employ the concept of experience, it does not follow that it is coherent. If the distinction between experiential and nonexperiential sources of justification cannot be coherently articulated, then at least part of the traditional framework of epistemic concepts must be rejected. The remaining conceptual hurdle is to provide a characterization of the distinction or, at a minimum, some reason to believe that one is forthcoming.

With respect to the existence of a priori knowledge, I argued that the leading arguments are inconclusive. The conceptual arguments, both for and against the a priori, involve implausible conditions on a priori justification. Supporting criterial arguments involve false epistemic premises, whereas deficiency arguments fail to show that radical empiricism has unacceptable consequences that are avoided by apriorism. Radical empiricist accounts of knowledge of propositions alleged to be knowable only a priori do not establish that those propositions are not known a priori. Finally, neither philosophical nor scientific naturalism supports the claim that a priori knowledge is incompatible with epistemic naturalism.

Two features of the arguments for and against the a priori emerge. They purport to reveal, largely on a priori grounds, deficiencies in the other position. Establishing the existence of a priori knowledge, however, requires more than revealing deficiencies in radical empiricist theories of knowledge. It requires offering supporting evidence for the claim that there are nonexperiential sources of justification. The remaining hurdle is to provide the requisite supporting evidence.

The goal of this chapter is to argue that the most promising approaches to resolving the two remaining issues require empirical investigation. In section 6.2, I identify the relevant concept of experience and examine a number of proposals for articulating it by using the traditional tools of conceptual analysis. I argue that none succeeds, and I propose viewing "experience" as a putative natural kind term whose extension is fixed by reference to the cognitive processes associated with the five senses. Whether those processes have important common properties, and, if so, what they are, are questions to be settled by empirical studies of human cognition. In short, uncovering the nature of experience is a matter for empirical, rather than a priori, investigation.

The primary theoretical claim of an apriorist theory of knowledge is that there are nonexperiential sources of justification. Hence, the primary challenge to proponents of the a priori is to offer supporting evidence for this central claim. In section 6.3, I argue that the most promising strategy for providing such supporting evidence consists of two related projects. The first, which is philosophical in character, involves more fully articulating the claim that there are nonexperiential sources of justification. Here I argue that there are three central issues that must be addressed before convincing support for this claim can be provided. The second involves providing empirical support for the articulated claim. Here I identify four areas where empirical investigation has the potential to provide significant support for apriorism. Section 6.4 addresses objections to the strategy of supporting the a priori by empirical investigation.

6.2   The Concept of Experience

In chapter 2, I argued that a priori justification is justification by a nonexperiential source but did not offer an analysis, or even a more informal characterization, of the distinction between experiential and nonexperiential sources of justification. If that distinction is not coherent, the traditional debate over the a priori is rooted in conceptual confusion. Hence, we now turn to the question of whether there is a coherent concept of nonexperiential justification.

Let us begin by focusing attention on the relevant target. Opponents of the a priori frequently complain that they find alleged a priori sources of justification, such as logical intuition, mysterious. Proponents offer a characteristic response. According to John Pollock, "Logically intuiting something is a phenomenologically unique *experience* which, although it may not be analyzable into other more familiar kinds of *experience*, is nevertheless a kind of *experience* a person can be quickly taught to recognize and label."[1] Laurence BonJour echoes this sentiment: "Contrary to the claim of mysteriousness, it is hard to see that there is anything in our cognitive *experience* that is, at first glance at least, any more transparently and pellucidly intelligible, any *less* mysterious than this."[2]

The sense of experience involved in these passages, call it the *broad* sense, is not the one that concerns us. This sense applies to any introspectively accessible state of a cognizer. As a consequence, logical intuitions and other cognitive states that allegedly justify a priori are broadly experiential. If the claim that logical intuitions are a source of nonexperiential justification is coherent, then there is another sense of experience, call it the *narrow* sense, in which they are *not* experiences. It is this narrow sense that is our primary concern.

There are two options for analyzing the narrow concept. The first is to offer an exhaustive list of the types of experience incompatible with a priori justification. The second is to provide a general characterization of the relevant type of experience. The enumerative approach faces three problems. The first is completing the list. Although there is general agreement that it includes sense experience (i.e., the experiences associated with the five senses), there is controversy over whether introspection, memory, and testimony should be included.[3] Assuming that the list is completed, the resulting analysis faces two more serious problems. Suppose that the list consists of three types of experience: sense experience, introspection, and memory. The resulting analysis has little explanatory value. For example, it yields the desired result that logical intuition is not a form of experience but offers no indication of why this is so. Since the analysis does not specify the general features by virtue of which sense experience, introspection, and memory qualify as experiences of the relevant type, it provides no rationale for dividing sources of justification into two fundamental categories: the experiential and the nonexperiential. Moreover, the analysis rules out the *possibility* that there are sources of experiential justification other than sense experience, introspection, and memory. If it should turn out, for example, that processes such as telepathy or clairvoyance are sources of justification, they automatically qualify as nonexperiential sources of justification. Hence, an analysis by enumeration is not very promising.

The second option attempts to circumvent these problems by providing a general characterization of the narrow concept. The paradigm of the rele-

---

1. Pollock, *Knowledge and Justification*, 321 (emphases mine).

2. BonJour, *In Defense of Pure Reason*, 108 (first emphasis mine; second BonJour's).

3. Pollock, *Knowledge and Justification*, 301–302, raises questions about introspection. Burge, "Content Preservation," raises questions about memory and testimony.

vant type of experience is sense experience in its various forms. A belief justified exclusively by sense experience is not justified a priori. Any general account of the relevant type of experience must identify some feature of sense experience that is possessed by all, and only, the other relevant types of experience. There are four features of sense experience that might provide the basis for such an account: (1) phenomenological features, (2) the content of beliefs justified by sense experience, (3) the objects of sense experience, and (4) the relation between cognizer and object of experience.

Proponents of the a priori frequently stress that the cognitive states that are alleged to justify a priori are familiar in the sense that they have a distinctive phenomenology that cognizers can easily be taught to recognize and label. The same is true of the experiences associated with the five senses. We readily distinguish between, say, auditory and visual experiences on the basis of differences in their phenomenological character. The fact that these different forms of experience (in the broad sense) have a unique phenomenological character is not sufficient to ensure that the difference between experiential (in the narrow sense) and nonexperiential states can be marked in terms of differences in their phenomenological character. For the distinction to be marked at the phenomenological level, there must be some general phenomenological feature that is (a) exemplified in the phenomenological states associated with all the various types of sense experience, and (b) is also exemplified in the phenomenological states associated with all the other forms of experience alleged to be incompatible with a priori justification. It is dubious that either condition obtains.

Roderick Chisholm, for example, characterizes the states associated with the five senses in terms of *sensible characteristics*.[4] Sensible characteristics, in turn, comprise the "proper objects," which are unique to each of the senses, along with the "common sensibles," which are common to all the senses. Chisholm illustrates the proper objects of each of the senses by providing examples of visual characteristics, auditory characteristics, and so on. The common sensibles are also illustrated by examples such as rest, number, figure, and magnitude. Hence, in the final analysis, Chisholm fails to provide a general characterization of the concept of a sensible characteristic. He fails to identify some general phenomenological feature common to sense experience in its various forms.[5]

Alvin Plantinga, on the other hand, draws attention to the *sensuous* character of sense perception:

> *Experience*, clearly enough, plays a crucial role in sense perception and in perceptual knowledge. First and most obviously, there is what we might call, appropriately enough, *sensuous* experience: in look-

4. Chisholm, *Theory of Knowledge*, 2nd ed., 77–78.
5. Sosa, "The Raft and the Pyramid," 188, maintains that "it is not clear that we can have a viable notion of sensible characteristic on the basis of examples so diverse as colors, shapes, tones, odors, and so on."

ing out at my backyard, perceiving grass, trees, sky, flowers, I am *appeared to* a certain way—greenly, or more accurately, greenly, brownly, bluely, redly, yellowly, and so on.[6]

He also maintains that one way to believe *p* a priori is to see that *p* is true, which requires forming the belief that *p* is necessarily true immediately and "not merely on the basis of memory or testimony."[7] Finally, he also acknowledges that for some individuals "memory seems to work with no sensuous phenomenology at all."[8] Hence, although justification by both sense perception and memory are incompatible with a priori justification, the experiences (in the broad sense) associated with them do not share some distinctive phenomenological characteristic.

Laurence BonJour provides an example of the second approach. He locates the difference between experiential and nonexperiential sources in the character of beliefs justified by each:

> I suggest that the relevant notion of experience should not be restricted to sense experience in a narrow sense, but should rather be understood to include any sort of cognitive factor or element which, whatever its other characteristics may be, provides or constitutes information, *input*, concerning the specific character of the actual world as opposed to other possible worlds.[9]

Experiential sources are those that provide information about only the actual world, whereas nonexperiential sources provide information about all possible worlds. Since experiential sources provide information about only the actual world, they justify only contingent propositions. Alternatively, since nonexperiential sources provide information about all possible worlds, they justify only necessary propositions. Hence, on BonJour's proposal, experiential justification reduces to justified belief in a contingent truth and nonexperiential justification reduces to justified belief in a necessary truth. The proposal faces two objections. First, it rules out the possibility of necessary truths being justified by experience, as well as the possibility of contingent truths being justified nonexperientially. Second, it lacks explanatory force. The proposal offers no indication of the difference, or even whether there is a difference, between the justification involved in believing a necessary truth as opposed to that involved in believing a contingent truth. As a consequence, it cannot explain the epistemic significance of the distinction between a priori and a posteriori justification.

6. Plantinga, *Warrant and Proper Function*, 91.
7. Ibid., 106.
8. Ibid., 59.
9. BonJour, *The Structure of Empirical Knowledge*, 192. BonJour uses the expression "experience in a narrow sense" to refer to what I call "sense experience." BonJour, *In Defense of Pure Reason*, offers a more sophisticated analysis of the relevant concept of experience, which is addressed later in this section.

The third approach draws attention to features of the object of experience. Sense experience in its various forms involves a relation between a cognizer and a physical object. Introspection involves a relation between a cognizer and a psychological state of that cognizer. Memory involves a relation to some earlier belief of the cognizer or, perhaps, some past events. The objects of the various forms of experience, according to the third approach, have a common feature: they are all concrete. Nonexperiential sources, by contrast, all involve a relation to abstract objects.[10] The primary epistemic consequence of the third approach is that experiential sources directly justify only beliefs about concrete objects, whereas nonexperiential sources directly justify only beliefs about abstract objects. This approach faces two objections analogous to those raised against the second approach. First, it rules out the possibility of beliefs about abstract objects being directly justified by experiential sources and the possibility of beliefs about concrete objects being directly justified by nonexperiential sources. Second, the approach also lacks explanatory force. It offers no explanation of how the justification involved in beliefs about concrete objects differs from the justification involved in beliefs about abstract objects. One might suggest that the fact that concrete, but not abstract, objects can stand in causal relations provides the resources for addressing the second alleged shortcoming. I address this suggestion in the ensuing discussion of the fourth approach.

The fourth approach to demarcating the experiential/nonexperiential distinction highlights the relation between cognizer and object of experience. We examine two versions of the approach. Colin McGinn rejects Kant's characterization of the a priori because it relies on "a vague and unanalyzed notion of 'experience'" and endorses the causal theory of perception as conceptually necessary: "The causal requirement spells out what is involved in having experiences of, or beliefs about, the world of particulars."[11] The conjunction of classical empiricism, which holds that empirical knowledge is "ultimately founded on and traceable to perception of the external world,"[12] and the causal theory of perception leads to the following analysis of a posteriori knowledge:

x knows that p *a posteriori* iff

    (i) x knows that p &
    (ii) $(\exists s)$ (s is x's ground or reason for believing that p &
    (iii) the subject-matter of s causes x to believe that p).[13]

On the other hand, x knows that p a priori if and only if (i) and (ii) and not-(iii). In the case of noninferential knowledge that p, "s" is replaced by the statement that p.

10. This view is suggested by Lewis, *On the Plurality of Worlds*, 108–115.
11. McGinn, "*A Priori* and *A Posteriori* Knowledge," 198.
12. Ibid.
13. Ibid., 196.

The proposed analysis accommodates some standard cases of a posteriori knowledge. Suppose, for example, that I am looking at my desk in normal circumstances and form the belief that there is a cup on my desk. Since my belief that there is a cup on my desk is caused by the subject matter of the belief, the cup, McGinn's analysis yields the result that the resulting knowledge is a posteriori. Consider a slightly modified situation. I am gazing out my window and something catches my eye. It looks familiar, but I'm not quite sure what it is. I gaze a bit longer and realize that it looks like a red geranium. I conclude that there is a red geranium in the garden. In this case my belief that there is a red geranium in the garden is based on a belief about how things look to me, and the latter belief provides my grounds for believing the former. Utilizing McGinn's notation, we can represent the situation as follows:

p = there is a red geranium in the garden.
s = the belief that there appears to be a red geranium in the garden.
Subject matter of s = being-appeared-to in a red-geranium-like way.

Since my being-appeared-to in a red-geranium-like way causes my belief that there is a red geranium in the garden, McGinn's analysis, once again, yields the result that the knowledge in question is a posteriori.

Unfortunately, there are cases that it does not accommodate as well. Suppose that I am a novice philosopher and encounter the claim that nothing can be both red and blue all over at the same time. I wonder whether it is true. Initially, I have some reservations. There are other statements with the same logical form that are false. Something can be both red and smooth all over at the same time. I also wonder whether purple objects are red and blue all over at the same time. Upon reflection, however, I come to believe that I now "see" that nothing can be both red and blue all over at the same time. Finally, on the basis of that belief, I conclude that nothing can be both red and blue all over at the same time. We can represent the situation as follows:

p = nothing can be both red and blue all over at the same time.
s = the belief that I "see" that nothing can be both red and blue all over at the same time.
Subject matter of s = "seeing" that nothing can be both red and blue all over at the same time.

Since my "seeing" that nothing can be both red and blue all over at the same time caused me to believe that I "see" that nothing can be both red and blue all over at the same time, the knowledge in question is a posteriori on McGinn's analysis. This case parallels the geranium case of the previous paragraph.

One might reply that in the former case the subject matter of p, the red geranium, causes me to be-appeared-to in a red-geranium-like way. In the latter case, however, the subject matter of p, redness and blueness, does not cause me to "see" that nothing can be both red and blue all over at the same time. Since properties are abstract entities, they cannot cause me to "see" or believe that certain propositions about them are true.[14] This response blocks the counterexample but requires that McGinn's analysis of a posteriori knowledge be revised to include an additional condition:

(iv) the subject matter of p causes the subject matter of s.

A corresponding change in the analysis of a priori knowledge is necessary: x knows that p a priori if and only if (i), (ii), (iii), and not-(iv).

The revision leaves the analysis of a posteriori knowledge open to two problems. First, it is vulnerable to some familiar counterexamples. Suppose I am sitting in front of the fireplace, see that there is a fire in the fireplace, and on this basis come to believe that there is smoke coming out of the chimney. Since the smoke did not cause the fire, (iv) is not satisfied. Hence, if I know that there is smoke coming out of the chimney, my knowledge is not a posteriori. Suppose that you tell me that you will visit me tomorrow, and on that basis I believe that you will visit me. Since your visit did not cause you to tell me that you will visit, (iv) is not satisfied. Hence, if I know that you will visit, my knowledge is not a posteriori. Second, it is incompatible with McGinn's desire to accommodate a posteriori knowledge of propositions knowable a priori:

> Thus suppose you come to know that the lines bisecting the interior angles of an equilateral triangle bisect the sides opposite by drawing many lines and noticing that they regularly display that geometrical property. Then, apparently, it is your causal contact, *via* perception, with those marks that is responsible (*inter alia*) for your inductively forming the belief in question.[15]

The subject matter of the knowledge in question is a geometrical property. Since, by hypothesis, properties are abstract entities, one cannot have causal contact, via perception, with geometrical properties. Hence, (iv) is not satisfied and the knowledge in question is a priori.

McGinn's defense of the causal condition is burdened by the fact that it is embedded within a causal theory of a posteriori knowledge, which is untenable on independent grounds. Laurence BonJour offers a more recent defense of the causal condition, which is free of this burden. His starting point is the traditional negative conception of an a priori justified belief as one that is justified independently of any appeal to experience. Two ques-

---

14. McGinn, ibid., 201, maintains, "Maybe one can come to know mathematical truths by 'perceiving relations between universals', but universals cannot cause such perception, on account of their abstractness."
15. Ibid., 199.

tions arise. What is the relevant sense of *independent*? What is the relevant sense of *experience*? BonJour contends that a priori justification must be independent of experience in the sense of not being based on experience and that experience should include any process that is perceptual in the sense of "(a) being a causally conditioned response to particular, contingent features of the world and (b) yielding doxastic states that have as their content putative information concerning such particular, contingent features of the actual world as contrasted with other possible worlds."[16] Hence, he concludes that *P* is justified a priori for someone if and only if "that person has a reason for thinking *P* to be true that does not depend on any positive appeal to experience or other causally mediated, quasi-perceptual contact with contingent features of the world, but only on pure thought or reason, even if the person's ability to understand *P* in question derives, in whole or in part, from experience."[17] Does BonJour's conception of experience avoid the problems plaguing McGinn's conception?

BonJour's official characterization of experience is straightforward. "Experience" is a predicate that applies primarily to belief-forming processes. A process is experiential if and only if it satisfies two conditions: (a) the causal-initiation condition and (b) the content-of-belief condition. Hence, a process is nonexperiential if and only if it fails to satisfy either (a) or (b).

Two issues complicate matters. First, BonJour's analysis of a priori justification appears to invoke a different conception of experience. The analysis involves two elements, one negative and one positive:

(N) Justification that does not depend on any positive appeal to experience or other causally mediated, quasi-perceptual contact with contingent features of the world;

(P) Justification that does depend only on pure thought or reason.

The characterization of experience in (N) refers only to (a), the causal-initiation condition, and not to (b), the content-of-belief condition. This suggests that the conception of experience involved here is wider, or less stringent, than that in BonJour's official account. A process is experiential if and only if it satisfies (a). The result is a narrower, or more stringent, conception of a nonexperiential process: failure to satisfy (a) is both necessary and sufficient for a process to be nonexperiential.

Second, the reference to "particular, contingent features" in (a) is unclear. According to BonJour's conception of a priori justification, one considers a proposition, such as that nothing can be both red and green all over at the same time, and, on the basis of understanding the proposition, apprehends that it is necessarily true. Presumably, an apprehension that *p* is necessarily true is a causally mediated response to considering the proposition in ques-

16. BonJour, *In Defense of Pure Reason*, 8.
17. Ibid., 11.

tion and understanding it, both of which are contingent features of the world.[18] If "particular, contingent features" includes these features, then (a) is satisfied by the process of apprehension. Consequently, in this reading, (a) does not distinguish experiential processes from nonexperiential processes.

There is an alternative reading, in which the "particular, contingent features" referred to in condition (a) are identical to those referred to in condition (b). The idea is that perceptual processes produce beliefs whose content is contingent. Moreover, in the case of true perceptual beliefs, the features of the world in virtue of which the belief is true play a role in shaping the content of those beliefs. In this reading, (a) is not satisfied by processes that yield doxastic states whose content is necessary since the necessary features of the world in virtue of which such states are true cannot play a role in shaping their content. Hence, the second reading of (a) appears to distinguish experiential processes from nonexperiential processes.

This reading, however, leaves BonJour vulnerable to Benacerraf's well-known problem.[19] Although BonJour denies that either justification or knowledge requires a causal connection between one's belief (or grounds for holding the belief) and the subject matter of the belief, he maintains that "if such a relation is *known* to be absent or impossible, as is allegedly the case for beliefs about Platonistic entities, then justification is ruled out as well."[20] BonJour, however argues that the necessary features of the world do play a role in shaping the content of our beliefs:

> If . . . I am to be justified on the basis of rational insight in believing that nothing can be red and green all over at the same time, then the properties redness and greenness must be capable of influencing or affecting my state of mind: what I think must be at least potentially responsive to the actual character of these properties. But it simply does not follow that redness and greenness themselves must be concretely involved in a causal chain of events connected to my state of mind. The obvious alternative is that such influence involves instead the presence in such a causal chain of an event or events involving concrete objects that *instantiate* these properties, where the fact that it is just those specific properties that are instantiated and not others affects the overall result.[21]

The "obvious alternative" indicates that an apprehension that nothing can be both red and green all over at the same time is a causally conditioned response to events involving concrete objects instantiating redness and greenness. Yet it is a particular, contingent feature of the world that certain con-

---

18. Since BonJour's rationalism is *moderate*, a priori justification requires only an *apparent* apprehension that p is necessarily true. The reader should regard the qualification as implicit.

19. Benacerraf, "Mathematical Truth."

20. BonJour, *In Defense of Pure Reason*, 158.

21. Ibid., 159–160.

crete objects instantiate redness and greenness. Moreover, and contrary to my earlier suggestion, the features of the world in virtue of which necessary propositions are true can influence or affect the content of beliefs based on apprehension. My apprehension that nothing can be both red and green all over is at least potentially responsive to the character of those properties. Consequently, in the second reading, (a) is satisfied by the process of apprehension.

The implications for BonJour's conception of a priori justification are clear. Since the process of apprehension satisfies (a), in either reading of the condition, justification derived from that process does not satisfy (N). Given the further assumption that no process of pure thought is experiential, apprehension does not satisfy (P) either. Hence, justification based on apprehension is not a priori.

To avoid this difficulty, BonJour might amend (N) to include both conditions (a) and (b). Since nonexperiential processes satisfy (a), the burden of distinguishing between them and experiential processes falls entirely on (b). Experiential processes are those that yield doxastic states that have as their content putative contingent propositions. Nonexperiential processes are those that yield doxastic states that have as their content putative necessary propositions.[22] This strategy has two negative consequences. First, it appears to entail that any justified belief whose content is a putative necessary truth is justified by a nonexperiential process and, hence, is justified a priori. But, as BonJour concedes, this result is implausible: "There is no reason to deny that propositions of mathematics can be justified and known by appeal to the output of a computer, even if no *a priori* justification is thereby obtained; nor any reason to rule out the possibility that at least some necessary propositions might be justified via empirical survey or investigation."[23] Moreover, it also appears to rule out the possibility of a priori justified beliefs whose content is a putative contingent truth. But, if the process of apprehension is fallible, as the moderate rationalist insists, there is no basis for denying that such insight might mistake a putative contingent truth for a necessary truth.[24]

There are two readings of BonJour's conception of experience, both of which have problematic consequences. Either the concept includes (a), the causal initiation condition, alone or it includes both (a) and (b), the content-

---

22. The expression "belief whose content is a *putative* necessary truth" is ambiguous since "putative" may refer to the truth value of the proposition, its general modal status, or both. On the first reading, such contents are always necessary but can be true or false. On the second reading, such contents are always true but can be necessary or contingent. On the third reading, such contents can be necessary or contingent, as well as true or false.

23. BonJour, *In Defense of Pure Reason*, 15.

24. Kant, *Critique of Pure Reason*, 54, for example, claimed that the proposition "that in all changes of the material world the quantity of matter remains unchanged," is necessary and a priori.

of-belief condition. If the former, then apprehension is a form of experience and beliefs justified by apprehension are not justified a priori. If the latter, then all justified beliefs that have as their content putative necessary truths are justified a priori.

I have articulated four approaches to a general characterization of the narrow concept of experience and have argued that none is successful. I have also argued that the alternative of characterizing the concept by enumeration fails. Where do these negative results leave us with respect to our original question about the cogency of the experiential/nonexperiential distinction? The failed attempts are a product of a priori reflection on introspectively accessible features of cognitive experience. Recent work on the semantics of natural kind terms suggests an alternative approach, which gives a more prominent role to empirical investigation.[25]

Many natural kind terms enter the language prior to the development of scientific theories about those kinds. Familiar examples are "water," "gold," and "horse." Such terms are introduced by using "local paradigms,"[26] prominent examples of the kind in question, which are identified by certain surface characteristics. For example, "water" might be introduced as the stuff in certain lakes, rivers, or oceans. This stuff is typically identified by characteristics, such as being a colorless, odorless liquid that quenches thirst. Although competent speakers of the language use these characteristics to identify samples of water, the characteristics do not fix the extension of "water." The extension of the term is fixed by the underlying nature of the paradigms. Moreover, that nature is discovered by scientific investigation rather than by a priori reflection. In the case of our example, scientific investigation discovered that the paradigms have a common chemical structure: they are composed of H_2O molecules. This underlying chemical structure fixes the extension of "water" in all possible worlds. In any possible world, something is water just in case it is H_2O.

This view has several important consequences. First, the surface characteristics that are used to identify samples of the kind in question are not necessary features of objects of that kind. It is possible that some H_2O samples lack one or more of those characteristics. Second, having those surface characteristics is not sufficient for being a sample of water. It is possible that some samples having the surface characteristics of water are not water because they are not samples of H_2O. Finally, there is no a priori guarantee that terms introduced by local paradigms are genuine natural kind terms since there is no a priori guarantee that there is in fact some underlying nature common to all, or even many, of the paradigms. The

25. These ideas were initially developed by Kripke, "Identity and Necessity" and *Naming and Necessity*, and Putnam, "The Meaning of 'Meaning.'"

26. Donnellan, "There Is a Word for That Kind of Thing," 155–171, introduces this expression in his presentation of the Kripke-Putnam account of natural kind terms. My discussion draws on features of his presentation.

paradigms for "witch," for example, fail to exemplify a distinctive set of common features.

My suggestion is that "experience" be viewed as a putative natural kind term whose reference is fixed by local paradigms. The local paradigms are the cognitive processes associated with the five senses, which are identified in terms of such characteristics as providing information about the actual world, involving a causal relation to physical objects, and perhaps having a distinctive phenomenology. Although the local paradigms are identified by these features, they do not fix the extension of "experience." Its extension is fixed by the underlying nature of the paradigms. In any possible world, something is an experiential process just in case it has certain important properties in common with the paradigms. The relevant properties are uncovered by empirical investigation rather than a priori reflection. Unlike the case of water, however, we do not presently have a theory of the nature of experience. Our present situation with respect to "experience" is analogous to that of sixteenth-century speakers of English with respect to "water." We are aware of some characteristic features of experience but not of its underlying nature. Consequently, the critical question for our purposes is whether the scientific study of human cognition will uncover some significant underlying properties that unify the local paradigms of experience and play some role in formulating laws and theories about how humans acquire knowledge.

If empirical investigation uncovers such properties, we will have the information necessary for determining whether alleged nonexperiential processes are different in nature from experiential processes. If the alleged nonexperiential processes differ in nature from the experiential processes, we will be in a position to articulate how they differ in terms of which essential properties of experience they lack or, alternatively, which they have in addition. We will have a characterization of nonexperiential processes that tells us not only *which* processes are nonexperiential but also *why* they are nonexperiential. Such investigations will also reveal whether the surface features that are used to identify the local paradigms are reliable guides to identifying experiential processes more generally. It is possible that those features are lacking in the case of some experiential processes or that they are present in the case of some nonexperiential processes. On the other hand, there is no guarantee that empirical investigation will uncover some significant set of properties that is distinctive of our paradigms and other alleged experiential processes. If such properties are not uncovered, then we have grounds for questioning the usefulness of the concept for theorizing about human cognition. If neither a priori analysis nor empirical investigation succeeds in providing a characterization of the concept, then there is little basis for being sanguine about its cogency or usefulness.

If "experience" is indeed a natural kind term, then it is neither surprising nor disturbing that prior attempts to provide a characterization of the nature of experience have failed. The most that can be achieved by a priori reflection is to identify the semantic rule associated with the term "experience." That rule, in turn, provides the local paradigms whose underlying nature fix the extension of the term and, perhaps, some salient surface features used to identify the paradigms. The failed attempts take as their starting point the local paradigms of experience. The attempts to provide an enumerative characterization fail because they propose to fix the extension of "experience" prior to identifying the underlying nature of the local paradigms. The attempts to provide a general characterization fail because they treat surface characteristics that are used to identify the local paradigms of experience as necessary and sufficient conditions for being an experience. The key to providing the desired characterization is to uncover the unifying properties of the paradigms, which requires empirical investigation. In conclusion, the alternative that I propose for analyzing the concept of experience both explains the failure of previous attempts to analyze the concept and offers the prospect of arriving at that goal by alternative means.

6.3   A Priori Justification

In chapters 4 and 5, I argued that neither proponents nor opponents of the a priori offer convincing arguments for their position. Moreover, my investigation revealed that their argument strategy is typically negative. Each side argues, primarily on a priori grounds, that the opposing position is deficient in some respect. The strategy is both ineffective and misguided. It is ineffective since it results in an impasse. Each side attempts to blunt the criticisms of the other while maintaining that the other is open to its criticisms. It is misguided since no evidence to the effect that one position does not accommodate a certain domain of knowledge can show that the other offers an adequate account of such knowledge. Advancing the debate beyond this impasse requires offering evidence in support of the adequacy of one position that is compelling to both parties. The goal of section 6.3 is to articulate a strategy for providing compelling supporting evidence for the a priori.

Providing compelling support for the a priori requires being clear about the parameters of the controversy. One must be clear about points of agreement, as well as points of disagreement. Radical empiricists are not skeptics in the traditional sense. Proponents of the a priori typically maintain that knowledge of logic, mathematics, and alleged synthetic a priori truths, such as that whatever is red is colored, provide the leading examples of such knowledge. Radical empiricists, unlike skeptics, do not deny that we have such knowledge. Their disagreement with apriorists is over its source. Radical empiricists, on the other hand, place an exclusive premium on empirical knowledge and, in particular, on the methods and results of the sciences. Apriorists, however, do not deny that we have scientific knowledge. Their disagreement with radical empiricists is over the claim that such knowledge is justified exclusively by experience. They insist that scientific theories involve elements, such as mathematical and logical principles, that are not so justified. Hence, the fundamental disagreement between apriorists and radical empiricists is not over the *scope* of human knowledge. There are broad areas, including mathematics, logic, and the sciences, where both agree that we have knowledge. Their disagreement is over the *source* of that knowledge.

The central claim in dispute between radical empiricists and apriorists is whether there are nonexperiential sources of justification. Advancing the case for the a priori requires offering evidence in support of the existence of such sources of justification that is compelling to both parties. A case that is compelling to both must be based on common ground. Fortunately, there is much common ground. Apriorists endorse the methodological principles central to scientific investigation, as well as the results of such investigations. Radical empiricists agree that we have knowledge in areas, such as logic and mathematics, that apriorists allege are beyond the purview of experience. Apriorists, however, have not fully exploited this common ground. In advancing their case, they have relied primarily on a priori arguments that purport to establish the limitations of empiricist theories. My primary contention is that, rather than offering a priori arguments against radical empiricism, apriorists should enlist empirical support for the claim that there are nonexperiential sources of justification.

This strategy recommends itself on two grounds. The first is dialectical. A case for the a priori that is based on evidence and methodological principles endorsed by radical empiricists is one that they must acknowledge by their own lights. Hence, it offers the prospect of engaging the radical empiricist and moving the philosophical debate forward. The dialectical advantage persists even if there is some competing, noncircular, a priori argument in the wings. The second is strategic. By limiting themselves to a priori arguments, proponents of the a priori place themselves in a needlessly handicapped position. They acknowledge that we have both a priori and a posteriori justified beliefs, yet they don't employ the latter when supporting their position. In the absence of some principled objection to employing a posteriori support, it is simply a mistake to overlook it.

My contention is that empirical evidence should be exploited to advance the case for the a priori. What empirical evidence is relevant in establishing such a claim? My earlier results highlight three primary concerns about alleged a priori sources of justification: (1) whether those sources exist, (2) whether they are truth conducive, and (3) whether there is available an explanation of their truth conduciveness. I briefly canvass the relevance of empirical investigation to each before turning to a more detailed account.

The defense of the claim that there are a priori sources of justification typically appeals to phenomenological considerations. Theorists, reflecting on their own cognitive situation, identify phenomenologically distinct states, which they claim justify certain beliefs a priori. They often allege that the states in question justify beliefs by providing cognitive access to abstract entities. Three questions arise here. Are the phenomenological states in question associated with a single belief-forming process or family of related belief-forming processes? Do the processes in question play any role in producing or sustaining the beliefs that they are alleged to justify? Do the processes provide cognitive access to the entities referred to by the truth conditions of the beliefs that they are alleged to justify? Empirical investigation is relevant to each of these concerns.

Concerns about truth conduciveness arise in three different ways. Many prominent apriorists maintain that truth conduciveness is a necessary condition for epistemic justification in general and, a fortiori, for a priori justification.[27] Moreover, on some apriorist accounts, a priori justification requires a connection with truth although justification in general does not.[28] The most

27. George Bealer, Alvin Plantinga, and Ernest Sosa endorse such a condition although there are differences in their positions. Bealer, "A Priori Knowledge and the Scope of Philosophy," 129, endorses a reliabilist conception of *basic sources of evidence*: "something is a basic source of evidence iff it has a certain kind of reliable tie to the truth." Plantinga, *Warrant and Proper Function*, 17, endorses a reliabilist constraint on *warrant*: "The module of the design plan governing its production must be such that it is objectively highly probable that a belief produced by cognitive faculties functioning properly according to that module (in a congenial environment) will be true or verisimilitudinous." Sosa, "Modal and Other *A Priori* Epistemology," 4, endorses a reliabilist condition on *epistemic justification*: "The epistemic justification of a belief B at a time t may thus require the production of B at t through a virtue V resident in that subject. What is required for a disposition V to be a virtue is that in normal circumstances V would yield a sufficient preponderance of true beliefs in subjects like S." Although BonJour, *In Defense of Pure Reason*, 1, rejects reliabilist accounts of epistemic justification, he does introduce truth conduciveness into his characterization of *epistemic reasons*: "Knowledge requires instead that the belief in question be justified or rational in a way that is internally connected to the defining goal of the cognitive enterprise, that is, that there be a reason that enhances, to an appropriate degree, the chances that the belief is *true*. Justification of this distinctive, truth-conducive sort will be here referred to as *epistemic justification*."

28. Another more recent example is Audi, *Belief, Justification, and Knowledge*, 115–116, who denies that reliabilism is plausible as a theory of justification but maintains,

> Justification by its very nature has some kind of connection with *truth*. One can see this by noting that there is something fundamentally wrong with supposing that a belief's being justified has nothing whatever to do with its truth. This is perhaps most readily seen with a priori justification. In the paradigm cases, as with beliefs of self-evident propositions and very simple proofs of theorems of logic, it is arguable that one's having a priori justification *entails* the truth of the beliefs so justified. These cases are unlike perceptual ones in that if a belief claimed to be so justified turns out to be false, there is at least normally a defect in the purported justification, say a careless error in the proof. But justification of empirical beliefs also seems connected with truth. If, for instance, we discovered that the sense of smell almost never yielded beliefs that corresponded to the facts (thus to truth) as determined by other sources of belief, we would have good reason to cease to regard olfactory impressions as a source of direct justification, or at least to consider it a far weaker source.

Two points are worth noting here. First, on Audi's view, a priori justification has a stronger connection with truth than perceptual justification. Second, at least with respect to the paradigm cases of a priori justification, Audi appears to endorse the strongest version of truth conduciveness: a priori justification that *p* entails the truth of *p*.

familiar example holds that, in the case of basic (or noninferential) a priori justified belief that p, understanding that p is sufficient to "see" that p is true. For such apriorists, establishing that there are nonexperiential sources of justified belief requires establishing that such sources are truth conducive. Finally, those who deny that truth conduciveness is a necessary condition for a priori justification concede that evidence that a source of beliefs is *not* truth conducive defeats whatever justification the source confers on the beliefs that it produces.[29] Hence, showing that some beliefs are justified by nonexperiential sources requires showing not only that the source satisfies the general conditions for epistemic justification but also that available evidence does not defeat the justification that the source confers on the beliefs that it produces. Empirical investigation is relevant in assessing claims about the truth conduciveness of alleged sources of justification.

Explanatory considerations play three distinct roles in advancing the case for the a priori. First, as I argued in chapter 5, the fact that causal-perceptual explanations appear to be of limited utility in explaining the reliability of alleged nonexperiential belief-forming processes, conjoined with the fact that no alternative models are available, exacerbates the concerns about the existence and reliability of such processes. Empirical investigation into human cognition offers the prospect of providing alternative models of reliable belief formation that can be utilized in the case of nonexperiential processes. Second, a theory of a priori knowledge involves both a descriptive and an explanatory component. The descriptive component articulates the sources of a priori justification and the range of beliefs justified by each source. The explanatory component explains how the sources in question provide access to the subject matter of the beliefs justified by each source. Empirical investigation into alleged nonexperiential sources offers the prospect of broadening our understanding of how those processes provide reliable information about the subject matter of the beliefs they produce. Third, although apriorists deny that epistemology is a chapter of science, they acknowledge that both epistemology and science contribute to our overall understanding of human knowledge. Establishing that the processes invoked by their epistemological theory are underwritten by their scientific commitments strengthens the apriorist's overall theory by demonstrating the coherence of its components.

I have identified three areas where empirical investigation offers the prospect of advancing the case for the a priori. I now develop the proposal in greater detail. Before proponents of the a priori can enlist empirical support for the claim that there are nonexperiential sources of justification, additional philosophical work remains to be done. The claim must be more fully articulated. Let us call this the *Articulation Project*:

---

29. Pollock, *Knowledge and Justification*, 329, acknowledges that justification based on logical intuitions is defeasible by empirically justified undermining defeaters.

> (AP) Provide (a) a generally accepted description, at least at the phenomenological level, of the cognitive states that noninferentially justify beliefs a priori, (b) the type of beliefs they justify, and (c) the conditions under which they justify the beliefs in question.[30]

The Articulation Project involves three related components: describing the cognitive states that confer noninferential a priori justification, delineating the scope of beliefs they justify, and specifying the conditions under which they justify the beliefs in question.

Much of the controversy over the a priori focuses on the cognitive states alleged to justify a priori. Radical empiricists claim that they find these states puzzling or even mysterious. Apriorists respond that they are familiar and offer phenomenological descriptions. If the cognitive states that justify a priori are indeed familiar, then it is reasonable to expect that descriptions of them offered by sympathetic proponents, who have carefully considered and reflected on the matter, should converge, at least in their broad outlines. Yet, if one surveys these descriptions, one finds enormous variation.

Panayot Butchvarov, for example, maintains, "Both primary a priori and primary a posteriori knowledge consist in the unthinkability of mistake in belief, and this unthinkability is due, in both cases, to the incompatibility of the falsehood of the belief with the context of the belief."[31] Concerning the source of a priori knowledge, he claims that "there is considerable truth in the traditional view that a priori knowledge is based on a certain kind of awareness, on intuition."[32] What is characteristic of such awareness?

> The point of using the word *intuitive* in describing primary knowledge of necessary truths has been to emphasize that such knowledge is like primary knowledge of contingent truths in one important respect: that while necessary and contingent truths have fundamentally different objects, in both cases such objects are, in a very general sense, *perceived*.[33]

Butchvarov is not alone in resorting to perceptual analogies to characterize the source of a priori knowledge. Indeed, it is the pervasive appeal to such analogies that fosters the appearance that proponents of the a priori are offering convergent descriptions of the state that noninferentially justifies a priori. Closer examination dispels the appearance. Alvin Plantinga, for example,

---

30. My focus here and in the subsequent discussion is on the sources of *noninferential*, or *basic*, a priori justification since inferential, or nonbasic, a priori justification results from applying inferential principles that are (noninferentially) justified a priori to other beliefs that are (noninferentially) justified a priori. Hence, in the final analysis, all a priori justified beliefs are ultimately justified by those sources.

31. Butchvarov, *The Concept of Knowledge*, 94–95.

32. Ibid., 178.

33. Ibid., 179.

claims that "*one* way to believe *p a priori* is to see that it is true."[34] Furthermore, this seeing "consists, first (I suggest), in your finding yourself utterly convinced that the proposition in question is *true*. It consists second, however, in finding yourself utterly convinced that this proposition is not only true, but *could not have been false*."[35]

Butchvarov and Plantinga agree on one point: the perceptual analogy can be articulated in terms of some more familiar cognitive state. Phenomenological reflection reveals that the "seeing" or "awareness" that underlies a priori justification is not at all mysterious. The problem, however, is that they point to different cognitive states in their respective articulations of the perceptual analogy. Being convinced that *p* is necessarily true, in the fashion required by Plantinga, need not involve finding mistake in believing that *p* unthinkable. Conversely, finding mistake in believing that *p* unthinkable need not involve being convinced that *p* is necessarily true since one might doubt that finding such a mistake unthinkable provides a reason to believe that *p* is necessarily true. Hence, although both invoke perceptual analogies, Butchvarov and Plantinga offer different accounts of noninferential a priori justification.

Laurence BonJour also appeals to perceptual analogies in articulating his account of a priori justification. He offers the following description of rational insight, the alleged source of such justification: "When I carefully and reflectively consider the proposition (or inference) in question, I am able simply to see or grasp or apprehend that the proposition is *necessary*, that it must be true in any possible world or situation (or alternatively that the conclusion of the inference must be true if the premises are true)."[36] Although he endorses the perceptual analogy, BonJour disagrees with both Butchvarov and Plantinga in a fundamental respect. He insists that a priori insights are apparently *irreducible*: "They are apparently incapable of being reduced to or constituted out of some constellation of discursive steps or simpler cognitive elements of some other kind."[37] The perceptual metaphor cannot be articulated in terms of some more familiar cognitive state. Butchvarov and Plantinga, alleges BonJour, simply misrepresent the phenomenological facts.[38]

Despite their significant differences, BonJour, Butchvarov, and Plantinga seem to agree on one point: the cognitive state that justifies a priori the belief that *p* includes the belief that *p*. George Bealer, however, disagrees even with this point. According to Bealer, a priori justification is rooted in a priori *intuition*:

We do not mean [by intuition] a magical power or inner voice or anything of the sort. For you to have an intuition that A is just for it to

34. Plantinga, *Warrant and Proper Function*, 106.
35. Ibid., 105.
36. BonJour, *In Defense of Pure Reason*, 106.
37. Ibid., 108.
38. Ibid., n. 12 and 13.

seem to you that A. Here 'seems' is understood, not as a cautionary or "hedging" term, but in its use as a term for a genuine kind of conscious episode. . . . Of course, this kind of seeming is *intellectual*, not sensory or introspective (or imaginative). The subject here is *a priori* (or rational) intuition.[39]

An intellectual seeming that p must be distinguished from a belief that p. For example, it may seem to one that the naive comprehension axiom of set theory is true although one does not believe that it is true. Conversely, there are mathematical theorems that one believes on the basis of having constructed a proof but that don't seem to be either true or false.

Although Ernest Sosa agrees with Bealer that an intuition that p need not involve the belief that p or, for that matter, any belief at all, he suggests that such seemings might be analyzable in terms of what one *would* believe in certain circumstances: "Seemings then, whether sensory or intellectual, might be viewed as inclinations to believe on the basis of direct experience (sensory) or understanding (intellectual) and regardless of any collateral reasoning, memory, or introspection—where the objects of *intellectual* seeming also present themselves as necessary."[40]

Sosa and Bealer differ in two significant respects. First, they offer different phenomenological descriptions of seemings. Sosa maintains that an intellectual seeming that p is an inclination to believe that p based on understanding that p. Bealer insists that "intuition is a *sui generis*, irreducible, natural propositional attitude which occurs episodically."[41] Hence, Bealer agrees with BonJour that the cognitive state that justifies a priori is irreducible but disagrees with him over the character of the state. Sosa, on the other hand, agrees with Butchvarov and Plantinga that the state is analyzable in terms of some more familiar cognitive state but disagrees with them over the character of that state. Second, although both agree that there are sensory and intellectual seemings, they disagree over how those seemings differ.[42] Bealer maintains that sensory seemings and intellectual seemings are phenomenologically distinct conscious states. According to Sosa, they do not differ phenomenologically. Both seemings involve an inclination to believe that p, but they differ in the basis of the inclination. Sensory seemings are based on direct experience, whereas intellectual seemings are based on understanding.

Apriorists are faced with a dilemma. Either we have direct introspective access to the cognitive states that provide noninferential a priori justification or we do not. If we do, sympathetic and sophisticated proponents of the position should be able to agree on the correct description of those states.

39. Bealer, "*A Priori* Knowledge and the Scope of Philosophy," 123.
40. Sosa, "Rational Intuition: Bealer on its Nature and Epistemic Status," 154.
41. Bealer, "*A Priori* Knowledge: Replies to William Lycan and Ernest Sosa," 169.
42. The Müller-Lyer illusion provides an example of a sensory seeming.

If we do not, some alternative rationale must be offered to support the claim that there are such states. The lack of consensus among proponents lends support to the claim of radical empiricists that more needs to be said here.

Turning to the second component of (AP), we find that there is also wide variation among apriorists over the scope of beliefs justified a priori. These differences are not typically seen within epistemological contexts since the focus is on stock examples such as elementary logical or mathematical propositions, simple analytic truths, and some familiar cases of alleged synthetic a priori truths. Since the primary goal in such contexts is to argue for the minimal claim that *some* knowledge is a priori, apriorists have rightly focused on uncontroversial cases where radical empiricists agree that we have the knowledge in question. Few apriorists, however, maintain that a priori knowledge is limited to those cases. In contexts in which the existence of a priori knowledge is not at issue, apriorists make bolder a priori claims. Consequently, unless they retract such claims, apriorists cannot effectively address the issue of the truth conduciveness of the cognitive states that are alleged to justify a priori by focusing exclusively on the noncontroversial cases. Instead, they must provide a more complete specification of the range of beliefs alleged to be justified by such states. A complete specification would include the different types of beliefs, such as mathematical and moral, justified by each source and the scope of beliefs justified within each type. In the absence of a more complete articulation of the scope of the a priori, the crucial issue of truth conduciveness will remain a subject of speculation, supported or rejected by bits of anecdotal evidence.

There is one issue regarding the scope of a priori justification that requires particular attention. The examples of a priori knowledge typically cited by apriorists are necessary truths. But, as I stressed in chapter 4, we must be careful to distinguish between knowledge of the *truth value* of a necessary proposition and knowledge of its *general modal status*. A critical question immediately arises. What is the target of a priori justification—the general modal status of a proposition, its truth value, or both? If a priori justification is limited to the general modal status of propositions, it loses much of its significance. Beliefs about the general modal status of propositions are largely confined to philosophers. The significance of the a priori, however, derives from the fact that beliefs about the truth value of some necessary propositions, such as logical and mathematical propositions, are among the most basic and universal beliefs of human cognizers. If a priori justification extends to the truth value of propositions, two further questions arise.

The first is whether beliefs about the truth value of necessary propositions and beliefs about their general modal status are justified by a single cognitive state or by different cognitive states. Few theorists offer a clear answer to the question. BonJour, Butchvarov, and Plantinga maintain that a priori justification involves a cognitive state whose content is that *p cannot be false*. Does such a content justify the belief that *p* or the belief that necessarily *p*? According to Butchvarov and Plantinga, it is the former. Yet they provide no account of the cognitive state that justifies the belief that *p* is necessary. BonJour is not explicit on this point. The examples he utilizes to illustrate his account include both modal propositions, such as that nothing can be both red and green all over at the same time, and nonmodal propositions, such as that 2 + 3 = 5. But he offers no explanation of why the state in question justifies belief in the general modal status of a proposition in some cases but not in others.

Bealer's account is more heterogeneous. He allows that there are logical, mathematical, conceptual, and modal intuitions. But he is not explicit about the content of each. Presumably, logical, mathematical, and conceptual intuitions are *nonmodal*. For example, for you to have the mathematical intuition that 2 + 2 = 4 is for it to seem to you that 2 + 2 = 4 is *true*. But what is it for you to have a *modal* intuition that 2 + 2 = 4? Is it for it to seem to you that 2 + 2 = 4 is *necessarily true*? Is it for it to seem to you that 2 + 2 = 4 is *necessary* (i.e., necessarily true or necessarily false)? Or are there modal intuitions of both kinds? Sosa is more explicit: to have an intellectual intuition that *p*, it must seem to you not only that *p* is *true* but also that *p* is *necessarily* true.[43] If Sosa is correct about the content of intellectual intuitions, then Bealer's logical, mathematical, and conceptual intuitions are *not* a priori intuitions since they are *nonmodal* intuitions. Sosa, however, is not explicit about whether an intellectual intuition that *p* justifies the belief that p or the belief that *p* is necessarily true.[44]

The second question is whether one can be justified a priori in believing that a contingent proposition is true. If such justification consists in apprehending that *p* is necessarily true, there is some basis for restricting it to necessary truths. The restriction is less plausible if one agrees with BonJour that "a moderate rationalism that abandons the indefensible claim of infallibility should hold instead that . . . it is *apparent* rational insight . . . that provides the basis for *a priori* epistemic justification."[45] If a priori justification is fallible, why can't one be justified a priori in believing some contingent proposition that *appears* to be necessarily true?[46] Similarly, if a priori justification consists in some proposition's intellectually seeming to be true, it is not evident that only necessary propositions can intellectually seem to be true. Even if one augments the account, as Sosa does, to include the fur-

---

43. Sosa, "Rational Intuition: Bealer on its Nature and Epistemic Status," 154. Sosa, "Minimal Intuition," introduces a weaker notion of intuition that drops the requirement that intuitions present themselves as necessary. Bealer, on the other hand, reports (in correspondence) that he claims elsewhere that a priori intuitions do present themselves as necessary. This shift in the views of both authors underscores my earlier point about the lack of consensus among apriorists about the character of the cognitive state that is alleged to justify a priori.

44. Sosa addresses this issue in "Modal and Other *A Priori* Epistemology."

45. BonJour, *In Defense of Pure Reason*, 113.

46. Plantinga, *Warrant and Proper Function*, 106–107, considers this question.

ther condition that the proposition presents itself as necessary, it is not evident that contingent propositions cannot so present themselves.

The third component of (AP) concerns the conditions under which beliefs are justified a priori. There are two distinct sets of issues here. The first is a specification of the conditions under which beliefs are prima facie justified by the proposed source of a priori justification. BonJour, for example, maintains that there are certain background conditions that must be satisfied for an apparent rational insight to have its justificatory force: the proposition must be considered with reasonable care, the person must have an approximate grasp of the concept of necessity, and one's reason must not be clouded by dogmatism or bias.[47] Two questions emerge. Is the list complete? Are the conditions sufficiently articulated so that it can be determined whether they are satisfied? One condition is that the cognizer have an *adequate grasp* of the concept of necessity. Does such a grasp require familiarity with the basic principles of modal logic? Does a modal skeptic lack all a priori knowledge?

The second set of issues is a specification of the conditions under which prima facie a priori justification is defeasible. Defeaters fall into two broad categories: overriding defeaters and undermining defeaters. There are two primary questions in the case of overriding defeaters. First, under what conditions, if any, do conflicts of rational insight undermine justification based on such insight? Second, can there be empirically justified overriding defeaters for beliefs justified a priori? Parallel questions arise in the case of undermining defeaters. Does a track record of conflicting beliefs or errors based on rational insight undermine justification based on such insight? Can a priori justified beliefs be defeated by empirically justified beliefs about the cognitive processes that underlie rational insight?

Once the main pieces of the Articulation Project are in place, the project of offering empirical supporting evidence for the a priori can be implemented. Let us call this the *Empirical Project*:

> (EP) Provide (a) evidence that the cognitive states identified at the phenomenological level are associated with processes of a single type or relevantly similar types, (b) evidence that the associated processes play a role in producing or sustaining the beliefs they are alleged to justify, (c) evidence that the associated processes are truth conducive, and (d) an explanation of how the associated processes produce the beliefs they are alleged to justify.

The Empirical Project highlights four areas of investigation: the relationship between cognitive states identified phenomenologically and underlying cognitive processes, the role of the underlying processes in our cognitive

---

47. BonJour, *In Defense of Pure Reason*, 133–137.

economy, the truth ratio of beliefs produced by the processes, and the means by which those processes produce beliefs.[48]

The first area of investigation addresses the claim that sources of justification are of two significantly different types: experiential and nonexperiential. Initially, this difference is marked at the phenomenological level. Apriorists identify certain phenomenologically distinct states as the source of a priori justification. The fact that the states are phenomenologically distinct, however, does not ensure either that they are produced exclusively by processes of a single type or, if they are, that those processes differ significantly from experiential processes. Yet the character of the processes that produce the state is relevant to whether the state justifies a priori.

Suppose, for example, that intellectual seemings have a distinctive and readily identifiable phenomenological character. Moreover, suppose that a child, under the supervision of a tutor, learns that $4 \times 4 = 16$ and that balls roll down inclined planes. The tutor utilizes techniques like those employed in the *Meno* to bring the child to "see" that $4 \times 4 = 16$, but the tutor also has the child perform experiments with balls and planes to see that balls roll down inclined planes. The training results in the child's having two beliefs, each produced by a different process. Finally, suppose that the child later forgets the tutor's lessons but, as a result of them, both propositions, when considered, appear to the child to be true. It is implausible to maintain that both beliefs are justified a priori for the child. The first is justified a priori since it is based on a "rational" or nonexperiential process, but the second is justified a posteriori since it is based on a perceptual or experiential process.

Two important points emerge. First, the fact that some cognitive states have a distinctive phenomenology, one different from those associated with familiar experiential processes such as perception, memory, or introspection, does not ensure either that those states are produced by a single type of process or that the process (or processes) producing them is nonexperiential. Second, the type of process responsible for producing and/or sustaining the cognitive state is directly relevant to the claim that such states justify a priori. This is evident in cases in which the states in question are produced by processes of significantly different types. But even if the state in question is produced only by processes of a single type, the further question remains of whether the processes differ in any epistemologically significant respect from experiential processes. If the cognitive processes associated with that state manifest no significant differences in their features or the manner in which they produce beliefs, then there will be legitimate questions about the significance of the experiential/nonexperiential distinction. For example, if such investigations were to show that Mill is correct in maintaining that what one

48. Goldman, "A Priori Warrant and Naturalistic Epistemology," argues that psychological studies are relevant to the existence of a priori knowledge. His focus is on whether such studies support the view that basic mathematical and logical skills are innate.

finds unthinkable is explained by experience and the laws of associationist psychology, this would cast doubt on the claim that the justification conferred on beliefs by such states is nonexperiential.

The second area of investigation assesses the claim that beliefs alleged to be justified a priori are produced and/or sustained by processes involving the cognitive state alleged to provide such justification. If an epistemic theory is to provide an account of how our beliefs are *in fact* justified, then the processes to which the theory appeals must actually play some role in acquiring or sustaining the beliefs in question. Empirical investigation can offer support for this claim. Although apriorists might rest content with the weaker claim that the processes in question *can* justify beliefs a priori, empirical considerations remain relevant in three ways. First, if the weaker claim involves more than an assertion of mere logical possibility, empirical evidence is necessary to show that the cognitive processes in question can, in some more robust sense, play a role in producing or sustaining the beliefs in question. Second, the epistemic status of our *actual* beliefs about the subject matter in question must be addressed. Do the processes that actually produce the beliefs in question also justify those beliefs? Are our actual beliefs epistemically overdetermined or unjustified? Third, some explanation of why the nonexperiential processes are not employed by cognizers is in order. Is it because the processes can be employed only by experts? Is it because the processes are cognitively dispensable? Answers to these questions are necessary to provide an accurate picture of the role of such processes in our cognitive economy.

The third area of investigation addresses the issue of truth conduciveness. The issue plays a dual role. First, if truth conduciveness is a necessary condition for epistemic justification, as many proponents of the a priori allege, or if it is a necessary condition for a priori justification, as others allege, then, if one is to offer evidence in support of the claim that a particular cognitive process is a source of a priori justification, one must offer evidence in support of the claim that beliefs based on that process are likely to be true. Even those who deny that truth conduciveness is a necessary condition for epistemic justification concede that evidence to the effect that a particular source of beliefs is error conducive defeats the justification such a source confers on the beliefs that it produces. If one is to offer evidence in support of the claim that a particular process is a source of a priori justification, one must offer evidence in support of the claim that defeating evidence that undermines the capacity of that process to justify any beliefs is not available. The claim that a process is truth conducive or, more minimally, that it is not error conducive is a contingent general claim that can only be supported by empirical investigation.

Empirical investigation can play a second important role in assessing the credentials of a cognitive process. To assess the truth conduciveness of a belief-forming process, one must have some approximation of the full range of beliefs that can be produced and/or sustained by the process in question.

The a priori is typically introduced and defended by using a narrow range of examples. Radical empiricists often attack the a priori by arguing that some of the examples, such as the principles of Euclidean geometry, have turned out to be false. Merely settling these disputes cannot either convincingly support or convincingly refute the a priori since the range of cases under consideration is so limited. Historical and psychological investigations, however, can provide a fuller picture of the range of beliefs produced by such processes.

In the case of areas of knowledge, such as mathematics and metaphysics, where there is documentation of appeals to nonexperiential sources of justification, historical investigations can reveal the scope of beliefs claimed to be justified by such sources, the extent to which there are conflicting claims, and whether there is a stable core of beliefs alleged to be justified a priori or widespread variation over time. Such investigations can also reveal whether alleged a priori sources play a significant role in the actual practices of areas of inquiry, such as mathematics, where apriorists claim that their role is significant.[49] Psychological studies, on the other hand, might be useful in determining whether alleged nonexperiential sources produce and/or sustain all and only those beliefs typically cited by apriorists. They might also reveal whether there is widespread variation among subjects with respect to beliefs produced and/or sustained by those sources. The main point to be emphasized, however, is that systematic studies that take into account the cognitive facts about a wide range of subjects, including those with no antecedent commitment to any particular epistemological theory, are necessary to make confident pronouncements about truth conduciveness. Reflection on one's own case or appeal to the experiences of a few like-minded theorists offers little prospect of making a plausible case for the truth conduciveness of such cognitive states.

The fourth area of empirical investigation, which focuses on explanatory considerations, offers the prospect of advancing the case for the a priori along several different fronts. First, if such investigation reveals that the cognitive processes associated with states alleged to justify a priori are of a single type or of relevantly similar types, then identification of the distinctive features of those processes might provide the basis for articulating the experiential/nonexperiential distinction. The net result would be a deeper understanding of the concept of a priori justification. Second, such investigations may provide a better understanding of how the processes in question produce true beliefs about their subject matter. This understanding, in turn, is the key to providing a non-causal-perceptual explanation of how the states in question provide cognitive access to the subject matter of the beliefs they produce and why they are truth conducive. Third, as we achieve a better

49. Kitcher, *The Nature of Mathematical Knowledge*, chaps. 7–10, provides a notable example of such an investigation. Penelope Maddy, *Realism in Mathematics*, chap. 4, provides an insightful case study of current mathematical practice.

understanding of these processes, our epistemological and psychological theories become more integrated. The fact that our epistemological theory coheres well with psychological theories for which we have independent support increases the overall support for the former theory.

6.4 Objections Considered

I conclude by addressing objections to the strategy of advancing the case for the a priori by offering empirical supporting evidence. The objections fall into two categories. Those in the first allege that empirical evidence *cannot* advance the case for the a priori. Those in the second allege that such evidence is *unnecessary* since alternative strategies are available. The objections in the first category center around two concerns: (1) that invoking empirical considerations to defend the a priori status of some beliefs thereby impugns their a priori status, and (2) that invoking empirical considerations is ultimately circular.

BonJour, in the context of arguing that the demand for supporting evidence for the truth conduciveness of rational insight is illegitimate, provides an example of an objection that falls into the first category. His objection is based on a particular conception of the role of such a demand: "The implicit suggestion is that one who accepts a claim on the basis of such insight must be appealing, at least tacitly, to a premise of this sort as an essential part of the alleged justifying reason in order for a justification that is genuinely epistemic in character to even putatively result."[50] If one's justification for believing that rational insight is truth conducive is indeed an essential part of one's justification for believing that *p* on the basis of rational insight, then if the former is empirical the latter is also empirical. Hence, concludes BonJour, to offer empirical evidence in support of the truth conduciveness of rational insight "is to abandon any claim to *a priori* justification."[51]

BonJour's dim assessment of the strategy of providing empirical supporting evidence for the truth conduciveness of rational insight is based on his conception of the demand. To see that it is his conception of the demand, rather than the strategy itself, that is problematic, let us distinguish between

(1) S's belief that *p* being justified by rational insight, and
(2) S's belief that S's belief that *p* is justified by rational insight being justified.

BonJour is correct in insisting that if

(3) Empirical evidence that rational insight is truth conducive

---

50. BonJour, *In Defense of Pure Reason*, 143.
51. Ibid., 143.

is an essential part of (1), then it would undercut the a priori status of S's justification for the belief that *p*. My case for the relevance of (3), however, does not depend on the assumption that (3) is an essential part of (1). On the contrary, the minimal conception of a priori justification that I have defended does not support that contention. Instead, on my proposal, (3) is relevant to (2). It is relevant to providing supporting evidence for the contention that rational insight is a source of justification. Although one need not be justified in believing that rational insight is a source of justification in order for one's beliefs based on rational insight to be justified, one must be justified in believing that rational insight is a source of justification in order to be justified in accepting moderate rationalism. Since, on my proposal, empirical evidence is relevant to (2) and not (1), such evidence does not undercut the a priori status of beliefs justified by rational insight. Instead, it provides moderate rationalism with the resources to support its primary theoretical claim.

The second type of objection that falls into the first category acknowledges the distinction between employing empirical evidence to support the claim that there are nonexperiential sources of justification as opposed to employing empirical evidence as part of one's alleged nonexperiential justification for holding some belief. Nevertheless, there is a residual concern that a proponent of the a priori lapses into circularity when using this strategy. The concern is based on two observations. First, the empirical methods necessary to establish the truth conduciveness of alleged nonexperiential sources of justification include logical and mathematical principles. Second, according to apriorists, such principles are justified a priori. Hence, by invoking logical and mathematical principles in advancing the claim that there are nonexperiential sources of justification, the apriorist is assuming that there are such sources of justification.

To address this concern, we need to keep in sharp focus the parameters of the debate. We must distinguish here between (a) *skeptics* who deny that we have justified logical and mathematical beliefs and (b) *radical empiricists* who maintain that such beliefs are justified but deny that the source of their justification is nonexperiential. One cannot invoke logical and mathematical principles in arguing against a skeptic who denies that such principles are justified without lapsing into circularity. The present debate, however, is with the radical empiricist and not the skeptic. Since apriorists and radical empiricists agree that we have justified logical and mathematical beliefs and disagree only over the source of their justification, both can employ such principles in advancing their respective positions *provided that* they make no claims about the source of justification of such principles. When using logical and mathematical principles to provide empirical support for the truth conduciveness of alleged a priori sources, one need not make any claims about how such principles are justified. Hence, in the context of advancing their position against radical empiricists, apriorists can avail themselves of such principles without lapsing into circularity. Radical empiricists cannot reject a case for the a priori solely on the grounds that it employs logical and mathematical principles without impugning their own epistemological theory.

The objections in the second category maintain that it is not necessary to introduce empirical considerations in order to advance the case for the a priori. For example, although BonJour maintains that a noncircular argument in support of rationalism is not possible, he offers some defense. There are three elements to his case: (B1) the arguments against radical empiricism, (B2) "an exhibition of the basic intuitive or phenomenological plausibility of the view in relation to particular examples,"[52] and (B3) responses to objections. (B1) and (B3) exemplify the negative strategy of offering criticisms of the opposing position while blunting those of opponents. Thus (B2) carries the burden of BonJour's positive argument.

Two questions arise at this point. What is involved in exhibiting the intuitive plausibility of rationalism? Can such an exhibition advance the case for rationalism? Exhibiting the intuitive plausibility of rationalism involves considering a proposition such as that nothing can be both red and green all over, noting that we are quickly convinced that it is true and asking ourselves why we are so convinced. For BonJour, the "overwhelmingly natural and obvious response" involves two elements:

> First, I *understand* the proposition in question. . . . Second, given this understanding of the ingredients of the proposition, I am able to see or grasp or apprehend in a seemingly direct and unmediated way that the claim in question cannot fail to be true. . . . It is this direct insight into the necessity of the claim in question that seems, at least *prima facie*, to justify my accepting it as true.[53]

Exhibiting intuitive plausibility is an exercise in reflection or introspection that is alleged to yield two primary results: (1) the identification of a cognitive state or process, and (2) the claim that it seems to justify the belief in question.

Such reflection offers little support for rationalism. Despite BonJour's claim that his answer is *natural* and *obvious*, we saw in section 6.3 that proponents of the a priori offer widely varying descriptions of the cognitive state they take to be the source of such justification. In the face of such disagreement, the claim that introspective appeals alone settle the issue is not compelling. Moreover, and more important, even if we concede that these differences can be reconciled, introspection reveals, at most, what one *takes* to be the justification for accepting the proposition in question. But can such reflection reveal that rational insight *in fact* justifies acceptance of the propositions in question? Reflection cannot carry that burden for two reasons. First, BonJour agrees that the defining characteristic of epistemic justification is

52. Ibid., 99.
53. Ibid., 101.

its essential connection with the epistemic goal of believing true propositions. A process or state justifies a belief only if beliefs based on it are likely
to be true. Reflectively examining a few stock examples of beliefs based on
rational insight does not provide grounds, even at the intuitive level, for
believing the *general* claim that beliefs based on rational insight are likely
to be true. Second, introspection cannot provide assurance that what one
takes to be the justification for believing a certain proposition is true is the
basis of one's conviction that it is true. If, as seems plausible, the basing
relation involves a counterfactual dependence of the belief on the alleged
ground of the belief, then introspection cannot provide such access. Hence,
the appeal to intuitive plausibility falls short of its goal.

The intuitive plausibility defense rests on a broad thesis about cognitive
access: reflection on the aspects of cognition revealed through introspection provides sufficient information to underwrite claims about the justificatory status of one's beliefs. Let us call this the *Epistemic Access Thesis*.
There are three aspects of the thesis that must be distinguished. The first is
that one can identify by introspection the cognitive states that justify beliefs. The second is that one can determine by introspection that certain
beliefs are based on those cognitive states. The third is that one can determine by introspection that such states are justifiers. I have argued that the
first is questionable and that the second and third are dubious. One response
to my contention is to deny the claims about the nature of epistemic justification and the basing relation that underlie the argument.

Roderick Chisholm offers an example of such an approach. He maintains
that the epistemologist is justified in making the following presupposition:

> (P2) I am justified in believing that I can improve and correct my
> system of beliefs. Of those beliefs that are about matters of
> interest or concern to me, I can eliminate the ones that are
> unjustified and add others that are justified, and I can replace
> less justified beliefs about those topics by beliefs about them
> that are more justified.[54]

Given this presupposition, it follows that epistemic justification is *internal*
and *immediate*: "One can find out directly, by *reflection*, what one is justified in believing at any time."[55]

Suppose that we grant the presupposition and the resulting conception
of internal justification. Do these concessions provide the resources necessary to advance the case for apriorism? The core of Chisholm's epistemological theory is a set of material epistemic principles that provide
logically sufficient conditions for the applicability of normative epistemic
concepts in terms of nonnormative concepts. An example of such a principle is

---

54. Chisholm, *Theory of Knowledge*, 3rd ed., 5.
55. Ibid., 7.

M1   If the property of being F is self-presenting, if S is F, and if S believes himself to be F, then it is certain for S that he is F.[56]

(M1) provides the basis for a posteriori knowledge.

In the case of the a priori, Chisholm does not provide any material epistemic principles. Instead, he offers the following definition of a priori knowledge:

D3   *h* is known *a priori* by S = Df   There is an *e* such that (i) *e* is axiomatic for S, (ii) the proposition, *e* implies *h*, is axiomatic for S, and (iii) S accepts *h*.[57]

A proposition is known a priori just in case it is axiomatic or an axiomatic consequence of something axiomatic. The following definitions complete the account:

D1   h is an axiom = Df   h is necessarily such [that] (i) it is true and (ii) for every S, if S accepts h, then h is certain for S.[58]

D2   h is *axiomatic* for S = Df   (i) h is an axiom and (ii) S accepts h.[59]

Although the following principle is true on Chisholm's account

C1   If h is an axiom and S accepts h, then h is certain for S,

it is not a material epistemic principle since the definition of "axiom" includes the normative epistemic of certainty. Let me introduce a material epistemic principle governing a priori justification:

M*   If S has an apparent rational insight that *p* is necessarily true, then S is justified in believing that *p*.

What justification can the apriorist offer in favor of principles such as (M*), given the resources of Chisholmian internalism?

Chisholm argues that it is not plausible to maintain that material epistemic principles are knowable a priori since many philosophers who understand them reject them. Instead, he invites us to consider *conditional material epistemic principles*: that is, conditional propositions whose antecedent is (P2) and whose consequent is some material epistemic principle. Consider, for example, "If (P2) then (M1)" and "If (P2) then (M*)": "I suggest that these conditional propositions *can* be known *a priori* to be true. This means that, for any subject S, for whom any such conditional is evident, the conse-

56. Ibid., 62.
57. Ibid., 29.
58. Ibid., 28.
59. Ibid.

quent of that conditional is at least as justified as is the antecedent."[60] Hence, according to Chisholm, the internal conception of epistemic justification provides the resources for offering a priori reasons in favor of epistemic principles such as (M*).

In assessing Chisholm's claim, I propose to sidestep issues about the epistemic status of (P2). Moreover, I also propose to bracket concerns about whether offering an a priori justification of conditional material epistemic principles governing a priori justification involves circularity. Instead, I draw attention to two other features of the Chisholmian defense. First, it is dialectically ineffective in advancing the case for the a priori against radical empiricism. Rather than exploiting common ground, it appeals to rational insight to justify the claim that rational insight is a source of justification. Hence, the defense presupposes an answer to the very question that is in dispute between the two camps. Second, the contention that conditional material epistemic principles are justified a priori is dubious even from a Chisholmian perspective. Chisholm rejects the claim that epistemic principles, such as (M1), are knowable a priori on the grounds that many philosophers who understand then reject them. But, surely, those who reject (M1) are not limited to those who reject (P2). There are internalist epistemologists who understand both (P2) and (M1), endorse (P2), but deny (M1). There are also theoretical grounds for rejecting the contention. A proposition is known a priori, according to Chisholm, just in case it is axiomatic or an axiomatic consequence of something that is axiomatic. He does not claim that conditional material epistemic principles are axiomatic consequences of other axiomatic propositions. Hence, if they are known a priori, they are axiomatic. If conditional material epistemic principles are axiomatic they are axioms and, as a consequence, certain for anyone who accepts them. If they are certain, then believing them is at least as reasonable as believing any other proposition. But it is implausible to maintain that believing some conditional material epistemic principle is at least as reasonable as believing that one exists or that $2 + 2 = 4$. Hence, conditional material epistemic principles are not known a priori.

Ernest Sosa also attempts to advance the case for the a priori on a priori grounds. He maintains that reflection on Descartes's strategy in the *Meditations* provides the resources for an a priori explanation of the truth conduciveness of a priori sources of justification. A priori justification, according to Sosa, ultimately derives from intellectual appearances. An appearance that p is true is a disposition to believe that p is true, independently of any support from first-level evidence of its truth. An intellectual appearance that p is true is one that derives from an understanding of the proposition in question. Sosa suggests that drills involving addition and multiplication

60. Ibid., 73.

tables promote the understanding of mathematical propositions in a manner that produces dispositions to believe that they are true.

Suppose that someone is disposed to believe a range of mathematical propositions on the basis of such drills. Is a belief that p based on the intellectual appearance that p always justified for such a person? Sosa's answer is negative. Consider a child who, under the tutelage of a careless nanny, learns the multiplication tables from a manual containing an unusually large number of errors. Suppose that it appears to the child that $9 \times 6 = 54$, and on that basis the child believes that $9 \times 6 = 54$. The belief is not justified since many other related false propositions appear true to the child. According to Sosa, "The epistemic justification of a belief B at a time t may thus require the production of B at t through a virtue V resident in that subject. What is required for a disposition V to be a virtue is that in normal circumstances V would yield a sufficient preponderance of true beliefs in subjects like S."[61] In short, intellectual appearances justify beliefs only if they are reliably connected to the truth in normal circumstances.

Sosa's concern with explaining the truth conduciveness of intellectual appearances arises from his bilevel epistemology, which distinguishes "*animal* knowledge, and its constitutive cognitive virtues, from a *reflective* knowledge that in addition requires one's beliefs to be defensible in the arena of reflection, wherein doubts may be raised as to the true reliability of one's supposed virtues."[62] The defensibility of one's a priori justified beliefs requires an explanation of their reliability. Sosa's primary contention is that explanations of reliability need not be a posteriori. The first step of his supporting argument notes that in the case of introspective knowledge of one's own mental life, and in the case of one's knowledge that one now thinks or that one now exists, "the explanation of reliability stays largely within the realm of the a priori in the fashion of Descartes. It is because we see how such beliefs are and must be infallible that we understand how perfectly reliable they are. No element of doubt here derives from our ignorance of causal mechanisms."[63] The next step is the suggestion that, through further a priori reflection on the conditions of thought, we can extend such a Cartesian-style a priori explanation of the reliability of our beliefs to the realm of the a priori.

Sosa, however, overestimates the resources of Cartesian methodology. To bring out the source of the difficulty, we must distinguish between

(RB) the reliability of S's *belief* that p, and
(RD) the reliability of the *disposition* that produces S's belief
     that p.

61. Sosa, "Modal and Other *A Priori* Epistemology," 4. I discuss Sosa's account in "Modal Epistemology."

62. Sosa, "Modal and Other *A Priori* Epistemology," 7.

63. Ibid., 9.

Consider now your favorite example of a cogito proposition: for example, that you now exist or that you now believe something (or other). Such propositions have the following feature:

(CP) It is not possible that (S believe that p and p is false).

What is so striking about each of these propositions is that if you believe it, it cannot be false. Moreover, you can become aware of this striking feature through a priori reflection. But, as striking as this feature may be, it has nothing to do with epistemic justification on Sosa's account. The justification of S's belief that p is a function of the reliability of the underlying *disposition* responsible for producing the belief that p: it is a function of the truth or falsehood of *all* beliefs produced by that disposition in normal circumstances. But, a cogito belief retains the logical feature that it cannot be false if believed however the belief is produced. It retains that feature whatever the underlying disposition that produces it.

Suppose, for example, that I join a cult that initiates its members by inducing a form of amnesia and then reeducates them by using training manuals. Inductees are instructed to carefully read their manuals and to believe everything that they read in the manual. Suppose that the manuals contain a mix of self-serving falsehoods about the cult and its members together with some harmless but true platitudes. One day I come across a page in my manual that includes the sentences "You now exist," "You now believe something," "You are thinking," and "To think you must exist," and I dutifully form the appropriate beliefs. My beliefs are not justified since they are acquired in a way that is not appropriately linked to truth.[64]

The fact that a cogito belief cannot turn out to be false does not ensure that the belief is justified or known. Animal knowledge that p requires the reliability of the process that produces and/or sustains the belief that p. The fact that a process produces some infallible beliefs is not sufficient to ensure that the process is reliable or, a fortiori, that those beliefs are justified. Moreover, reflective knowledge that p requires an explanation of the reliability of the underlying process that produces and/or sustains the belief that p. In Sosa's words, we need to understand how our beliefs are "arrived at in ways that put us in touch with the truth not accidentally but reliably."[65] Showing that a cogito belief cannot be false no more explains how it was arrived at in a way that reliably puts us in touch with the truth than show-

64. Goldman, "What Is Justified Belief?," offers the example of a student who studies pseudologic with Elmer Fraud, whom the student has no reason to trust as a logician. The student believes, on the basis of Fraud's testimony, that any disjunctive proposition involving at least 40 disjuncts is very probably true. The student encounters a contingent proposition with 40 disjuncts and, on the basis of his pseudological training, believes that it is true. As it turns out, one of the disjuncts is "I exist." The student's belief is infallible but, nevertheless, epistemically suspect.

65. Sosa, "Modal and Other *A Priori* Epistemology," 8.

ing that a belief that $2 + 2 = 4$ cannot be false explains how it was arrived at in a way that reliably puts us in touch with the truth.

The upshot is that in order to assess the epistemic credentials of any belief, cogito or otherwise, I must first identify the process that produces and/or sustains it. To certify animal knowledge, I must determine that the process is virtuous, or truth conducive. Finally, to meet the higher standard of reflective knowledge, I must explain how the process reliably produces true beliefs. Rehearsing the cogito achieves none of these goals. Moreover, there are reasons to doubt that these goals can be achieved exclusively by a priori means. First, knowledge of the acquisition and/or sustaining conditions of one's beliefs presumably involves knowledge of cause and effect, but it is implausible to maintain that causal knowledge is a priori. Second, it is difficult to see how one could know a priori that the process that produces and/or sustains some belief is reliable since such knowledge involves a contingent general truth. Finally, any explanation of the reliability of the process that produces and/or sustains some belief will involve contingent facts about human cognition, both particular facts about the cognizer in question and general psychological laws about the normal functioning of the process.

6.5 Conclusion

The two deepest challenges to proponents of the a priori are the contentions that the concept of a priori knowledge is incoherent and that, even granting its coherence, such knowledge does not exist. In chapter 2, I argued that given the conceptual framework of traditional epistemology, there is indeed a coherent conception of a priori justification. A priori justification is non-experiential justification. In chapters 4 and 5, I argued that neither the arguments purporting to show that there is a priori knowledge nor those purporting to show that such knowledge does not exist are compelling. Two residual issues remained. Is the experiential/nonexperiential distinction cogent? Is there any reason to believe that there is a priori knowledge? The present chapter addresses these two remaining issues.

My answers to both involve a common theme: the relevance of empirical investigation. The standard approach of apriorists is to employ a priori methods to address both questions: conceptual analysis to address the first, and a priori arguments that highlight alleged deficiencies of radical empiricism to address the second. I argue that attempts to articulate the experiential/nonexperiential distinction by means of conceptual analysis fail and that a more fruitful approach is to treat "experience" as a putative natural kind term whose extension is fixed by the processes associated with the five senses. Empirical investigation will determine whether there is some interesting set of features common to these processes and other alleged experiential processes, and whether dividing cognitive processes into two categories based on the presence or absence of those features is fruitful for theorizing about human cognition.

Concerning the second question, the primary challenge to apriorists is to offer compelling evidence in support of the central claim that there are nonexperiential sources of justification. Compelling evidence is evidence that is acknowledged by both apriorists and their radical empiricist opponents. I argue for two theses. First, there is a wide range of agreement between proponents and opponents of the a priori about the scope of human knowledge. Hence, there is much common ground that can be exploited in arguing for the existence of a priori knowledge. Second, apriorists have not exploited this common ground. They have relied almost exclusively on a priori arguments to support their claim, ignoring entirely the alternative of offering empirical support. To remedy this shortcoming, I identify four central issues bearing on the existence of a priori knowledge that can be addressed by such investigation and contend that, rather than persisting in the largely negative strategy of offering a priori arguments against their radical empiricist opponents, apriorists should embrace the more promising strategy of enlisting empirical support for their position.

PART III

WHAT ARE THE RELATIONSHIPS?

7

A Priori Knowledge and Necessary Truth

7.1 Introduction

Kant's investigation of the a priori takes place within a framework that includes two nonepistemic distinctions: the metaphysical distinction between necessary and contingent propositions, and the semantic distinction between analytic and synthetic propositions. Utilizing these distinctions, he raises two *relational* (or *external*) questions: What is the relationship between the a priori and the necessary? What is the relationship between the a priori and the analytic? Kant's answers to these questions play a central role in his overall theory of a priori knowledge. His primary argument for the existence of such knowledge is based on a premise about the relationship between the a priori and the necessary. The claim that there is synthetic a priori knowledge sets the stage for his major theoretical contribution.

Kant's two questions, as well as his answers to them, remain controversial. My goal in the remaining two chapters is to address these questions. My primary goal, however, is not to answer them, although they will be answered to some extent. Rather, my primary goal is to raise a question about the questions themselves: How important are they?

The questions are important in several respects. First, a complete theory of a priori knowledge must address them. Second, they are intrinsically interesting from a theoretical perspective. Third, they are historically significant. Indeed, much, if not most, of the traditional literature pertaining to the a priori has as its primary focus one or both of these questions. Hence, on the face of it, the answer to my question is obvious. Yes, they are important.

My concern, however, is somewhat narrower. My goal is to assess whether answers to the relational questions are necessary in order to answer the two *internal* (or *nonrelational*) questions about the a priori: What is a priori knowledge? Is there a priori knowledge? The impressive body of literature addressing the relational questions is not motivated primarily by their intrinsic theoretical interest or by the desire to fill a gap in a virtually complete theory of a priori knowledge. The primary motivation is the belief that answering them is relevant to answering one or both of the internal questions. I argue in chapters 7 and 8 that the results of parts I and II reveal that this belief is rooted either in conceptual confusion or in a misguided strategy for addressing the internal questions.

7.2   Kant's Strategy

The relationship between the a priori and the necessary plays a central role in Kant's account of a priori knowledge for two related reasons. His analysis of the concept of a priori knowledge is incomplete. Although he characterizes a priori knowledge as absolutely independent of all experience, he does not articulate the respect in which knowledge must be independent of experience in order to be a priori. The immediate consequence of this shortcoming is that Kant is not in a position to offer a conceptual argument for the existence of a priori knowledge. Conceptual arguments offer an analysis of the concept of a priori knowledge and maintain that there is knowledge that satisfies the conditions in the analysis. Instead, he must offer a criterial argument. Criterial arguments propose sufficient conditions for a priori knowledge, which are not claimed to be constituents of the concept, and maintain that some knowledge satisfies the proposed conditions. Hence, for Kant, the contention that necessity is a criterion of the a priori is the key to establishing that there is such knowledge.

Two questions arise at this juncture. What is Kant's view about the relationship between the a priori and the necessary? How successful is his strategy? Kant famously argues, "Experience teaches us that a thing is so and so, but not that it cannot be otherwise. First, then, if we have a proposition which in being thought is thought as *necessary*, it is an *a priori* judgment."[1] Utilizing this criterion, he quickly establishes that there is a priori knowledge: "Mathematical propositions, strictly so called, are always judgments *a priori*, not empirical; because they carry with them necessity, which cannot be derived from experience."[2] Kant's official statement of his criterion is provided in the first passage:

(K1) All knowledge of necessary propositions is a priori.

---

1. Kant, *Critique of Pure Reason*, 43.
2. Ibid., 52.

In the second passage, Kant makes the stronger claim that all knowledge of necessary propositions *must* be a priori. My subsequent discussion utilizes the official, weaker formulation of the criterion. Nothing in the subsequent argument turns on this choice.

Does Kant also maintain that necessity is a *necessary* condition for a priori knowledge? This question is more vexing. He does not endorse such a principle in the introduction to the *Critique of Pure Reason*. The only claim of which I am aware that supports such a contention comes from the preface to the first edition: "Any knowledge that professes to hold *a priori* lays claim to be regarded as absolutely necessary."[3] Here Kant appears to endorse the converse of (K1):

(K2) All propositions known a priori are necessary.

Two issues complicate matters. First, in this context, Kant is making a claim about the nature of his inquiry. Although his inquiry is an a priori one, these remarks are not part of that inquiry. Since they are not part of the inquiry, it is not obvious that they should be considered part of his official view. Second, these remarks raise a significant interpretive question. The passage in which the previous quote appears reads as follows:

> As to *certainty*, I have prescribed to myself the maxim, that in this kind of investigation it is in no wise permissible to hold *opinions*. Everything, therefore, which bears any manner of resemblance to an hypothesis is to be treated as contraband; it is not to be put up for sale even at the lowest price, but forthwith confiscated, immediately upon detection. Any knowledge that professes to hold *a priori* lays claim to be regarded as absolutely necessary. This applies still more to any *determination* of all pure *a priori* knowledge, since such determination has to serve as the measure, and therefore as the [supreme] example, of all apodeictic (philosophical) certainty.[4]

Kant moves freely from "certainty" to "necessary" and back to "certainty" in this passage. The concepts, however, are distinct, and Kant offers no rationale that underwrites the move from one to the other. Hence, it is unclear whether he fails to distinguish between the two concepts or whether he thinks that there are defensible principles that allow him to move between them.

7.3   Kripke's Reaction

Recent interest in the relationship between the a priori and the necessary is due largely to the influence of Saul Kripke, who argues for three related theses:

3. Ibid., 11.
4. Ibid.

(T1) The concepts of a priori truth and necessary truth are
      different; they are not interchangeable.

(T2) It is a substantive philosophical thesis, one that requires
      philosophical argument to establish, that everything
      necessary is a priori or that everything a priori is necessary.

(T3) The a priori and the necessary are not coextensive; there are
      examples of necessary a posteriori truths and probably
      contingent a priori truths.[5]

Kripke's primary theoretical motivation is to block a potential epistemological objection to the metaphysical thesis that identity statements between
coreferential proper names are necessarily true. There are examples of identity statements, such as "Hesperus is Phosphorus," that appear to be known
a posteriori. If the concepts of a priori truth and necessary truth are different and there is no substantive philosophical argument connecting them,
then alleged counterexamples to the thesis that they are coextensive can be
evaluated on their own merits. But, as we saw in section 7.2, although Kant
agrees that the a priori and the necessary are different concepts, he also
maintains that there is at least one important relationship between them.
Hence, the question we must address is whether Kripke's results conflict
with the traditional Kantian position.

Let us begin by considering Kripke's discussion of essential properties
in order to introduce the necessary distinctions. According to the essentialist view, the properties of an object fall into two categories, those that are
essential and those that are accidental. The essential properties of an object
are those that it must have if it exists. Kripke offers the example of a lectern.
Suppose that the lectern is in fact made of wood. Could the very same lectern
have been made from ice? Kripke acknowledges that one could have made a
lectern from ice and put it in place of the lectern in question. But if one had
done so, the resulting object would have been a *different* object. Hence, it
appears that the lectern in question could not have been made of ice.

What are the epistemic implications of essentialism? According to Kripke,
"If the essentialist view is correct, it can only be correct if we sharply distinguish between the notions of a posteriori and a priori truth on the one
hand, and contingent and necessary truth on the other hand, for although the
statement that this table, if it exists at all, was not made of ice, is necessary, it
certainly is not something that we know a priori."[6] We don't know it a priori
because the evidence of the senses, such as how it looks or how it feels, is
necessary to know that it is not made of ice. But, given that it is not made of
ice, it is necessarily not made of ice. Kripke summarizes his position as follows:

In other words, if *P* is the statement that the lectern is not made of ice,
one knows by a priori philosophical analysis, some conditional of the

---

5. Kripke, *Naming and Necessity*, 34–38.
6. Kripke, "Identity and Necessity," 152–153.

form "if P, then necessarily P." If the table is not made of ice, it is necessarily not made of ice. On the other hand, then, we know by empirical investigation that P, the antecedent of the conditional, is true—that this table is not made of ice. We can conclude by *modus ponens*:

$$P \supset \Box P$$
$$\underline{P }$$
$$\Box P$$

The conclusion—'$\Box P$'—is that it is necessary that the table not be made of ice, and this conclusion is known a posteriori, since one of the premises on which it is based is a posteriori.[7]

If the essentialist view is correct, then the proposition that necessarily the table is not made of ice is known a posteriori. Essentialism has the consequence that there is a posteriori knowledge of necessary propositions.

In chapter 4, I noted that the expression "know a necessary proposition" is ambiguous, and I introduced the following distinctions:

(A) S knows the *general modal status* of p just in case S knows that p is a necessary proposition (i.e., either necessarily true or necessarily false) or S knows that p is a contingent proposition (i.e., either contingently true or contingently false).

(B) S knows the *truth value* of p just in case S knows that p is true or S knows that p is false.

(C) S knows the *specific modal status* of p just in case S knows that p is necessarily true or S knows that p is necessarily false or S knows that p is contingently true or S knows that p is contingently false.

I also noted that although (A) and (B) are logically independent of one another, (C) is not independent of (A) and (B). One can know the truth value of a proposition but not know its general modal status. Alternatively, one can know the general modal status of a proposition but not know its truth value. One cannot, however, know the specific modal status of a proposition without knowing both its truth value and its general modal status.

Some additional consequences of these distinctions are worth noting here. First, since knowledge of the general modal status of a proposition and knowledge of its truth value are independent of each other, the evidence that justifies one of them need not be the same as the evidence that justifies the other. A philosopher may know that the Goldbach conjecture is a necessary proposition without knowing whether it is true because the metaphysical considerations relevant to justifying the former belief are not the same

7. Ibid., 153.

as the mathematical considerations relevant to justifying the latter. Alternatively, a mathematician may know the truth of certain theorems of number theory without knowing that they are necessary because the proofs that suffice to justify the former beliefs do not suffice to justify the latter.

Second, since the evidence that justifies a belief about the truth value of a proposition need not be the same as the evidence that justifies a belief about its general modal status, there is no guarantee that if one belief is justified a priori (a posteriori) then the other is also justified a priori (a posteriori). For example, a mathematician may know the truth of some theorem on the basis of a proof but know that the resulting theorem is a necessary proposition on the basis of the testimony of a philosopher. Conversely, a philosopher may know, on the basis of metaphysical considerations, that a mathematical theorem is a necessary proposition but know, on the basis of the testimony of a mathematician, that it is true.

Third, since knowledge of the specific modal status of a proposition is the conjunction of knowledge of its general modal status and knowledge of its truth value, it follows that if *either* one's knowledge of the general modal status of a proposition *or* one's knowledge of its truth value is a posteriori, then one's knowledge of its specific modal status is also a posteriori. However, from the fact that one's knowledge of the specific modal status of a proposition is a posteriori, it does not follow that one's knowledge of its general modal status is also a posteriori. Analogously, from the fact that one's knowledge of the specific modal status of a proposition is a posteriori, it does not follow that one's knowledge of its truth value is also a posteriori.

Kripke observes that if essentialism is correct, then there is a posteriori knowledge of necessary propositions. This observation, however, is ambiguous. Consider the proposition that the table is not made of ice. Does essentialism require

(EA) A posteriori knowledge that the proposition that the table is not made of ice is a necessary proposition, or

(EB) A posteriori knowledge that the proposition that the table is not made of ice is true?

In other words, does essentialism require a posteriori knowledge of the general modal status or the truth value of necessary propositions?

Kripke's argument entails only that essentialism requires a posteriori knowledge of the truth value of necessary propositions. Knowing whether the table is made of wood or ice or cotton candy requires the evidence of the senses. Hence, knowledge that the table is not made of ice is a posteriori. However, from the fact that knowledge of the truth value of that proposition is a posteriori, it does not follow that knowledge of its general modal status is also a posteriori. Moreover, Kripke explicitly denies that it is a posteriori. He tells us that "if *P* is the statement that the lectern is not made of ice, one knows by *a priori philosophical analysis*, some conditional of the form 'if *P*, then necessarily *P*.'"[8] Hence, essentialism requires (EB) but not (EA).

The contention that essentialism does not require (EA) appears to conflict with Kripke's claim that the conclusion that it is *necessary* that the table not be made of ice is known a posteriori. To dispel this appearance, it is necessary to distinguish between knowledge of the *general modal status* of a proposition and knowledge of its *specific modal status*. More specifically, we need to distinguish between

(EA) A posteriori knowledge that the proposition that the table is not made of ice is a necessary proposition, and

(EC) A posteriori knowledge that the proposition that the table is not made of ice is necessarily true.

Knowledge that it is necessary that the table not be made of ice is knowledge of the necessary truth, or specific modal status, of the proposition. Since knowledge of the specific modal status of a proposition is the conjunction of knowledge of its truth value and knowledge of its general modal status, it follows that if knowledge of its truth value is a posteriori, knowledge of its specific modal status is also a posteriori. It does not follow, however, that if knowledge of the specific modal status of a proposition is a posteriori, knowledge of its general modal status is also a posteriori. Hence, essentialism requires (EB) and, a fortiori, (EC) but not (EA).

If we turn to the case of identity statements between proper names, the situation is analogous in all respects. First, if Kripke's account is correct, then it follows that knowledge of the truth value of such identity statements is a posteriori: "So two things are true: first, that we do not know a priori that Hesperus is Phosphorus, and are in no position to find out the answer except empirically."[9] Second, although such identity statements cannot be known to be true a priori, they are nevertheless necessary: "We have concluded that an identity statement between names, when true at all, is necessarily true, even though one may not know it *a priori*."[10]

But how does Kripke arrive at the latter conclusion? How does he know the general modal status of such identity statements? Here he offers the same answer that he offers in the case of essential properties: "Certain statements—and the identity statement is a paradigm of such a statement on my view—if true at all must be necessarily true. One does know a priori, by philosophical analysis, that *if* such an identity statement is true it is necessarily true."[11] Once again, Kripke does not maintain that knowledge of the general modal status of necessary statements is a posteriori. On the contrary, he endorses the view that such knowledge is a priori. What is a posteriori, according to

8. Ibid. (emphasis mine).
9. Kripke, *Naming and Necessity*, 104.
10. Ibid., 108.
11. Ibid., 109.

Kripke, is knowledge of the truth value of such statements. Hence, it follows that knowledge of their specific modal status is also a posteriori.

How do Kripke's claims bear on the traditional Kantian account of the relationship between a priori and necessary propositions? The question cannot be answered straightforwardly since Kant, like Kripke, fails to make the appropriate distinctions. Kant's leading claim

(K1) All knowledge of necessary propositions is a priori

is ambiguous. There are two ways of reading it:

(KT) All knowledge of the *truth value* of necessary propositions is a priori.
(KG) All knowledge of the *general modal status* of necessary propositions is a priori.

Kant's argument for the claim that mathematical knowledge is a priori conjoins (K1) with the additional premise

(P1) Mathematical propositions, such as that 7 + 5 = 12, are necessary,

and concludes that

(C1) Knowledge of mathematical propositions, such as that 7 + 5 = 12, is a priori.

This argument is valid only if (K1) is read as (KT). Kant, however, supports (K1) with the observation that although experience teaches us that something is true, it does not teach us that it cannot be otherwise. Taken at face value, this observation states that experience teaches us that a proposition is true but not that it is necessary. Hence, Kant's argument for (K1), if cogent, supports (KG) but not (KT).

So where does this leave us? (K1) is ambiguous and can be read in two ways. The argument Kant offers for (K1) supports (KG), not (KT), but his argument for the existence of a priori knowledge is valid only if (K1) is read as (KT). Kripke's leading claim—that there is a posteriori knowledge of the truth value of necessary propositions—contravenes (KT) but not (KG). Kripke does not dispute, and indeed endorses, Kant's claim that knowledge of the general modal status of necessary propositions is a priori. Hence, Kripke's claims challenge one reading of (K1) but provide support for the alternative reading.

In the addenda to *Naming and Necessity*, Kripke explicitly discusses Kant's account of the relationship between the a priori and the necessary. Moreover, he appreciates that (K1) is ambiguous and distinguishes between knowing that a proposition is *true* and knowing that it is *necessary*. Nevertheless, he argues that Kant's position cannot be partially vindicated by means of such a distinction:

Kant thus appears to hold that if a proposition is known to be *necessary*, the mode of knowledge not only *can* be *a priori* but *must* be.

On the contrary, one can learn a mathematical truth *a posteriori* by consulting a computing machine, or even by asking a mathematician. Nor can Kant argue that experience can tell us that a mathematical proposition is *true*, but not that it is *necessary*; for the peculiar character of mathematical propositions . . . is that one knows (*a priori*) that they cannot be contingently true; a mathematical statement, if true, is necessary.[12]

Kripke's argument can be reconstructed as follows:

(P2) We can learn mathematical truths a posteriori.

(P3) We know a priori that a mathematical statement, if true, is necessary.

(C2) Kant cannot argue that (E) Experience cannot tell us that a mathematical proposition is necessary.

The argument, however, is inconclusive because Kripke fails to distinguish between knowing the *general* modal status of a proposition and knowing its *specific* modal status.

The failure to make this distinction introduces an ambiguity into (C2). More specifically, there are two readings of (E):

(G) Knowledge of the *general modal status* of mathematical propositions cannot be a posteriori.

(S) Knowledge of the *specific modal status* of mathematical propositions cannot be a posteriori.

Kripke, I suggest, reads (E) as (S). On this reading, the argument is valid, for (P2) entails

(T) We can know a posteriori the *truth value* of mathematical propositions,

which, in conjunction with (P3), entails the negation of (S). Since knowledge of the specific modal status of a proposition is the conjunction of knowledge of its general modal status and knowledge of its truth value, if knowledge of its truth value is a posteriori it follows that knowledge of its specific modal status is a posteriori as well. If (E) is read as (G), however, the argument is invalid since the conjunction of (T) and (P3) does not entail the negation of (G).

In conclusion, neither Kant nor Kripke draws the distinctions required to cogently address the relationship between the a priori and the necessary. As a consequence, each position involves a significant error. Kant fails to distinguish between knowledge of the truth value of a proposition and knowledge of its general modal status. This oversight results in his failure to recognize that his leading premise, that experience does not teach us that something must be the case, supports only (KG) and not (KT). Kripke fails

12. Ibid., 159.

to distinguish between knowledge of the general modal status of a proposition and knowledge of its specific modal status. As a consequence, he fails to recognize that his examples of necessary a posteriori propositions call into question (KT) but not (KG).

7.4   Complications

I argued in section 7.3 that Kripke's examples of the necessary a posteriori, propositions involving essential properties and identity statements between names, show that

(KT) All knowledge of the *truth value* of necessary propositions
is a priori

is false but leave untouched

(KG) All knowledge of the *general modal status* of necessary
propositions is a priori.

The prior discussion, however, masks an important feature of Kripke's examples. To unveil this feature, let us recast (KT) as

(ST) If p is a necessary proposition and S knows that p, then S
knows a priori that p.

Kripke maintains that cases of knowing the truth of a mathematical proposition on the basis of consulting a mathematician or a computer show that (ST) is false. He also points out that if such cases were the only counterexamples to (ST), (ST) could be replaced with the weaker

(WT) If p is a necessary proposition and S knows that p, then S
can know a priori that p.

It is plausible, however, to maintain that the truth value of propositions involving essential properties and identity statements are knowable *only* a posteriori.[13] Hence, Kripke's examples show that both (ST) and (WT) are false.

Analogous considerations apply to (KG). (KG) can be recast as

---

13. Kripke, "Identity and Necessity," 153, is explicit on this point in the case of essential properties: "So we have to say that though we cannot know a priori whether this table was made of ice or not, given that it is not made of ice, it is *necessarily* not made of ice." Kripke, 153–154, is more cautious about identity statements: "One can hold that certain statements of identity between names, though often known a posteriori, and maybe not knowable a priori, are in fact necessary, if true." In *Naming and Necessity*, 104, Kripke makes a somewhat stronger claim on behalf of identity statements: "So two things are true: first, that we do not know *a priori* that Hesperus is Phosphorus, and are in no position to find out the answer except empirically."

(SG) If p is a necessary proposition and S knows that p is a
necessary proposition, then S knows a priori that p is a
necessary proposition.

If cases of testimonial knowledge that a mathematical proposition is true
show that (ST) is false, then cases of testimonial knowledge that a mathematical proposition is necessary show that (SG) is false. If such cases were the
only counterexamples to (SG), (SG) could be replaced with the weaker

(WG) If p is a necessary proposition and S knows that p is a
necessary proposition, then S *can* know a priori that p is a
necessary proposition.

C. Anthony Anderson, however, argues that if Kripke's examples establish
that (WT) is false, they also establish that (WG) is false.[14] Hence, if Anderson is correct, then Kripke's examples also establish that the stronger (KG)
is false, contrary to the conclusion of section 7.3.

Anderson provides an elegant proof for his conclusion couched within
the framework of a modal-epistemic logic. I will present his case in a more
intuitive fashion. Let me begin with the following propositions:

(n) Hesperus is Phosphorus.
(c) The president of the United States in 2020 will be a woman.

The two propositions differ in their general modal status. The first is either
necessarily true or necessarily false; the second is either contingently true
or contingently false. Now consider their disjunction: (n or c). If (n) is true,
then (n or c) is a necessary proposition, for if (n) is true, then (n) is necessarily true and if (n) is necessarily true then (n or c) is necessarily true. If (n) is
false, however, then (n or c) is a contingent proposition, for if (n) is false
then (n) is necessarily false. Since (c) is contingent, (c) is true in some worlds
but false in others. Hence, if (n) is false, (n or c) is also contingent since it is
true in some worlds but false in others.

Let us now assume that (n) is true and that the truth value of (n) is known
a posteriori but is not knowable a priori. Since (n) is true, (n or c) is a necessary proposition. (WG), however, entails that

(A*) If (n or c) is a necessary proposition and S knows that (n or c)
is a necessary proposition, then S can know a priori that
(n or c) is a necessary proposition.

To know whether (n or c) is a necessary proposition or a contingent proposition, one must know the truth value of (n). Although (n or c) is a necessary
proposition if (n) is true, (n or c) is a contingent proposition if (n) is false.
Since the truth value of (n) is not knowable a priori, it is not the case that
one can know a priori that (n or c) is a necessary proposition. Yet one who
knows a posteriori that (n) is true and knows that if (n) is true then (n or c)

14. Anderson, "Toward a Logic of A Priori Knowledge."

is a necessary proposition also knows, by elementary inference, that (n or c) is a necessary proposition. Since one's knowledge that (n or c) is a necessary proposition is based on a posteriori knowledge that (n) is true, it is also a posteriori. Consequently, if (WT) is false, that is, if there are necessary propositions whose truth value is known but is not knowable a priori, then (WG) is also false; that is, there are necessary propositions whose general modal status is known but is not knowable a priori.

Anderson's contention is surely correct. Kripke's examples of necessary a posteriori propositions challenge (WG), as well as (WT). Yet there is something puzzling about the situation. The very argument that purports to show that one cannot know a priori the general modal status of (n or c) rests on a priori justified premises about its modal status. To locate the source of this paradoxical result, let me fully articulate the a priori justified premises regarding modal status involved in the argument. With respect to (n), we know a priori that

(n1) If (n) is true then (n) is necessarily true.
(n2) If (n) is false then (n) is necessarily false.

With respect to (c), we know a priori that

(c1) If (c) is true then (c) is contingently true.
(c2) If (c) is false then (c) is contingently false.

Finally, with respect to the disjunctive proposition (n or c), we know a priori that

(d1) If (n) is true and (c) is true, then (n or c) is necessarily true.
(d2) If (n) is true and (c) is false, then (n or c) is necessarily true.
(d3) If (n) is false and (c) is true, then (n or c) is contingently true.
(d4) If (n) is false and (c) is false, then (n or c) is contingently false.

Hence, our list indicates that, with respect to each of the three propositions in question, our a priori modal knowledge is complete. We know a priori, with respect to each of these three propositions, whether it is necessary or contingent for any given assignment of truth values to its simple components. But if our a priori modal knowledge is complete, how can we fail to know a priori the general modal status of (n or c)?

The articulation of these three cases reveals that we need to look more deeply into how we acquire knowledge of the general modal status of a proposition. The two initial propositions, (n) and (c), exemplify a feature, which I call *modal symmetry*. A truth functionally simple proposition is modally symmetric just in case it has the same modality regardless of its truth value. In other words, a truth functionally simple proposition is modally symmetric just in case either (a) if it is true then it is necessarily true and if it is false then it is necessarily false or (b) if it is true then it is contingently true and if it is false then it is contingently false. More generally, a truth functional proposition is modally symmetric just in case it has the same modality regardless of the truth values of its simple components. In other words, a truth functional proposition is modally symmetric just in case, for all assignments of truth values to its simple components, it is either (a) necessarily true or necessarily false or (b) contingently true or contingently false.

Modal symmetry stands in an important relationship to the general modal status of a proposition. Associated with each truth functionally simple proposition is a pair of conditional propositions: one provides the specific modal status of the proposition given that it is true; the other provides its specific modal status given that it is false. Associated with each truth functionally compound proposition is a series of conditional propositions, one for each assignment of truth values to its simple components. Each conditional proposition provides the specific modal status of the proposition given that assignment of truth values. Let us call these propositions *conditional modal propositions* and say that S knows the *conditional modal status* of *p* just in case S knows all the conditional modal propositions associated with *p*.[15]

If S knows the conditional modal status of *p* and *p* is modally symmetric, then S can know the general modal status of *p* via a simple process of deductive reasoning. In the case where *p* is truth functionally simple, S can reason as follows:

(i) If *p* is true then *p* is necessarily (contingently) true.
(ii) If *p* is false then *p* is necessarily (contingently) false.
(iii) Either *p* is true or *p* is false.
(iv) Therefore, either *p* is necessarily (contingently) true or p is necessarily (contingently) false.
(v) Therefore, *p* is a necessary (contingent) proposition.

In cases in which *p* is truth functionally compound, there are analogous but more complex arguments, where the first two premises of the above argument are replaced by a series of premises, one for each assignment of truth values for its simple components. The process of deductive reasoning involved, however, remains essentially the same. Consequently, if S knows *a priori* the conditional modal status of *p* and *p* is modally symmetric, then S can also know *a priori* the general modal status of *p*.

Returning to Anderson's example, we see that modal symmetry is satisfied in the case of (n) and (c). Since "Hesperus" and "Phosphorus" are rigid designators, that is, since they refer to the same object in all possible worlds, if it is true that Hesperus is Phosphorus, then it is necessarily true. But, by parity of reasoning, if it is false, then it is necessarily false. Whether or not a woman is president of the United States in 2020 depends on a large number of contingent facts about campaign finances, delegate selection procedures, voting preferences of eligible voters, and ultimately the ballots cast on election day. As a consequence, if it is true that the president of the United

---

15. I owe the expression "conditional modal status" to David Chalmers.

States in 2020 will be a woman, it is contingently true. If it is false, it is contingently false. Kripke's examples of propositions that involve essential properties also satisfy this condition. If the substance of which an object is made is an essential property of that object, then if it is true that the lectern is made of wood, it is necessarily true. But, if it is false that it is made of wood, it is necessarily false. Hence, in these cases, one can know a priori the general modal status of the proposition in question, regardless of how one knows (or can know) their truth values.

In the case of (n or c), however, modal symmetry fails. Although one can know a priori, on the basis of one's a priori knowledge of the conditional modal status of (n) and one's a priori knowledge of the conditional modal status of (c), that (n or c) is necessarily true if (n) is true but contingently false if (n) is false, one cannot know a priori its general modal status. To know whether (n or c) is a necessary proposition or a contingent proposition, one needs to know whether (n) is true or false. If one cannot know a priori the truth value of (n), however, one cannot know a priori the general modal status of (n or c). Hence, in cases where modal symmetry fails, (WG) is not generally true.[16]

What general moral can we draw from this discussion? The examples we have considered suggest that our basic modal knowledge involves conditional modal propositions and that our knowledge of general modal status derives from this basic modal knowledge. This point is illustrated by the following passage from Kripke:

> If the Goldbach conjecture is false, then there is an even number, n, greater than 2, such that for no primes p_1 and p_2, both $< n$, does $n = p_1 + p_2$. This fact about n, if true, is verifiable by direct computation, and thus is necessary if the results of arithmetical computations are necessary. On the other hand, if the conjecture is true, then every even number exceeding 2 is the sum of two primes. Could it then be the case that, although in fact every such even number is the sum of two primes, there might have been such an even number which was not the sum of two primes? What would that mean? . . . Goldbach's conjecture, then, cannot be contingently true or false; whatever truth-value it has belongs to it by necessity.[17]

We don't know the truth value of the Goldbach conjecture. We don't know whether it is true or false. Yet we can determine its general modal status.

---

16. There are cases in which modal symmetry fails, but (WG) is not impugned. Consider, for example,

   (b) There is a prime number between 5 and 10.

The conjunctive proposition (b or c) is identical in conditional modal status to (n or c). If (b) is true, then (b or c) is necessarily true. If (b) is false, then (b or c) is contingently false. However, since one can know a priori whether (b) is true or false, one can also know a priori the general modal status of (b or c).

17. Kripke, *Naming and Necessity*, 36–37.

How is this possible? According to Kripke, we determine the general modal status of the Goldbach conjecture by first assuming that it is false and asking whether it could be true and then assuming that it is true and asking whether it could be false. The two thought experiments reveal that if the conjecture is true it is necessarily true and if it is false it is necessarily false. On the basis of our knowledge of these two conditional modal propositions, we derive a conclusion about the general modal status of the conjecture: "whatever truth-value it has belongs to it by necessity."[18]

Once we recognize the role of knowledge of conditional modal propositions in acquiring knowledge of the general modal status of a proposition, we can address Anderson's problem by revising (WG) to reflect the primacy of such knowledge:

> (WG*) If p is a necessary proposition and S knows the conditional modal status of p, then S can know a priori the conditional modal status of p.

(WG*) is not vulnerable to Anderson's example. As we saw earlier, even if we grant that Kripke has established that (n) is a necessary proposition whose truth value is knowable only a posteriori, we still can know a priori

> (d1) If (n) is true and (c) is true, then (n or c) is necessarily true.
> (d2) If (n) is true and (c) is false, then (n or c) is necessarily true.
> (d3) If (n) is false and (c) is true, then (n or c) is contingently true.
> (d4) If (n) is false and (c) is false, then (n or c) is contingently false.

The assumption that the truth value of (n) is knowable only a posteriori does not preclude one from knowing a priori the conditional modal status of (n or c). Hence, (WG*) survives Anderson's example.

Our investigation of Anderson's argument reveals that understanding the nature of modal knowledge requires introducing a further distinction between knowledge of the conditional modal status of a proposition and knowledge of its general modal status. In cases of modally symmetric propositions, if one knows a priori the conditional modal status of the proposition, one can also know a priori the general modal status of that proposition. But, in cases where modal symmetry fails, a priori knowledge of the conditional modal status of the proposition does not ensure that one can know a priori the general modal status of that proposition. Our investigation also reveals that the conclusion of section 7.3 requires revision. There is a version of the traditional account of the relationship between the a priori and the necessary that is immune to Kripke's examples of necessary a posteriori propositions. That version is not (KG), as I argued in section 7.3, but (WG*).

18. Ibid.

7.5   Kant Revisited

Sections 7.3 and 7.4 offer an analysis of the differences between Kant and Kripke on the relationship between the a priori and the necessary. The analysis introduces the distinctions necessary for identifying points of agreement and points of disagreement. My primary goal, however, is not to resolve the disagreements but to determine whether such a resolution is necessary in order to provide an analysis of the concept of a priori knowledge or to determine whether such knowledge exists.

The primary disagreement between Kant and Kripke is over

(K1) All knowledge of necessary propositions is a priori.

Within Kant's framework, the theoretical significance of (K1) is a direct consequence of his strategy for demonstrating that there is a priori knowledge. Since he does not offer a fully articulated analysis of the concept of a priori knowledge, Kant cannot offer a conceptual argument for the existence of such knowledge. He cannot show that some knowledge satisfies the conditions in his analysis of the concept of a priori knowledge. Instead, he must offer a criterial argument for the existence of such knowledge. Hence, (K1) is theoretically significant since it is the leading premise of Kant's only argument for the existence of a priori knowledge.

Kripke maintains that some necessary propositions are known a posteriori. The primary examples he offers are propositions that involve essential properties and identity statements between names. His contention that there is a posteriori knowledge of necessary propositions bears on the more general question of whether there is a priori knowledge because it challenges (K1). Hence, it appears that the cogency of Kant's supporting argument for the existence of a priori knowledge turns on whether Kripke's examples of necessary a posteriori knowledge are genuine.

Although Kripke's examples challenge (K1), the cogency of Kant's argument does not depend on whether they are genuine. This contention is based on two related observations. First, Kant's indirect strategy for arguing in support of a priori knowledge involves an incoherence. To establish that there is a priori knowledge, Kant must first establish that necessity is indeed a criterion of the a priori. The only way to establish this is to show that any knowledge that satisfies the criterion also satisfies all the necessary conditions on a priori knowledge. But, in the absence of a fully articulated concept of a priori knowledge, he is not in a position to do so. Consider, for example, the observation Kant offers in support of the claim that necessity is a criterion of the a priori: experience does not teach us that something cannot be otherwise. This observation, even if cogent, is not sufficient to underwrite the claim that knowledge of necessity is a priori. He must also show that justification is the only respect in which knowledge must be independent of experience in order to be a priori. If, for example, indefeasibility by experience is also necessary, the observation falls short of its goal.

Kant now faces a dilemma. Either he has available a fully articulated concept of a priori knowledge or he does not. If he does not, then he cannot show that necessity is indeed a criterion of the a priori. If he does, then he can argue directly for the existence of such knowledge without utilizing the criterion. He can show that the knowledge in question satisfies the conditions on a priori knowledge. Since (K1) is either indefensible or unnecessary, the indirect strategy is incoherent. Kant's argument fails whether or not Kripke's examples are genuine.

Moreover, even if we assume that Kant's indirect strategy is coherent, the cogency of his argument still does not turn on whether Kripke's examples are genuine examples of necessary a posteriori propositions. For, as I argued in section 7.3, (K1) is ambiguous. If Kripke's examples are genuine examples of necessary a posteriori knowledge, they are examples of a posteriori knowledge of the truth value of necessary propositions but they are not examples of a posteriori knowledge of the general modal status of necessary propositions. They show that

(KT) All knowledge of the *truth value* of necessary propositions is a priori

is false but not that

(KG) All knowledge of the *general modal status* of necessary propositions is a priori

is false.[19] Hence, the cogency of Kripke's examples is not sufficient to undermine Kant's case for the existence of a priori knowledge.

Kant ties the question of whether a priori knowledge exists to the question of the relationship between the a priori and the necessary. His criterial argument for the existence of such knowledge is based on the premise that all knowledge of necessary propositions is a priori. The argument fails since the premise is either indefensible or unnecessary. It fails regardless of whether Kripke's examples of necessary a posteriori knowledge are genuine. Moreover, if the strategy were coherent, Kripke's examples, even if genuine, would not blunt Kant's conclusion that there is a priori knowledge. Hence, the differences between Kant and Kripke on the relationship between the a priori and the necessary do not bear directly on the more general question of whether there is a priori knowledge.

This discussion of the differences between Kant and Kripke on the relationship between the a priori and the necessary has focused exclusively on (K1). I have not addressed

(K2) All propositions known a priori are necessary.

There are two reasons for not discussing (K2) in this context. First, it is not clear that Kant endorses the principle. Second, and more important, (K2)

19. I am ignoring here the complications introduced in section 7.4.

does not play an important role in his argument strategy. It does not play any role in his analysis of the concept of the a priori, his arguments for the existence of a priori knowledge, or his arguments for the existence of synthetic a priori knowledge. As a consequence, little turns on whether (K2) is true within the Kantian framework.

(K1) is important within the Kantian framework because it provides the key to establishing that there is a priori knowledge, but (K2) plays no comparable role because it is a thesis about the *scope* of a priori knowledge. If Kripke is correct in maintaining that there is a priori knowledge of some contingent propositions, the net result is that the scope of a priori knowledge is greater than Kant alleged. But, clearly, this has no negative impact on either the Kantian conception of a priori knowledge or the claim that such knowledge exists. Conversely, if Kripke is wrong on the matter, there is no negative impact on either the concept or the existence of a priori knowledge. (K2) introduces a pleasing symmetry into the Kantian framework, but no more. If (K2) is false and the symmetry is lost, the answers to the two central questions remain unchanged. The importance of (K2) derives not from the Kantian framework but from the commitments of rationalism. Hence, we now turn to the commitments of rationalism with respect to the relationship between the a priori and the necessary.

7.6   Rationalism

Traditional rationalism introduces a *conceptual* connection between the a priori and the necessary. To revert to the taxonomy of chapter 1, traditional rationalists favor a positive characterization of a priori justification,

> (P1) S's belief that p is justified a priori if and only if S's belief is justified by Φ,

where "Φ" designates some particular source of justification. BonJour offers the following version of the traditional rationalist conception:

> (TR)   S's belief that p is justified a priori if and only if S is able "to intuitively 'see' or apprehend that its truth is an invariant feature of all possible worlds, that there is no possible world in which it is false."[20]

(TR) involves a single condition with two components: the source of a priori justification, or intuitive apprehension, and the content of beliefs so justified, or necessary truths. This condition straightforwardly entails that if S's belief that p is justified a priori then p is necessarily true.

The traditional rationalist conception of a priori justification entails

---

20. BonJour, *The Structure of Empirical Knowledge*, 192. BonJour no longer endorses this conception.

(TR1) If S's belief that p is justified a priori then p is necessarily true

and, a fortiori,

(K2) All propositions known a priori are necessary.

As a consequence, the question of whether there is contingent a priori knowledge is of much greater import within the traditional rationalist framework than within the Kantian framework. The falsehood of (K2) does not negatively affect either Kant's conception of a priori knowledge or his strategy for demonstrating that there is such knowledge. For traditional rationalism, the stakes are much higher. If (K2) is false, then its conception of a priori knowledge is inadequate.

Kripke maintains that (K2) is false. He offers the following example of contingent a priori knowledge.[21] Suppose that someone stipulates that "one meter" is to be the length of stick S at t_0. Kripke maintains that the statement that S is one meter long at t_0 is contingently true because the person is using the definite description to fix the reference, and not to give the meaning, of "one meter." Since the definite description is used to fix the reference of "one meter," "one meter" designates S's actual length in all possible worlds even though there are worlds in which S has a length different from its actual length. Nevertheless, Kripke maintains that anyone who fixes the reference of "one meter" in this fashion knows a priori that S is one meter long at t_0: "It would seem that he knows it *a priori*. For if he used stick S to fix the reference of the term 'one meter', then as a result of this kind of 'definition' . . . he knows automatically, without further investigation, that S is one meter long."[22] Hence, the reference fixer has a priori knowledge of a contingent truth.

If Kripke's example is cogent, then (K2) is false and (TR) is untenable. BonJour, however, argues that the traditional rationalist conception of a priori justification is unnecessarily strong and favors a more moderate rationalism:

(MR) S's belief that p is justified a priori if and only if S has an *apparent* intuitive apprehension that p is necessarily true.

He observes that since having an apparent intuitive apprehension that p does not entail that p is true, (MR) does not entail (TR1). Hence, it appears that once (TR) is rejected in favor of (MR), Kripke's example of contingent a priori knowledge no longer threatens the rationalist conception of a priori justification.

Unfortunately, the appearances are deceiving. There is a another issue lurking in the background. Although BonJour maintains that the source of a

---

21. Kripke offers some other examples as well. See Geirsson, "The Contingent *A Priori*."
22. Kripke, *Naming and Necessity*, 56.

priori justification, intuitive apprehension, is fallible with respect to the *truth value* of necessary propositions, he does not indicate whether it is fallible with respect to the *general modal status* of such propositions. If the source is *not* fallible in this respect, then moderate rationalism is committed to

(MR1) If S's belief that p is justified a priori, then p is either necessarily true or necessarily false.

However, (MR1) straightforwardly entails that no contingent propositions are justified a priori.

Alvin Plantinga, who also endorses a moderate rationalist conception of a priori justification, addresses this issue. As we saw in chapter 1, he maintains that noninferential a priori justification consists in seeing that p is true which in turn involves finding yourself convinced that p is true and could not have been false, where the belief is formed immediately but not on the basis of memory or testimony and is accompanied by a distinctive phenomenology. Plantinga, however, allows that God could design cognizers that form such convictions with respect to contingent truths: "Would such creatures have *a priori* knowledge of those contingent propositions, despite their mistakenly thinking them necessary? I should think so: no doubt I know that $2 + 1 = 3$ even if, contrary to what I believe, Mill is right in supposing that proposition contingently true."[23] If Plantinga's answer is correct, then moderate rationalism must allow that the source of a priori justification is fallible with respect to both the truth value and the general modal status of necessary propositions. Such a moderate rationalism does not entail (MR1) and, as a consequence, does not appear to exclude the possibility of contingent propositions that are justified a priori.

There is, however, a further complication. Plantinga's moderate rationalism entails

(MR2) If S's belief that p is justified a priori, then S believes that p is necessarily true.

Yet one who fixes the reference of "one meter" by using stick S need not believe that the statement "S is one meter long at t_0" is necessarily true. Hence, Kripke's example is incompatible with any form of moderate rationalism that entails (MR2).

BonJour is not explicit on the question of whether his version of moderate rationalism entails either (MR1) or (MR2). He maintains that even an apparent rational insight "must involve a genuine awareness by the person in question of the necessity or apparent necessity of the proposition."[24] The reference to "apparent necessity" appears to allow for the possibility of a contingent proposition that appears to someone to be necessary. Hence, we have

23. Plantinga, *Warrant and Proper Function*, 107, n. 7.
24. BonJour, *In Defense of Pure Reason*, 114.

(MR3) If S's belief that p is justified a priori, then p appears to S to be necessarily true.

Since BonJour does not address the issue of whether such an appearing either takes the form of a belief that necessarily p or entails such a belief, it is difficult to assess whether (MR3) entails (MR2). Nevertheless, (MR3) is also incompatible with Kripke's example since the contingent statement "S is one meter long at t_0" need not appear to the reference fixer to be necessary.

In summary, since traditional rationalism entails that only necessary truths are justified a priori, it excludes the possibility of contingent a priori knowledge. Moderate rationalism, however, appears to allow for the possibility of such knowledge since it does not entail that if S's belief that p is justified a priori then p is true. The issue, however, is more complex. Although moderate rationalism does not entail that a priori justification is infallible with respect to the *truth value* of beliefs justified a priori, it is unclear whether it entails that a priori justification is infallible with respect to the *general modal status* of beliefs so justified. If a priori justification is infallible with respect to general modal status, then moderate rationalism entails (MR1), which is incompatible with the possibility of contingent a priori knowledge. If a priori justification is fallible with respect to the general modal status of propositions but moderate rationalism entails either (MR2) or (MR3), then there is logical space for the contingent a priori *provided that* S believes, or it appears to S, that the contingent proposition in question is necessary. Nevertheless, since it is not necessary that the reference fixer believe, or that it appear to the reference fixer, that "S is one meter long at t_0" is necessary, Kripke's example, if cogent, shows that both the strong and the moderate rationalist conceptions of a priori justification are inadequate.

The question of whether there is a priori knowledge of contingent propositions takes on prominence against the background of rationalism. Since the rationalist conception of a priori knowledge introduces a conceptual connection between the a priori and the necessary, the existence of such knowledge entails that the conception is inadequate. I argued, however, in chapter 1 that the rationalist conception of a priori justification should be rejected on the basis of considerations that are independent of the alleged existence of contingent a priori knowledge. Given that the rationalist conception of a priori justification, in both forms, is untenable on independent grounds, the question of whether there is contingent a priori knowledge need not be resolved in order to articulate or defend the concept of a priori knowledge.

7.7 The Contingent A Priori

Although the cogency of Kripke's examples of contingent a priori knowledge need not be resolved for my purposes, I conclude with a brief discussion whose goal is to locate more precisely the epistemic issues that they raise. Kripke's claims about the epistemic implications of reference fixing introduce a tension into his position concerning the relationship between the a priori and the necessary. Discussions of his examples tend to focus on the fact that a *contingent* truth is known a priori. The epistemic questions raised by reference fixing, however, extend to *necessary* truths. Suppose that a student is asked to determine the sum of 117 and 386. Rather than calculating the sum, the student stipulates that "Alpha" is to be the sum of 117 and 386. If Kripke is correct, then, as a result of the stipulation, the student knows a priori that Alpha is the sum of 117 and 386. Since "Alpha" is a rigid designator of the number that is the sum of 117 and 386, it designates the same number in all possible worlds. Since being the sum of 117 and 386 is an essential property of Alpha, if Alpha is the sum of 117 and 386 in the actual world, it is the sum of 117 and 386 in all possible worlds. Hence, the student has a priori knowledge of a *necessary* truth via reference fixing.[25]

The possibility of necessary a priori knowledge based on reference fixing undermines Kripke's claims about the import of his examples of the necessary a posteriori. Identity statements and propositions involving essential properties are alleged to be knowable *only* a posteriori. They are alleged to show that

(WT)   If *p* is a necessary proposition and S knows that *p*, then S
        can know a priori that *p*

is false. The contention that reference fixing generates a priori knowledge is incompatible with this claim. This consequence is clearest in the case of the lectern example. Suppose that S stipulates that "wood" is to be the substance out of which lectern L is made. If Kripke is correct, then S knows a priori that L is made of wood.[26] The case of identity statements is more controversial since it involves difficult questions about the semantic contribution of names and the content of beliefs expressed by using them. But, on the face of it, if S stipulates that "Hesperus" is to be the planet identical to Phosphorus, then S knows a priori that Hesperus is Phosphorus. Hence, if Kripke is correct about the epistemic implications of reference fixing, he has no basis for rejecting (WT).

There is a tension between Kripke's claims about the possibility of a priori knowledge of contingent propositions and his claims about the impossibility of a priori knowledge of some necessary propositions. Although the tension does not show that the former are incorrect, it does indicate that further investigation is necessary. Robert Stalnaker provides an analysis of the meter

---

25. For additional examples, see Jeshion, "Ways of Taking a Meter." Kripke, *Naming and Necessity*, 60, notes that a reference-fixing description may pick out an essential property of an object.

26. Strictly speaking, the example should read "*If* L *exists*, then L is made of wood." For ease of exposition, I presuppose rather than state the antecedent when providing examples of alleged contingent a priori statements.

stick example from the perspective of two-dimensional semantics. If I leave aside the technical presentation, the essentials are as follows:

> An a priori truth is a statement that, while perhaps not expressing a necessary proposition, expresses a truth in every context. . . . Suppose that in worlds i, j, and k, a certain object, a metal bar, is one, two and three meters long, respectively, at a certain time t. Now suppose an appropriate authority fixes the reference of the expression *one meter* by making the following statement in each of the worlds i, j, and k: *This bar is one meter long* . . . . The proposition expressed by the authority is one that might have been false, although he couldn't have expressed a false proposition in that utterance.[27]

Although the meter stick statement does not express a proposition that is true in all possible worlds, it express a true proposition in every context of utterance. Following Stalnaker, one can call statements that have that feature *a priori truths*. But it remains an open question whether a priori truths are known (or knowable) a priori in the primary epistemic sense of that term.[28]

Let us grant that the meter stick statement is an a priori truth in Stalnaker's sense:

(AP) S expresses a truth in every context.

The question before us is this: Does the fact that one believes a statement satisfying (AP) ensure that one's belief is justified a priori?[29] Section 6.4 addressed a related issue. Cogito propositions have the following feature:

(CP) It is not possible that (S believe that p and p is false).

If someone believes a cogito proposition, then that belief cannot be false. Nevertheless, the fact that one believes a cogito proposition does not ensure that one's belief is justified, for a cogito proposition can be believed for bad reasons. A similar point applies to a priori truths. Since one can believe an a priori truth for bad reasons, the fact that one believes such a truth does not ensure that one's belief is justified.

Suppose that Sam belongs to a cult that promulgates the view that naming celestial objects is a divine right. Moreover, according to the cult, that right is given to humans under certain circumstances, one of which is be-

---

27. Stalnaker, "Assertion," 83–84.

28. Stalnaker acknowledges this point in his "Introduction," 14.

29. Donnellan, "The Contingent *A Priori* and Rigid Designators," maintains that the reference fixer knows that the statement expresses a true proposition but not the truth of the proposition expressed by the statement. He argues that if there were such knowledge, it would be *de re*. But a reference-fixing stipulation is not sufficient for the reference fixer to have a *de re* belief about the designated entity. Evans, "Reference and Contingency," disputes this argument. I propose to grant that the reference fixer has the requisite belief in order to examine its epistemic status.

coming officially initiated into the cult. Suppose that Sam is initiated into the cult and given the right to name a celestial object. Sam is told by the cult leaders that, upon her stipulating that "X" is to be the Φ, it will be true, as a matter of divine law, that X is the Φ. Sam stipulates that "Starbright" is to be the brightest star at t_0 and now believes that Starbright is the brightest star at t_0. Since Sam believes the statement solely on the basis of unjustified beliefs promulgated by the cult, Sam's belief is not justified despite the fact that the statement that she believes satisfies (AP). Sam is not cognizant of the semantic implications of her reference-fixing stipulation. Sam does not recognize that, as a result of her reference-fixing stipulation, her statement that Starbright is the brightest star at t_0 expresses a truth in every context. Although the statement that she believes satisfies (AP), she is not cognizant of this semantic fact.

Believing an a priori truth does not ensure that one knows it, a priori or otherwise, since one may believe it on the basis of reasons that have little epistemic merit. What is required in order to know an a priori truth? The preceding example indicates that for S to know an a priori truth that p, S's belief that p must be based on a recognition of the semantic implications of introducing a term by using a reference-fixing description; that is, it must be based on the semantic knowledge that if the reference of "X" is fixed by using the description "the Φ," then "X is the Φ" expresses a truth in every context. Moreover, if S can know a priori the requisite semantic information, then S can know a priori that if S stipulates that "X" is to be the Φ, then S's statement X is the Φ expresses a truth in every context.

Kripke, however, maintains that stipulative reference fixing is the exception rather than the rule. For most speakers, terms like "one meter" do not refer by virtue of an associated definite description. Such terms refer instead by virtue of a chain of communication within the speaker's linguistic community that connects, in the appropriate way, the speaker's use of the term with its referent. For such speakers, the statement that S is one meter long at t_0 does not express a truth in every context. Hence, to know that one's statement that S is one meter long at t_0 expresses a truth in every context, one must know that one has stipulated that "one meter" is to be the length of S at t_0. Since one cannot know a priori that one has fixed the reference of "one meter" by stipulation, one cannot know a priori that one's statement that S is one meter long at t_0 expresses a truth in every context.

Kripke's supporting argument for the claim that such knowledge is a priori rests on the observation that the reference fixer knows "automatically, without further investigation," that S is one meter long at t_0. Here we need to distinguish between S knows without further investigation that p and S knows a priori that p. The reference fixer knows at t_0, without further investigation, that S is one meter long at t_0, for the reference fixer knows at t_0 that he has stipulated that "one meter" is to be the length of S at t_0. Nevertheless, since the latter piece of knowledge is a posteriori, the reference fixer's knowledge that S is one meter long at t_0 is not a priori.

Two points emerge about Kripke's examples of contingent a priori knowledge: the first pertains to the claim that they are cases of *knowledge*; the second pertains to the claim that they are cases of *a priori* knowledge. First, to know that X is the Φ on the basis of a reference-fixing stipulation, one must know that (1) if the reference of "X" is fixed by using the description "the Φ," then "X is the Φ" expresses a truth in every context, and (2) one has fixed the reference of "X" by using "the Φ." Second, to know a priori that X is the Φ on the basis of a reference-fixing stipulation, a further condition must be satisfied. One must know a priori that (1) and (2). Since one cannot know a priori that one has stipulatively introduced "X" as "the Φ," one cannot know a priori that X is the Φ.

7.8   Conclusion

Two theses, traditionally associated with Kant, concerning the relationship between the a priori and the necessary have received considerable attention because of the work of Kripke: (K1) All knowledge of necessary propositions is a priori, and (K2) All propositions known a priori are necessary. The primary conclusion of this chapter is that resolving the controversies surrounding (K1) and (K2) is not essential to answering either of the two internal questions about a priori knowledge.

The significance of (K1) derives from Kant's strategy of arguing for the existence of a priori knowledge via criteria. That strategy is flawed since Kant cannot establish that necessity is a criterion of the a priori without offering an analysis of the concept of a priori knowledge. But, once such an analysis is offered, he can argue directly for the existence of such knowledge without need of the criterion. Since (K1) is either indefensible or unnecessary, the disagreement between Kant and Kripke over (K1) need not be resolved in order to address the question of whether a priori knowledge exists. Moreover, if Kant's strategy is sound, the success of his case for the existence of a priori knowledge does not turn on whether Kripke's examples of necessary a posteriori propositions are genuine. Even if Kripke's examples are genuine, they only establish that it is false that all knowledge of the truth value of necessary propositions is a priori. They do not, however, affect the claim that all knowledge of the general modal status of necessary propositions is a priori.

Although (K2) does not play a role either in Kant's remarks about the concept of the a priori or in his arguments for the existence of such knowledge, it bears on the rationalist conception of a priori knowledge. Both the traditional and moderate rationalist conceptions of a priori knowledge are incompatible with Kripke's examples of contingent a priori knowledge. If the examples are genuine, both conceptions must be rejected. Since chapter 1 provides independent grounds for rejecting both rationalist conceptions, the question of whether Kripke's examples are genuine need not be settled in order to provide an analysis of the concept of a priori knowledge.

8

A Priori Knowledge and Analytic Truth

8.1   Introduction

Kant's most enduring contribution to the controversies surrounding the a
priori are the introduction of the analytic/synthetic distinction and the claim
that there is synthetic a priori knowledge. The latter claim sets the stage for
his major theoretical contribution, which is to answer this question: How is
synthetic a priori knowledge possible? Dissatisfaction with his answer fueled
the debate over the existence of such knowledge and ultimately led to the
more general question of the cogency of his distinction. These two controversies have dominated discussion of the a priori.

My primary goal in this chapter is not to resolve the disputes generated
by the synthetic a priori. My goal is to argue that a resolution of these disputes has little bearing on the two internal questions: What is a priori
knowledge? Is there a priori knowledge? Much of the literature devoted to
the synthetic a priori is rooted in two assumptions. First, such knowledge
poses explanatory problems that are more significant than those posed by
analytic a priori knowledge. Second, the incoherence of the analytic/syn-
thetic distinction casts doubt on the coherence of the a priori/a posteriori
distinction. I contend that both assumptions are false and that, as a consequence, it is not necessary to resolve the disputes over the existence of
synthetic a priori knowledge and the cogency of the analytic/synthetic
distinction in order to address the internal questions about a priori knowledge. Moreover, preoccupation with these disputes obscures both the most
pressing issue concerning the cogency of the a priori/a posteriori distinction and the legitimate explanatory problems that must be addressed by a
theory of a priori knowledge.

8.2   Kant's Assumptions

Kant's treatment of the relationship between the a priori and the analytic involves two elements. He first introduces the distinction between analytic and synthetic propositions, and he then offers two theses about the relationship between the a priori and the analytic. Kant introduces the distinction with respect to propositions of the form "All *A* are *B*":

> Either the predicate B belongs to the subject A, as something which is (covertly) contained in this concept A; or B lies outside the concept A, although it does indeed stand in connection with it. In the one case I entitle the judgment analytic, in the other synthetic. . . . The former, as adding nothing through the predicate to the concept of the subject, but merely breaking it up into those constituent concepts that have all along been thought in it, although confusedly, can also be entitled explicative. The latter, on the other hand, add to the concept of the subject a predicate which has not been in any wise thought in it, and which no analysis could possibly extract from it; and they may therefore be entitled ampliative.[1]

Two issues immediately arise. First, presumably, every proposition is either analytic or synthetic yet Kant's account applies only to universal categorical propositions. Second, even within this restricted domain, Kant appears to offer two different accounts of the distinction:

(A1)   An analytic (synthetic) proposition is one in which the predicate is *covertly contained* in (lies outside) the subject.

(A2)   An analytic (synthetic) proposition adds nothing (a predicate) to the subject that has not been *thought* in it.

The first refers solely to the *content* of the concepts involved, whereas the second refers to what the subject *thinks* when entertaining the concept.

Kant's account of the relationship between the a priori and the analytic opens with the following contention: "Judgments of experience, as such, are one and all synthetic. For it would be absurd to found an analytic judgment on experience. Since, in framing the judgment, I must not go outside my concept, there is no need to appeal to the testimony of experience in its support."[2] In this passage, Kant appears to endorse

(K3)   All knowledge of analytic propositions is a priori.

His supporting argument, however, establishes only the weaker claim that all analytic propositions are knowable a priori. From the fact that there is no need to appeal to experience in support of an analytic proposition, it does not follow that one cannot or does not appeal to experience.

---

1. Kant, *Critique of Pure Reason*, 48.
2. Ibid. 49.

Kant also endorses

(K4) Some propositions known a priori are synthetic.

Here he maintains that all mathematical propositions are synthetic and offers two supporting arguments. The first involves the arithmetic proposition that $7 + 5 = 12$: "The concept of 12 is by no means already thought in merely thinking this union of 7 and 5; and I may analyse my concept of such a possible sum as long as I please, still I shall never find the 12 in it."[3] The second involves a proposition of geometry: "That the straight line between two points is the shortest, is a synthetic proposition. For my concept of *straight* contains nothing of quantity, but only of quality."[4] Although Kant does not address this point, his arguments appear to employ different conceptions of analyticity. The first appeals to the fact that in thinking the union of seven and five, one is not thinking of twelve, whereas the second appeals to the fact that the concept of straight does not contain the concept of shortest.

Within the Kantian framework, neither (K3) nor (K4) has a direct bearing on the two internal questions about the a priori. Both questions are addressed prior to the introduction of the analytic/synthetic distinction. Kant first provides a characterization of a priori knowledge, then argues that necessity is a criterion of the a priori, and finally utilizes that criterion to argue that mathematical knowledge is a priori. The order of argument mirrors the order of presentation. The analytic/synthetic distinction plays no role in Kant's characterization of the a priori, in his account of the relationship between the a priori and the necessary, or in his argument for the existence of a priori knowledge. On the contrary, his argument that there is synthetic a priori knowledge rests on his earlier argument that mathematical knowledge is a priori, which in turn rests on his contention that necessity is a criterion of the a priori.

Kant regards the analytic/synthetic distinction as significant despite the fact that it does not directly bear on the two internal questions. The distinction is necessary to frame his major theoretical question: How is synthetic a priori knowledge possible? The project of the *Critique of Pure Reason*, which is to answer this question, patently presupposes that there is synthetic a priori knowledge. Hence, (K4) sets the stage for Kant's primary theoretical undertaking.

Kant's approach to framing his project is puzzling in one respect. Having established that there is a priori knowledge, he is in a position to pose the question: How is a priori knowledge possible? The fact that he deems it necessary to draw the analytic/synthetic distinction and to defend (K4) indicates that he does not think that a priori knowledge *in general* is problematic. More specifically, he does not regard analytic a priori knowledge as problematic or, at a minimum, not as problematic as synthetic a priori knowledge. As a consequence, (K3) is viewed as unremarkable and not in

3. Ibid., 53.
4. Ibid.

need of further discussion. It is not sufficient to motivate the project of the *Critique of Pure Reason.*

If the existence of synthetic a priori knowledge is of such great epistemic import, whereas the existence of analytic a priori knowledge is epistemically mundane, there must be some difference between analytic a priori knowledge and synthetic a priori knowledge. If there were no such difference, then it would be hard to see how the latter could raise difficult epistemic questions whereas the former did not. If there is such a difference, then it must be in the source of justification. If we require some explanation of how synthetic a priori knowledge is possible but not of how analytic a priori knowledge is possible, then the source of justification for both cannot be the same. If it were, then whatever explained the possibility of analytic a priori knowledge would also explain the possibility of synthetic a priori knowledge. So the theoretical problem raised by the existence of synthetic a priori knowledge ultimately rests on the assumption that the source of such knowledge is not the same as the source of analytic a priori knowledge.

Kant endorses the view that the source of analytic a priori knowledge is different from the source of synthetic a priori knowledge. In the case of an analytic proposition, such as that all bodies are extended, he offers the following account: "I have already in the concept of body all the conditions required for my judgment. I have only to extract from it, in accordance with the principle of contradiction, the required predicate."[5] Such knowledge requires the principle of contradiction and an analysis of the subject concept. Kant does not regard this explanation as exceptional or problematic. The explanation of analytic a priori knowledge raises no significant epistemic questions. The case of synthetic a priori knowledge, however, is different. Such knowledge raises a significant question: "What is here the unknown = X which gives support to the understanding when it believes that it can discover outside the concept A a predicate B foreign to this concept, which it yet at the same time considers to be connected with it?"[6] Synthetic a priori knowledge introduces the problem that the *Critique of Pure Reason* must resolve: What is the = X? That is, what is the source of such knowledge?

Kant offers an initial answer to this question. Upon concluding that "7 + 5 = 12" is a synthetic proposition, he claims, "We have to go outside these concepts, and call in the aid of the intuition which corresponds to one of them."[7] He concludes his discussion of the geometrical example with a similar observation: "Intuition, therefore, must here be called in; only by its aid is the synthesis possible."[8] Synthetic a priori knowledge requires the aid of intuition; analytic a priori knowledge does not. Synthetic a priori knowledge raises special epistemological questions because of its alleged source in intuition.

5. Ibid., 49.
6. Ibid., 51.
7. Ibid., 53.
8. Ibid.

The significance of (K4) derives from two epistemic assumptions:

(EA1) The source of synthetic a priori knowledge is different
from the source of analytic a priori knowledge.

(EA2) The source of synthetic a priori knowledge is more problematic than the source of analytic a priori knowledge.

It is striking, however, that Kant does not explicitly defend either assumption. In his view, knowledge of analytic propositions requires knowledge of
the principle of contradiction and the content of concepts. Yet he never
addresses the source of such knowledge. In the absence of such an account,
there is no basis for assuming that the source of analytic a priori knowledge
is different from the source of synthetic a priori knowledge, let alone that
the latter is more epistemically problematic than the former. Since Kant does
not defend the assumption that the analytic/synthetic distinction marks two
distinct sources of a priori knowledge, the epistemic significance of (K4) is
presupposed rather than established.

8.3   Three Reactions

Reactions to (K4) fall into three broad categories. Those in the first endorse
(K4) but take issue with some of Kant's examples. Frege, for example, agrees
that the truths of geometry are synthetic a priori but maintains that the truths
of arithmetic are analytic. Those in the second category reject (K4). Some,
such as A. J. Ayer, argue that alleged examples of synthetic a priori propositions are either analytic or a posteriori. Others, such as Anthony Quinton
and R. G. Swinburne, offer general arguments in support of the claim that
all a priori knowledge is of analytic truths. The reactions in the third category, drawing their inspiration from W. V. Quine, deny the cogency of the
analytic/synthetic distinction and, a fortiori, the cogency of (K4).

My goal is not to offer a comprehensive assessment of these different
reactions. My primary goal is to look at some representative examples and
to argue that, even if they establish that Kant's view is incorrect, this result
has little bearing on the two internal questions regarding the a priori. Appearances to the contrary derive from two errors: assuming, without supporting argument, that the analytic/synthetic distinction is epistemically
significant, and offering accounts of the distinction that trivialize the claim
that there exists some significant relationship between the a priori and the
analytic.

Frege's reaction to (K4) falls into the first category. He agrees with Kant
on several key points: there is synthetic a priori knowledge, geometry provides a leading example of such knowledge, and synthetic a priori knowledge has its source in intuition. Frege does not regard the general claim that
some a priori knowledge is grounded in intuition as problematic. His concern is a species of epistemic laziness: "We are all too ready to invoke inner

intuition, whenever we cannot produce any other ground of knowledge."[9] Hence, Frege is not disputing either Kant's framework for addressing the a priori or the general claims that Kant makes within that framework. His disagreement with Kant is over the proper placement of arithmetic within that framework. The truths of arithmetic are, according to Frege, analytic, and as a consequence, intuition is not the ground of such knowledge.

Despite Frege's agreement with the general features of Kant's framework, there are some significant departures. For example, he holds that "these distinctions between a priori and a posteriori, synthetic and analytic, concern, as I see it, not the content of the judgement but the justification for making the judgement."[10] Although Frege claims to be articulating what earlier writers—in particular, Kant—meant by these terms, there is a striking difference. Both distinctions are drawn along the same dimension. Both pertain, according to Frege, to the *justification* for making a judgment. Hence, it appears that Frege treats both distinctions as fundamentally *epistemic*, which represents a radical departure from Kant.

When we turn to Frege's treatment of mathematical propositions, a new twist emerges. Here he maintains that the question of justification pertains to the proof of the proposition:

> The problem becomes, in fact, that of finding the proof of the proposition, and of following it up right back to the primitive truths. If, in carrying out this process, we come only on general logical laws and on definitions, then the truth is an analytic one, bearing in mind that we must take account also of all propositions upon which the admissibility of any of the definitions depends. . . . For a truth to be a posteriori, it must be impossible to construct a proof of it without including an appeal to facts, i.e., to truths which cannot be proved and are not general, since they contain assertions about particular objects. But if, on the contrary, its proof can be derived exclusively from general laws, which themselves neither need nor admit of proof, then the truth is a priori.[11]

Frege's notion of proof is tied to a conception of mathematics as a hierarchical structure of propositions in which each is either primitive or derived from the primitive propositions. Both the analytic/synthetic distinction and the a priori/a posteriori distinction are explicated in terms of features of the proof of the proposition in question. Frege's notion of proof, however, is silent about the issue of how one knows primitive general laws and proofs based on those laws. Hence, contrary to the appearances, Frege's notion of justification is not fundamentally epistemic.

Three points emerge. First, Frege's conception of analyticity is broader than Kant's. It does not restrict analytic propositions to those in which the

9. Frege, *The Foundations of Arithmetic*, 19[e].
10. Ibid., 3[e].
11. Ibid., 4[e].

predicate is contained in the subject. Instead, any proposition derivable from general logical laws in conjunction with definitions qualifies as analytic. Second, Frege's conception of the a priori also differs from Kant's. Here the change is more radical. Kant's conception is fundamentally epistemic: it pertains to the role of experience in one's justification for believing a proposition. Frege's conception is fundamentally nonepistemic: it pertains to features of the proof of the proposition in question. Third, by drawing both the analytic/synthetic distinction and the a priori/a posteriori distinction in terms of the proof of the proposition, Frege trivializes the claim:

(F1) All analytic truths are a priori.

Frege's conception of analyticity mentions only two features of a proof: general logical laws and definitions. Any proposition whose proof involves only those features is analytic. Frege's conception of the a priori mentions one feature: general laws. Any proof involving only that feature is a priori. Presumably, the failure to include definitions in the characterization of the a priori is an oversight. If so, then it is a trivial consequence of a proposition's being analytic that it is also a priori since any proof involving only general logical laws and definitions involves only general laws and definitions.

Frege's leading claim is

(F2) All arithmetic truths are analytic.

(F2) faces a number of technical obstacles, which I shall ignore in order to assess its epistemic implications.[12] My contention is that they are minimal. The fact that all arithmetic truths can be proved from general logical laws and definitions, taken by itself, tells us little about knowledge of those truths since it is silent about knowledge of general logical laws and definitions. (F2) is compatible with the epistemic claim that the truths of arithmetic are knowable only a posteriori. One might contend that Frege's conception of the a priori underwrites (F1) and that the conjunction of (F2) and (F1) entails that all arithmetic truths are a priori. Frege's conception of a priori truth, however, is nonepistemic. Hence, it does not support the epistemic conclusion that the truths of arithmetic are knowable a priori. It entails only that all arithmetic truths can be proved from primitive general laws but is silent about the source of knowledge of such laws.

One might suggest that my bleak assessment fails to take account of the context of Frege's discussion. Frege, the suggestion continues, accepts without independent argument the broad outlines of Kant's account of the a priori and focuses exclusively on the one issue with which he disagrees. Since he takes it for granted that logicosemantic and arithmetic knowledge are a priori, the only issue he addresses explicitly is the source of arithmetic knowledge. Frege defends (F2) in order to establish that the source of such knowledge

12. For a discussion of these issues, see Hempel, "On the Nature of Mathematical Truth," and Steiner, *Mathematical Knowledge*, chaps. 1 and 2.

is not intuition. Even if we endorse the suggestion, the epistemic implications of (F2) are limited. At most, (F2) establishes that if logicosemantic knowledge is not grounded in intuition, then arithmetic knowledge is not grounded in intuition. Since, as I argued in section 8.2, Kant does not demonstrate, but simply assumes, that logicosemantic knowledge is not grounded in intuition, (F2) is insufficient to establish that arithmetic knowledge is not grounded in intuition.

One might insist, nevertheless, that although Frege does not establish that arithmetic knowledge is not grounded in intuition, he makes progress toward resolving the issue of the source of such knowledge. He shows that if logicosemantic knowledge does not have its source in intuition, then arithmetic knowledge does not have its source in intuition. By contrast, Kant maintains that even if logicosemantic knowledge does not have its source in intuition, arithmetic knowledge does. In short, Frege shows that logicosemantic knowledge and arithmetic knowledge derive from the same source (whatever it is). This result is epistemically significant since it establishes that there is a uniform explanation of logicosemantic and arithmetic knowledge.

The claim that (F2) establishes that there is a uniform explanation of logicosemantic and arithmetic knowledge rests on an unsubstantiated assumption: the only avenue to arithmetic knowledge is via proof from general logical laws and definitions. This assumption has a significant unwelcome epistemic consequence. It entails a wide-ranging, if not complete, skepticism regarding the truths of simple arithmetic. If arithmetic knowledge is possible only via proof from general logical laws and definitions, then few if any have such knowledge. Certainly no one had it prior to Frege, and Frege admits that not even he has provided the requisite proofs.[13] If there is such knowledge, then it is restricted to a small number of specialists in the foundations of mathematics. Even most mathematicians lack such knowledge.

Kant took for granted that most literate adults know a priori that $7 + 5 = 12$ and set out to provide an account of such knowledge. If most literate adults have such knowledge, then there must be an avenue to it other than the type of proof envisioned by Frege. Therefore, Frege fails to show that there is a uniform explanation of logicosemantic and arithmetic knowledge of the nonspecialist. There are two options concerning the nonspecialist's a priori knowledge of arithmetic: either its source is the same as the source of logicosemantic knowledge or it is different. If it is the same, then Frege's program for establishing (F2) is otiose. If it is different, then we are still faced with the problem of explaining how such knowledge is possible. In the final analysis, Frege's program offers the prospect of a uniform explanation of logicosemantic and arithmetic knowledge only by drastically reducing the scope of, and perhaps entirely eliminating, such knowledge. If Kant is right about the scope of a priori arithmetic knowledge, Frege fails to provide an explanation of such knowledge.

13. Frege, *The Foundations of Arithmetic*, 102ᵉ.

8.4   Rejecting the Synthetic A Priori by Cases

I have argued that Frege's program for demonstrating that arithmetic is analytic is of little epistemic consequence. First, it is silent about the source of arithmetic knowledge since it does not address the source of logicosemantic knowledge. Second, it offers an implausible account of arithmetic knowledge. What is necessary to remedy these two shortcomings is a conception of analyticity that is broad enough to (1) include logical and semantic truths and (2) provide an account of elementary arithmetic knowledge without the need of complex proofs.

The reactions that fall into the second category propose broader conceptions of analyticity. Their goal is to reject the synthetic a priori. There are two general approaches. The first proceeds by examining alleged cases of synthetic a priori knowledge. A. J. Ayer, for example, focuses on the truths of arithmetic, geometry, and logic. In each case, he attempts to show that, given his conception of analyticity, the truths in question are analytic. Anthony Quinton and R. G. Swinburne favor a different approach. Their goal is to provide a general proof that there is no synthetic a priori knowledge.

Ayer's discussion takes place within a broader epistemological context. His goal is to defend a form of empiricism whose central thesis is

> (E) Truths about the world are knowable only on the basis of experience.

The primary obstacle to empiricism, according to Ayer, is to provide an account of knowledge of necessary truths. The obstacle arises because no general proposition based on experience can be shown to be necessary or certain, but the truths of mathematics and logic do appear to be necessary and certain. There are two options for the empiricist. Radical empiricists, such as Mill, deny that the truths of mathematics and logic are necessary and certain, which allows them to maintain that they are known on the basis of experience. Logical empiricists, such as Ayer, deny that necessary truths are about the world. Instead, they maintain that

> (LE) All propositions known a priori are analytic.

Since logical empiricism does not deny the existence of a priori knowledge, it is often referred to as moderate empiricism.

Ayer is also explicit about the motivation for empiricism. If empiricism is false, then we must admit that

> there are some properties which we can ascribe to all objects, even though we cannot conceivably observe that all objects have them. And we shall have to accept it as a mysterious inexplicable fact that our thought has this power to reveal to us authoritatively the nature of objects which we have never observed. Or else we must accept the Kantian explanation which, apart from the epistemological difficul-

ties which we have already touched on, only pushes the mystery a stage further back.[14]

Ayer's contention is that by showing that necessary truths are analytic, he can provide an explanation of a priori knowledge that is free of the mystery plaguing Kant's account. So we are faced with three questions. What is Ayer's conception of analyticity? What is his argument in support of the claim that truths of arithmetic, geometry, and logic are analytic? Does the resulting account offer a less mysterious explanation of arithmetic, geometric, and logical knowledge?

Ayer rejects Kant's account of the distinction between analytic and synthetic propositions on the grounds that (A1) and (A2) provide two different ways of marking the distinction. Propositions that are synthetic according to (A2) need not be synthetic according to (A1): "It is possible for symbols to be synonymous without having the same intensional meaning for anyone: and accordingly from the fact that one can think of the sum of seven and five without necessarily thinking of twelve, it by no means follows that the proposition '7 + 5 = 12' can be denied without self-contradiction."[15] Since he maintains that the latter logical conception is important for epistemological purposes, Ayer introduces an alternative formulation of the distinction: "A proposition is analytic when its validity depends solely on the definitions of the symbols it contains, and synthetic when its validity is determined by the facts of experience."[16] Since validity is a property of arguments rather than individual propositions, let us replace "validity" by "truth." The resulting conception of analyticity is broader than that of Kant or Frege since it does not require that an analytic proposition be an instance of the law of identity or derivable from laws of logic. It requires only that it be true in virtue of the definitions of the symbols it contains.

Ayer's defense of (LE) proceeds by examining cases. His most explicit argument is presented in the context of discussing logical truths:

> Thus, the proposition "There are ants which have established a system of slavery" is a synthetic proposition. For we cannot tell whether it is true or false merely by considering the definitions of the symbols which constitute it. We have to resort to actual observation of the behaviour of ants. On the other hand, the proposition "Either some ants are parasitic or none are" is an analytic proposition. For one need not resort to observation to discover that there either are or are not ants which are parasitic. If one knows what is the function of the words "either," "or," and "not," then one can see that any proposition of the form "Either p is true or p is not true" is valid, independently of experience. Accordingly, all such propositions are analytic.[17]

14. Ayer, *Language, Truth and Logic*, 73.
15. Ibid., 78.
16. Ibid.
17. Ibid., 78–79.

The argument can be stated as follows:

> (P1) One need not resort to observation to discover that there either are or are not ants which are parasitic.
>
> (C1) Therefore, the proposition "Either some ants are parasitic or none are" is an analytic proposition.

Two observations are in order here. (P1) is an epistemic premise. It is equivalent to the claim that one can know a priori that there either are or are not ants which are parasitic. However, (C1) is a semantic conclusion, but Ayer provides no intermediate premise that links the two. Hence, he assumes, but does not demonstrate, that there is a connection between the epistemic concept of the a priori and the semantic concept of the analytic. Second, the obvious intermediate premise that is necessary in order to move from (P1) to (C1) is

> (P2) All propositions knowable a priori are analytic.

Hence, as an attempt to partially vindicate (LE), the argument fails dismally. It is patently circular.

Suppose we grant (C1). Does (C1) provide an explanation of a priori knowledge of logical truths? If we return to the previously cited passage, Ayer offers the following premise in support of (P1):

> (P3) If one knows what is the function of the words "either," "or," and "not," then one can see that any proposition of the form "Either p is true or p is not true" is valid, independently of experience.

A priori knowledge of logical truths is explained in terms of an ability to *see* their truth independently of experience. Since the seeing involved in a priori knowledge is nonexperiential, the explanation appeals to some metaphorical sense of "see" that is not further explained. Consequently, like Kant's appeal to intuition, the explanation "only pushes the mystery a stage further back."

If we turn to Ayer's remarks about arithmetic and geometry, he offers even less. He maintains that the propositions of arithmetic need not be reducible to truths of logic in order to be analytic:

> For even if it is the case that the definition of a cardinal number as a class of classes similar to a given class is circular, and it is not possible to reduce mathematical notions to purely logical notions, it will still remain true that the propositions of mathematics are analytic propositions. They will form a special class of analytic propositions, containing special terms, but they will be none the less analytic for that. For the criterion of an analytic proposition is that its validity should follow simply from the definition of the terms contained in it, and this condition is fulfilled by the propositions of pure mathematics.[18]

18. Ibid., 82.

Ayer does not offer an argument in support of the claim that the truths of arithmetic follow from the definitions of arithmetic terms and does not address the issue of how we know such truths. In the case of geometry, Ayer appears to deny that we have a priori knowledge of either the axioms or theorems of geometry. He claims that, in light of the discovery of non-Euclidean geometries, "We see now that the axioms of a geometry are simply definitions, and that the theorems of a geometry are simply the logical consequences of these definitions. A geometry is not in itself about physical space; in itself it cannot be said to be 'about' anything."[19] The primary consequence of this view of geometry is this: "All that the geometry itself tells us is that if anything can be brought under the definitions, it will also satisfy the theorems. It is therefore a purely logical system, and its propositions are purely analytic propositions."[20] A priori geometric knowledge is limited to knowing that the theorems of a geometric theory are logical consequences of its axioms.

To explore the epistemic implications of Ayer's account of geometric knowledge, let us turn to a more fully developed version of the view by Carl Hempel. The basic idea is to treat pure geometry as an uninterpreted axiomatic system. The postulates or axioms of the system are accepted without proof. The remaining propositions, the theorems, are accepted on the basis of proof from the postulates. The key to understanding the special character of geometric truths is an understanding of the nature of geometric proof:

> What the rigorous proof of a theorem . . . establishes is not the truth of the proposition in question but rather a conditional insight to the effect that that proposition is certainly true *provided that* the postulates are true; in other words, the proof of a mathematical proposition establishes the fact that the latter is logically implied by the postulates of the theory in question. Thus, each mathematical theorem can be cast into the form
>
> $$(P_1 \cdot P_2 \cdot P_3 \cdot \ldots \cdot P_n) \to T$$
>
> where the expression on the left is the conjunction (joint assertion) of all the postulates, the symbol on the right represents the theorem in its customary formulation, and the arrow expresses the relation of logical implication or entailment.[21]

The conditional character of geometric truths underwrites their analytic status:

> A truth of this conditional type obviously implies no assertions about matters of empirical fact and can, therefore, never get into conflict with

19. Ibid.
20. Ibid., 83.
21. Hempel, "Geometry and Empirical Science," 240.

any empirical findings, even of the most unexpected kind. . . . Any theorem of geometry, therefore, when cast into the conditional form described earlier, is analytic in the technical sense of logic, and thus true *a priori*; i.e., its truth can be established by means of the formal machinery of logic alone, without any reference to empirical data.[22]

Thus, Hempel, like Ayer, establishes that geometric knowledge is a priori by limiting it to knowledge that the theorems of a geometric theory are logically implied by its postulates.

The obvious objection to this account of geometric truth is that it is incomplete since a geometric theory unconditionally asserts the truths of its postulates and consequently, in conjunction with the theorems in conditional form, also unconditionally asserts the truth of its theorems. In response, Hempel draws attention to the character of the primitive terms of a geometric theory. The primitive terms of a geometric theory are not defined within the theory, but all other terms of the theory are defined in terms of the primitives. With respect to the primitive terms, Hempel maintains that "no specific meaning has to be attached to the primitive terms of an axiomatized theory; and in a precise logical presentation of axiomatized geometry the primitive concepts are accordingly treated as so-called logical variables."[23] If the primitive terms are treated as logical variables, "geometry cannot be said to assert the truth of its postulates, since the latter are formulated in terms of concepts without any specific meaning; indeed, for this very reason, the postulates themselves do not make any specific assertion which could possibly be called true or false!"[24] Since the primitive terms of pure geometry are uninterpreted, the postulates and theorems of pure geometry are not propositions but propositional functions. Hence, they are neither true nor false.

This strategy for demonstrating the analyticity of geometry, as W. V. Quine argues, comes at a high price.[25] First, even if we concede that the conditional theorems are analytic, there remains the question of the status of the unconditional theorems taken in their customary meaning. Hempel maintains that the theorems of geometry, in their unconditional interpreted form, have factual import but do not belong to the theory of *pure* geometry. They are part of the theory of *physical* geometry, which is a branch of physics. Thus, Hempel vindicates the view that all truths of geometry are analytic by restricting geometry to pure geometry. Second, whatever the merits of the view as an account of geometric truth, it is completely implausible as an explanation of a priori knowledge of such truths. It explains too much. Any axiomatizable theory, including quantum mechanics, biology, and even sociology, can be treated in a parallel fashion. If we let "P_s," stand for the

22. Ibid., 241.
23. Ibid., 244.
24. Ibid.
25. Quine, "Truth by Convention," 82–84.

postulates of sociology and "T_{s1}, T_{s2}, . . . ," stand for the theorems of sociology, then each theorem of sociology can be cast in the form "$P_s \rightarrow T_{s1}$,"
"$P_s \rightarrow T_{s2}$,". . . . Since the theorems of sociology are logical consequences of
the postulates of sociology, the theorems of sociology in conditional form
are analytic in the same sense as the theorems of geometry. The upshot is
that if this sense of analytic explains the a priori status of geometry, it also
explains the a priori status of sociology. According to logical empiricism,
however, the epistemology of geometry and the epistemology of sociology
are different—the former is a priori and the latter is empirical—and the
analytic character of geometric truth is supposed to explain the difference.

However, another avenue is open to Hempel and Ayer, one that Ayer
suggests in the context of his discussion of arithmetic. The previous approach
treats the primitive terms of geometry as uninterpreted. The second approach
provides them with a meaning by stipulating that the axioms of geometry
are to be true. The stipulation assigns to the primitive terms whatever meanings make the axioms true. Hence, the axioms of geometry are true by virtue
of meaning, by virtue of the meaning assigned to the primitives by the stipulation. Since both the axioms of geometry and the theorems of geometry in
conditional form are true, the theorems of geometry in unconditional form
are also true. This approach can be extended to the case of arithmetic. Instead of explicitly defining the primitive terms of arithmetic by using only
logical terms, one can implicitly define them by stipulating that the axioms
of arithmetic are to be true. The axioms of arithmetic will then be true in
virtue of the stipulatively assigned meaning of its primitive terms.

Once again, whatever the merits of the stipulative approach as an account
of mathematical truth, it fails as an explanation of a priori knowledge of such
truths. As Quine argues, the explanation that it offers of the a priori status
of arithmetic and geometry can be extended to any axiomatizable theory.[26]
Given an axiomatization of quantum mechanics, biology, or even sociology,
one can stipulate that the axioms of the theory are to be true, thus assigning
meanings to its primitive terms, with the result that the axioms are true in
virtue of the meanings of those terms. Therefore, the stipulative approach
does not explain the difference between our alleged a priori knowledge of
arithmetic and geometry and our empirical knowledge of quantum mechanics, biology, and sociology.

Moreover, the stipulative approach presupposes rather than explains one's
knowledge of the axioms in question. Consider the following uninterpreted
axiom of geometry:

(UA) If a segment AB is R the segment $A'B'$ and also is R the segment $A''B''$, then the segment $A'B'$ is R the segment $A''B''$.[27]

26. Ibid., 98–102.
27. (UA) is the second axiom of congruence of Hilbert, *The Foundations of Geometry*, 12–13. To make the argument clearer, I treat only "congruent to" as a primitive
geometric term and, to explicitly indicate that it is uninterpreted, replace it by "R."

Suppose that I stipulate that the axioms of geometry are to be true, thus implicitly endowing its primitive terms with meaning. The stipulation does not explain my knowledge of the interpreted axiom:

(IA) If a segment AB is congruent to the segment $A'B'$ and also is congruent to the segment $A''B''$, then the segment $A'B'$ is congruent to the segment $A''B''$.

To know that the interpreted axiom is true, I need to know *which* meaning has been assigned to the primitive term "R" by the stipulation. But, to know that "R" means "congruent to" rather than, say, "larger than," I need to know that (IA) is true but that

(IB) If a segment AB is larger than the segment $A'B'$ and also is larger than the segment $A''B''$, then the segment $A'B'$ is larger than the segment $A''B''$

is false. Hence, the stipulative approach presupposes, rather than explains, my knowledge of (IA).[28]

Ayer offers an account of analyticity that is broad enough to encompass logical and semantic truths, and he does not require that arithmetic truths be reducible to logical truths in order to be analytic. Utilizing this broader conception, Ayer attempts to defend (LE) and offer an account of a priori knowledge that does not invoke intuition or other mysterious faculties. Ayer falls short on both counts. He does not offer compelling support for the claim that the propositions of arithmetic, geometry, and logic are analytic. His most explicit argument is patently circular. Moreover, and more important, he fails to show that his conception of analyticity offers a transparent explanation of a priori knowledge. His explanation of logical knowledge appeals to an unarticulated, metaphorical sense of "see." The explanation of arithmetic and geometric knowledge, which I extrapolated through my discussion of Hempel, fails to explain how it differs from scientific knowledge.

8.5   Rejecting the Synthetic A Priori by General Argument

Anthony Quinton notes that the strategy of defending (LE) by rejecting alleged cases of synthetic a priori knowledge is not optimal. Its proponents regard (LE) as an a priori truth. Hence, by their lights, (LE), if true, is an analytic truth. Quinton contends that "they did not treat it as if it were. Instead of attempting to prove it they put it forward more as an hypothesis, supporting it with representative pieces of favourable evidence and attempting to dispose of apparent counter-examples."[29] The limitations of the strat-

---

28. Butchvarov, *The Concept of Knowledge*, 109–110, and BonJour, *In Defense of Pure Reason*, 50–51, offer versions of this argument.
29. Quinton, "The *A Priori* and the Analytic," 89.

egy are clear if we consider again Ayer's case for (LE). A demonstration that arithmetic and geometric truths are analytic, if successful, establishes that Kant failed to provide convincing examples of synthetic a priori propositions. But, in the absence of some reason for believing that Kant had provided the *only* plausible examples, it is not sufficient to establish (LE). The controversy merely shifts to other examples, such as that nothing can be both red and green all over. Quinton, therefore, opts for an alternative strategy. He offers a general proof of (LE).

Although Ayer and Quinton employ different strategies to defend (LE), both strategies involve a common theme. Ayer maintains that the primary obstacle to (LE) is providing an account of knowledge of necessary truths. He attacks the problem by arguing that particular examples of necessary truths—arithmetic, geometric, and logical truths—are analytic. Quinton, as we shall see, employs the alternative strategy of arguing that all necessary truths are analytic. The common theme of both strategies is that the connection between the a priori and the analytic is indirect; it is mediated by the concept of necessity.

Quinton's goal is to prove the *analytic thesis*:

(AT) All a priori statements are analytic.

(AT) is the conjunction of two theses:

(AT1) All a priori statements are necessary, and
(AT2) All necessary statements are analytic.

Quinton identifies two different senses of "a priori": "'*A priori*' means either, widely, 'non-empirical' or, narrowly, following Kant, 'necessary,'"[30] as well as four different senses of "analytic":

(1) An analytic statement is one true in virtue of the meanings of the terms it contains;
(2) An analytic statement is an instance of the law of identity whose denial is an explicit contradiction;
(3) An analytic statement is one that is true in virtue of the conventions of language;
(4) An analytic statement is a truth of logic or reducible to one with the help of definitions.[31]

He endorses the narrow sense of a priori, contending that "the essential content of the [analytic] thesis is that all *necessary* truths are analytic."[32] His endorsement, however, has the consequence of trivializing (AT1).

There are four versions of (AT2), one for each sense of analytic. Quinton endorses all four versions. His strategy for defending them is to first estab-

30. Ibid., 90.
31. Ibid., 90–91.
32. Ibid., 93.

lish that (AT2) is true in sense (1) of analytic and then to show that the other three versions of (AT2) are consequences of the first. Since the first version of (AT2),

> (AT2.1) All necessary truths are true in virtue of the meaning of the terms they contain,

forms the basis of Quinton's defense of the others, I focus on it. In support of (AT2.1), he offers the following argument: "A necessary truth is one that is true in itself, true, in Lewis's phrase, 'no matter what', must be true and cannot be false. . . . Since there is nothing more to the statement than the words it is composed of and the meaning they are given and since the words do not determine its truth, if it is true in itself it must be true in virtue of its meaning."[33]

Quinton offers three characterizations of necessary truth in his opening remarks. The burden of his argument, however, is carried by the initial characterization. The idea of a statement being true in itself is by no means clear but, presumably, is intended to convey the idea that the truth conditions of the statement do not refer to features external to it. This characterization of a necessary truth is not equivalent to the other two, more orthodox characterizations. From the fact that a statement must be true and cannot be false, or is true no matter what, it does not follow that its truth conditions do not refer to features external to it. Although the concept of a necessary truth does entail that its truth conditions cannot refer to contingent features of the world, it does not entail that they cannot refer to necessary features of the world. Hence, Quinton's argument for (AT2.1) fails since it rests on his unorthodox characterization of necessary truth.

Quinton offers a second consideration in support of (AT2.1). He maintains that it is universally accepted; not even defenders of the synthetic a priori deny it. In support of this contention, he cites the views of a number of authors. For example, "Broad says that an *a priori* proposition is either one that can be seen to be true 'by merely inspecting it and reflecting on its terms and their mode of combination' or else the logical consequence of such a proposition. . . . Ewing says that the truth of an *a priori* proposition 'depends wholly on the meaning of the terms used.'"[34] On the basis of his survey, Quinton concludes that "no philosopher who has seriously considered the question is prepared to dispute the view that necessary truth is determined by meaning."[35] Hence, (AT2.1) is uncontroversial.

The passages Quinton cites in support of his contention are instructive. Although he claims that they all endorse the view that "necessary truth is determined by meaning," closer examination reveals that two different

33. Ibid., 91–92.
34. Ibid., 94. The first quotation in the passage is from Broad, "Are There Synthetic *A Priori* Truths?" 102. The second is from Ewing, "The Linguistic Theory of *A Priori* Propositions," 231.
35. Quinton, "The *A Priori* and the Analytic," 94.

senses of *determination* are involved. Broad and Ewing endorse, respectively, the following positions:

(B1) An a priori proposition is one whose truth *can be seen* solely by reflecting on its meaning.

(E1) An a priori proposition is one whose truth *depends* wholly on its meaning.

Even if, following Quinton, we read "a priori" as "necessary," (B1) and (E1) assert two different relationships between meaning and truth. (B1) asserts an *epistemic* relationship: the truth of a necessary proposition *can be known* solely by reflecting on its meaning; (E1) asserts a *semantic* relationship: the truth of a necessary proposition *depends* solely on its meaning. Hence, Quinton fails to show that (AT2.1) is universally accepted.

Quinton fails to provide compelling support for (AT2.1). Let us, however, concede (AT2.1) in order to assess its epistemic significance. Does (AT2.1) remove any of the mystery alleged to plague synthetic a priori knowledge? Consider the position of Bertrand Russell, who, Quinton contends, endorses (AT2.1): "Russell says, 'all *a priori* knowledge deals exclusively with the relations of universals.' . . . Since universals are at any rate the meanings of general terms this amounts to an acceptance of the present form of the [analytic] thesis."[36]

The thesis that all necessary truths are true in virtue of their meaning has no immediate epistemological implications. Any epistemological implications are mediated by a further premise regarding the source of one's knowledge of meanings. Russell offers the following epistemic premise:

> Thus the statement 'two and two are four' deals exclusively with universals, and therefore may be known by anybody who is acquainted with the universals concerned and can perceive the relation between them which the statement asserts. It must be taken as a fact, discovered by reflecting upon our knowledge, that we have the power of sometimes perceiving such relations between universals, and therefore of sometimes knowing general *a priori* propositions such as those of arithmetic and logic.[37]

Russell's explanation of a priori knowledge of necessary truths appeals to two cognitive capacities: the capacity to become acquainted with universals and the capacity to perceive relations among the universals with which we are acquainted. But these are the very sort of cognitive capacities that detractors of the synthetic a priori find mysterious.

(AT2.1) does not yield the epistemic payoff desired by logical empiricists. Nevertheless, it is possible that one of the other three versions of (AT) is more successful. I argued earlier that senses (2) and (4) of analytic are too

---

36. Ibid., 93–94. The quotation in the passage is from Russell, *The Problems of Philosophy*, 103.

37. Russell, *The Problems of Philosophy*, 105.

narrow to offer an explanation of all a priori knowledge. Neither offers a nontrivial explanation of logical knowledge. Hence, I conclude by examining briefly the third version of (AT2):

> (AT2.3) All necessary truths are true in virtue of the conventions of language.

Quinton maintains that (AT2.3) is a consequence of (AT2.1). The argument is straightforward: "A statement is a necessary truth because of the meaning of the words of which it is composed. The meaning that words have is assigned to them by convention. Therefore it is a linguistic convention that makes a form of words express a necessary truth."[38] The conclusion of the argument is unobjectionable. It is because of the conventions of English that the words "two" and "four" refer, respectively, to the numbers 2 and 4 and, hence, that the sentence "Two and two are four" expresses a necessary truth. However, (AT2.3) involves a stronger claim. It states that necessary truths are true in virtue of linguistic conventions. But it is not clear how the claim that it is a matter of convention that a sentence expresses a truth shows that the truth of what it conventionally expresses is also a matter of convention. In the case of contingent truths, we are not tempted to think that from the fact that it is a matter of convention that the word "birds" refers to birds and, hence, that the sentence "Birds fly" expresses a truth that the truth of what it conventionally expresses is also a matter of convention. Moreover, I argued in section 8.4 that the clearest version of (AT2.3), the view that necessary truths are true by stipulation, fails to provide a plausible account of knowledge of such truths since it fails to explain the difference between knowledge of (necessary) mathematical truths, which is alleged to be a priori, and knowledge of (contingent) scientific truths, which is alleged to be empirical.

R. G. Swinburne also offers a general argument that connects the a priori and the analytic. Moreover, like Quinton, he maintains that the connection is indirect; it is mediated by the concept of necessity. His strategy is to defend two theses:

> (S1) A proposition is a priori if and only if it is necessary and can be known to be necessary; and
> (S2) A proposition is a priori if and only if it is analytic and can be known to be analytic.[39]

(S2) is both stronger and weaker than Quinton's (AT). It is stronger in that the connection between the a priori and the analytic involves a biconditional rather than a conditional. It is weaker in that it connects the a priori with *knowable* analytic propositions.

Swinburne's defense of (S1) is superior to Quinton's defense of (AT1) in one crucial respect. He rejects Quinton's identification of "a priori" and "necessary" and endorses Kant's characterization of a priori knowledge as absolutely independent of all experience. Hence, (S1) is not trivially true; it involves a substantive claim about the relationship between the epistemic and the metaphysical. Since (S1) is not trivially true, it also faces a potential objection. It appears vulnerable to Kripke's examples of necessary propositions whose truth value is knowable only a posteriori.[40] I return to this issue after introducing Swinburne's conception of analyticity.

Swinburne maintains that definitions of analyticity fall into three categories: (1) those in terms of logical truth and synonymy, (2) those in terms of truth deriving solely from the meanings of words, and (3) those in terms of self-contradictoriness or incoherence of its negation. He rejects those in the first category on two counts: (a) there is no satisfactory definition of the notion of logical truth, and (b) they are too narrow. He maintains that there is one satisfactory definition that falls into the second category,

> (SA1) A proposition is analytic if and only if any sentence which
> expresses it expresses a true proposition and does so
> solely because the words in the sentence mean what
> they do,

and two that fall into the second category,

> (SA2) A proposition is analytic if and only if its negation entails
> an explicitly self-contradictory proposition, and
> (SA3) A proposition is analytic if and only if its negation is not
> coherent.[41]

Moreover, Swinburne argues that all three definitions are equivalent.

To complete his argument for (S2), Swinburne must offer a general argument connecting the concept of necessity with the concept of analyticity. He must show that

> (S3) A proposition is necessary if and only if it is analytic

in the three (allegedly equivalent) senses of analytic he endorses. Here Swinburne introduces four definitions of necessity, two of which are drawn from philosophical theology and are not relevant for our purposes. According to the first,

> (A) A proposition is necessary if and only if it is analytic.[42]

The second definition, inspired by the work of Kripke, holds that

> (B) A proposition is necessary if and only if it is incoherent to
> suppose that the individuals in fact picked out by the
> referring expressions in the sentence which expresses it do

---

40. (S1) is also vulnerable to Kripke's examples of the contingent a priori. Swinburne does not address this problem.

41. Swinburne, "Analyticity, Necessity, and Apriority," 173–175.

42. Ibid., 178.

>not have the properties and/or relations claimed by the
>proposition.[43]

Since Swinburne is not prepared to reject the cogency of Kripke's examples
of necessary a posteriori propositions, he endorses definition (A). Although
Kripke's examples are necessary in sense (B), they are not necessary in sense
(A). Since Kripke's examples are not necessary in sense (A), they do not pose
a threat to (S1). The cost of blocking Kripke's challenge to (S1), however, is
a trivialization of (S3). Swinburne has not offered a substantive argument
connecting the metaphysical concept of necessity with the semantic concept of analyticity but, instead, has offered a semantic characterization of
the concept of necessity.

Let us assume that Swinburne can provide a nontrivial defense of (S3)
and (S2). Does this result have any significant epistemic implications? The
answer, once again, is clearly negative. To bring out the limited epistemic
import of (S2), let us consider (SA2). Swinburne offers the following demonstration that "All bachelors are unmarried" is analytic: "Assuming the
existential commitment of 'all' the entailment can be demonstrated as follows. 'It is not the case that all bachelors are unmarried', entails 'some unmarried men are not unmarried' which entails that there are certain persons,
call them xs such that 'xs are unmarried and it is not the case that xs are
unmarried'."[44] The entailment from "It is not the case that all bachelors are
unmarried" to "Some unmarried men are not unmarried" is mediated by
the definition of "bachelor" as "unmarried man" and other logical truths
such as the law of double negation. Hence, (SA2) explains one's knowledge
that all bachelors are unmarried in terms of one's knowledge of definitions
and logical truths but offers no explanation of one's knowledge of the definitions and logical truths. Moreover, it offers no explanation of one's knowledge of the law of contradiction or of the principle that whatever entails a
contradiction is false. Hence, (SA2) is of limited explanatory value.

Both Quinton and Swinburne offer general arguments in support of the
conclusion that all propositions known a priori are analytic. Both argue that
there is an indirect connection between the a priori and the analytic: a connection mediated by the concept of necessity. For such an argument to
nontrivially establish its conclusion, it must acknowledge that the concepts
of the a priori, the necessary, and the analytic are all different and offer substantive arguments connecting the a priori with the necessary and the necessary with the analytic. The arguments offered by Quinton and Swinburne fall
short on this score. Quinton identifies the a priori and the necessary, whereas
Swinburne identifies the necessary and the analytic. Moreover, even if we
concede that all propositions known a priori are analytic in the proposed sense,
the epistemic implications are minimal. Either the conception of analyticity
offers no explanation of how we know such propositions or explains how we

43. Ibid., 179.
44. Ibid., 174.

know such propositions in terms of our knowledge of some other propositions, typically logical truths, for which it offers no explanation.

8.6   Denying the Cogency of the Distinction

I have examined two responses to Kant's contention that there is synthetic a
priori knowledge. The first agrees with Kant that there is such knowledge but
disputes some of his examples. The second denies that there is such knowledge. All parties to the debate agree on two points: the question of whether
there is synthetic a priori knowledge is cogent, and providing an answer to it
is of central importance to epistemology. I have argued against the second
claim. W. V. Quine argues against the first. Although he is not explicit on this
point, his arguments are widely viewed as impugning the existence of a priori
knowledge. We are faced with two questions. Are Quine's arguments sound?
If so, what are the implications for questions about the nature and existence
of a priori knowledge. My focus is on the second question.

Quine's attack is directed at a variant of Frege's conception of analyticity: a statement is analytic if it can be turned into a logical truth by replacing synonyms with synonyms.[45] His primary target is the notion of *synonymy*,
and his leading contentions can be summarized as follows:

- (Q1) Definition presupposes synonymy rather than explaining it.
- (Q2) Interchangeability *salva veritate* is a sufficient condition of
  cognitive synonymy only in relation to a language containing an intensional adverb "necessarily."
- (Q3) Semantic rules do not explain "Statement *S* is analytic for
  language *L*," with variable "*S*" and "*L*," even if "*L*" is
  limited to artificial languages.
- (Q4) The verification theory of meaning provides an account of
  statement synonymy that presupposes reductionism.
  Radical reductionism fails, but reductionism survives as the
  view that individual statements admit of confirmation or
  infirmation.
- (Q5) Any statement can be held to be true come what may. No
  statement is immune to revision.

There are two strands to Quine's argument. The first three contentions focus
directly on the cogency of semantic concepts such as synonymy. The final
two are directed toward reductionism. I begin by considering the claim that
synonymy and related semantic concepts are not cogent and, as a consequence, that the concept of analyticity is not cogent. What are the implications for the a priori?

Consider first the concept of a priori knowledge. If the concept of a priori
knowledge involves one of the semantic concepts, then it is also incoher-

45. Quine, "Two Dogmas of Empiricism," 23.

ent. There are two ways in which the concept of a priori knowledge might involve semantic concepts: explicitly or implicitly. I argued in chapters 1 and 2 for a reductive analysis of a priori knowledge in terms of the concept of a priori justification and for a minimal conception of a priori justification as nonexperiential justification. The concept of nonexperiential justification is not semantic. Hence, the concept of a priori knowledge does not explicitly involve any semantic concepts.

The only plausible case for maintaining that the concept of a priori knowledge implicitly involves semantic concepts is based on two premises. The first alleges that the concept of a priori knowledge involves the concept of necessity. The second contends that the concept of necessity is analyzable in terms of the concept of analyticity. In sections 8.4 and 8.5, I cast doubt on the second premise. But even if the second premise is conceded, the first involves an endorsement of a rationalist conception of a priori knowledge. I argued, however, in chapter 1 that the rationalist conception is untenable on independent grounds. Hence, the concept of a priori justification does not implicitly involve any semantic concepts.

The only other routes to the conclusion that the concept of a priori knowledge implicitly involves semantic concepts are based in conceptual confusion. The first fails to distinguish between the epistemic sense of a priori, which has its primary application to knowledge or justification, and the nonepistemic sense of a priori, which has its primary application to grounds of truth and, as a consequence, equates the a priori and the necessary. The second fails to distinguish Kant's claim that necessity is a *criterion* of the a priori from the stronger claim that necessity is a *constituent* of the a priori. Both routes lead to the conclusion that the concept of a priori knowledge involves the concept of necessity, which, in conjunction with the claim that necessity is analyzable in terms of analyticity, entails the further conclusion that the concept of a priori knowledge involves the concept of analyticity.

Consider now the existence of a priori knowledge. Since the concept of a priori knowledge does not involve any semantic concepts, the question of whether there exists a priori knowledge is cogent. The remaining question is whether the incoherence of semantic concepts, such as synonymy, negatively affects the traditional arguments for the a priori. In chapter 4, I identified three types of argument for the existence of a priori knowledge. Arguments of the first type offer an analysis of the concept of a priori knowledge and maintain that some knowledge satisfies the conditions in the analysis. Arguments of the second type identify criteria of the a priori and show that some knowledge satisfies the criteria. Arguments of the third type maintain that radical empiricist theories of knowledge are deficient in some respect and that the only remedy for the deficiency is to embrace the a priori. Since the concept of a priori knowledge does not involve any semantic concepts, arguments of the first type are not negatively affected by the incoherence of semantic concepts. Since arguments of the third type draw out the implications of radical empiricist theories of knowledge and the concept of analyticity plays no significant role in such theories, they are not negatively affected by the incoherence of semantic concepts. Finally, none of the arguments of the second type explicitly appeals to the concept of analyticity or any other semantic concepts. Hence, the only remaining option is that some argument involves a semantic concept implicitly.

The only plausible case for maintaining that some argument involves a semantic concept implicitly draws attention to the Argument from Necessity and maintains that the concept of necessity is analyzable in terms of the concept of analyticity. Even if we concede this contention, the epistemic damage is minimal. The concession entails that the premises of the argument are incoherent since they involve the concept of necessity. I have distinguished, however, two versions of the argument. The Kantian Argument, which purports to establish that knowledge of the truth value of necessary propositions is a priori, fails on independent grounds. Hence, if it were the case that its premises are incoherent, there would be no further epistemic damage. The Modal Argument, which purports to establish that knowledge of the general modal status of necessary propositions is a priori, also fails on independent grounds. But here there is additional damage. Since the conclusion of the Kantian Argument makes no reference to the modal status of mathematical propositions, proponents of the a priori are free to offer a more compelling argument for that conclusion from premises that do not involve the concept of necessity. The conclusion of the Modal Argument, however, refers to the general modal status of mathematical propositions. If the concept of necessity is not coherent, then the conclusion of the argument is not coherent and there is no possibility of offering an alternative argument for that conclusion. Hence, if the concept of necessity is analyzable in terms of the concept of analyticity and the latter is not coherent, then there cannot be knowledge of the general modal status of a proposition and, a fortiori, the route of defending the existence of a priori knowledge via knowledge of general modal status is closed. Here there is epistemic damage but, I suggest, minimal damage since the primary goal of all major proponents of the Argument from Necessity is to establish that the truth value of necessary propositions is known a priori.

I have argued that the incoherence of the concept of analyticity has minimal impact on questions about the nature and existence of a priori knowledge because the concept of a priori knowledge does not involve the concept of analyticity either explicitly or implicitly. It might be argued, however, that there is an epistemically significant nonconceptual connection between the a priori and the analytic and, moreover, that as a consequence of this connection the incoherence of the concept of analyticity has significant epistemic implications. Here we face two questions. What is the connection? Is it epistemically significant?

Kant's primary objective is to provide an explanation of how synthetic a priori knowledge is possible. Logical empiricists find Kant's explanation unsatisfactory since it invokes the mysterious cognitive faculty of intuition.

Establishing that all propositions known a priori are analytic offers the prospect of providing an explanation of such knowledge that is not shrouded in mystery. If, indeed, the concept of analyticity offers the only prospect for providing a nonmysterious explanation of a priori knowledge and the concept is incoherent, then proponents of the a priori are in the position of endorsing a theory that postulates a type of knowledge for which it can offer no explanation.

The final challenge to the a priori via the concept of analyticity is based on three premises. First, a theory of knowledge that postulates a type of knowledge for which it can offer no explanation is unacceptable. Second, the only available explanation of a priori knowledge involves the concept of analyticity. Finally, the concept of analyticity is incoherent. Therefore, theories endorsing the a priori are unacceptable. This challenge rests on the contention that the connection between the a priori and the analytic is explanatory. The concept of analyticity is alleged to provide a compelling explanation of how a priori knowledge is possible. I argued in sections 8.4 and 8.5, however, that none of the available conceptions of analyticity offer much in terms of explaining a priori knowledge. They offer either incomplete explanations or none at all. Hence, whether the concept of analyticity proves to be coherent or not is of little epistemic consequence since it cannot discharge the explanatory burden. Nevertheless, the general problem posed by the final challenge remains. Any acceptable theory of knowledge endorsing the a priori must offer some explanation of how such knowledge is possible. The problem, however, is more general than the final challenge allows. By conceding that the concept of analyticity has explanatory power, the final challenge mistakenly elevates its status within the theory of knowledge. Once we recognize that the concept of analyticity offers little in terms of explanatory power, we are in a position to recognize that the problem goes beyond the analytic/synthetic distinction. The more general problem that must be addressed is how a priori knowledge is possible.

My initial assessment of the epistemic import of Quine's argument focused on his claim that semantic concepts, such as definition and synonymy, are suspect. Hilary Putnam and Philip Kitcher maintain that this focus is misplaced. Putnam rejects what he regards as the orthodox reading of "Two Dogmas": "Quine was attacking the analytic/synthetic distinction. His argument was simply that all attempts to define the distinction are *circular*."[46] The orthodox reading is too simplistic because Quine's arguments are not all directed at the same concept. Some target the linguistic notion of analyticity—a sentence is analytic if it can be obtained from a truth of logic by putting synonyms for synonyms—others "the notion of an analytic truth as one that is *confirmed no matter what*."[47] Putnam dismisses the attack on the former since "Quine's argument is little more than that Quine cannot

46. Putnam, "'Two Dogmas' Revisited," 87.
47. Ibid.

think how to define 'synonymy'."[48] With respect to the latter, Putnam makes two points. First, the targeted concept is epistemic not semantic:

> But why should this concept, the concept of a statement which is confirmed no matter what, be considered a concept of *analyticity*? Confirmation, in the positivist sense, has something to do with rational belief. A statement which is highly confirmed is a statement which it is rational to believe, or rational to believe to a high degree. . . . On the face of it, then, the concept of a truth which is confirmed no matter what is not a concept of *analyticity* but a concept of *apriority*.[49]

Putnam's second point is that Quine's argument against the latter is different from his argument against the former: "Quine's argument against the notion of a truth which is *confirmed no matter what*, is not an argument from the circularity of definitions. Quine's argument is an argument from what is clearly a normative description of the history of modern science."[50] Putnam locates the argument in the following trenchant passage:

> Any statement can be held true come what may, if we make drastic enough adjustments elsewhere in the system. . . . Conversely, by the same token, no statement is immune to revision. Revision even of the logical law of the excluded middle has been proposed as a means of simplifying quantum mechanics; and what difference is there in principle between such a shift and the shift whereby Kepler superseded Ptolemy, or Einstein Newton, or Darwin Aristotle?[51]

Putnam endorses the argument and locates the importance of "Two Dogmas" in its rejection of the a priori.

Philip Kitcher echoes Putnam's view about the locus of Quine's most important argument:

> Defenders of analyticity have often construed the main thrust of Quine's most famous attack, "Two Dogmas of Empiricism," as arguing that the concept of analyticity is undefinable in notions Quine takes to be unproblematic. . . . I locate Quine's central point elsewhere. The importance of the article stems from its final section, a section which challenges not the existence of analytic truths but the claim that analytic truths are knowable a priori.[52]

According to Kitcher, the argument for this claim is located in the same passage highlighted by Putnam. Kitcher elaborates the argument as follows:

> Quine connects analyticity to apriority *via* the notion of unrevisability. If we can know a priori that *p* then no experience could deprive us of our warrant to believe that *p*. . . . But "no statement is immune from

48. Ibid.
49. Ibid., 90.
50. Ibid.
51. Quine, "Two Dogmas of Empiricism," 43; quoted by Putnam, ibid.
52. Kitcher, *The Nature of Mathematical Knowledge*, 80.

revision." It follows that analytic statements, hailed by Quine's empiricist predecessors and contemporaries as a priori, cannot be a priori.[53]

Hence, like Putnam, Kitcher maintains that the target of Quine's most important argument is the a priori and not the analytic.

On the Putnam-Kitcher reading, in contrast to the orthodox reading, the argument of "Two Dogmas," if sound, does have significant epistemic implications because, according to that reading, if Quine's argument is sound there is no a priori knowledge. There are, however, two crucial points to note about the Putnam-Kitcher reading. First, the epistemic implications of the reading rest essentially on the premise that if someone knows a priori that p, then p is indefeasible by experiential evidence. This premise does not assert that the concept of a priori knowledge involves or entails a *semantic* condition. It asserts that the concept of a priori knowledge involves or entails a weak indefeasibility condition, which is an *epistemic* condition. Second, the Putnam-Kitcher reading does not challenge the cogency of the concept of a priori knowledge. If successful, it establishes that the concept is vacuous; there are no items of knowledge that meet the standards imposed by the concept. Although Quine maintains in this context that "it becomes folly to seek a boundary between synthetic statements, which hold contingently on experience, and analytic statements, which hold come what may,"[54] this claim cannot be read as disputing the cogency of the distinction. Since the leading claim of his supporting argument is that no statement is immune to revision, if his argument is coherent, the distinction is also coherent.

Let us take stock. I have identified two lines of argument in "Two Dogmas," one that targets the cogency of semantic concepts such as synonymy and one that challenges the claim that some statements are indefeasible by experiential evidence. If the first line is sound, it does cast doubt on the cogency of the analytic/synthetic distinction and the question of whether there is synthetic a priori knowledge. The epistemic implications of these results are rather minimal since neither the leading conceptions of a priori knowledge nor the leading arguments in support of the existence of such knowledge employ the concept of analyticity. The second line of argument, if sound, does have significant epistemic implications. These implications, however, depend on the claim that the concept of a priori knowledge involves or entails a weak indefeasibility condition. I argued in chapter 2 that the concept of a priori knowledge does not involve such a condition and, in chapter 5, that it does not entail such a condition. Hence, even if Quine is right in maintaining that all statements are revisable in light of experience, the epistemic implications are minimal. But it is also important to recognize that even if I am wrong about the concept of a priori knowledge and Quine's second line of argument does establish that there is no a priori knowl-

53. Ibid.
54. Quine, "Two Dogmas of Empiricism," 43.

edge, the argument does not rest on the premise that the analytic/synthetic distinction is not cogent.

8.7   Conclusion

Underlying the debate over the synthetic a priori are two formidable challenges that must be addressed by any theory of a priori knowledge: How is a priori knowledge possible? Is the concept of a priori knowledge cogent? The focus on the synthetic a priori, however, mislocates the sources of these challenges and, as a consequence, becomes an obstacle to effectively addressing them. Kant took it for granted that there is no special problem in explaining the possibility of analytic a priori knowledge, but he maintained that there is a special problem in explaining the possibility of synthetic a priori knowledge, which requires an appeal to intuition. Kant's logical empiricist critics found the explanation unsatisfactory and responded by offering broader conceptions of analyticity that were alleged to encompass all a priori knowledge. The underlying assumption was that restricting a priori knowledge to analytic truths removed the obstacles to explaining how a priori knowledge is possible. In this chapter, I argue that no conception of analyticity provides a complete explanation of how a priori knowledge is possible. Some provide no explanation of how such knowledge is possible; others leave unexplained how logical and semantic knowledge is possible.

The focus on the question of how synthetic a priori knowledge is possible masks the scope of the explanatory problem: it overlooks the need for an explanation of analytic a priori knowledge. The more general problem that must be addressed is how a priori knowledge is possible. I argued in section 6.3 that empirical investigation is relevant in addressing the explanatory issues raised by the a priori. This result extends to the questions raised by the synthetic a priori. Empirical investigation is relevant in determining whether there are two distinct sources of a priori knowledge and, if so, whether the content of the beliefs produced by each source coincides with some version of the analytic/synthetic distinction. Moreover, if there are two distinct sources of a priori knowledge, one that produces beliefs whose content is analytic and one that produces beliefs whose content is synthetic, empirical investigation is relevant in explaining how each of the sources produces those beliefs and in determining whether the cognitive processes employed by each source differ significantly.

Quine's arguments against the cogency of the analytic/synthetic distinction are widely viewed as challenging the cogency of the a priori/a posteriori distinction. But because of his focus on the attempts of logical empiricists to defend the view that all a priori truths are analytic, Quine mislocated the source of the problem. The relevant question is not whether *semantic* concepts, such as synonymy, are cogent. The concept of a priori knowledge neither involves nor entails any conditions involving the concepts of synonymy or analyticity. The relevant question is whether the *epistemic* concept of nonexperiential justification is cogent. In section 6.2, I proposed articulating the experiential/nonexperiential distinction by treating experience as a natural kind whose underlying nature can be uncovered only by empirical investigation.

The debate over the synthetic a priori raises a significant conceptual issue and a significant explanatory issue. The conceptual issue cannot be effectively addressed by defending the cogency of the analytic/synthetic distinction, and the explanatory question cannot be effectively addressed by demonstrating that a priori knowledge is limited to analytic truths. The concept of a priori justification does not involve or entail the concept of analyticity, and the concept of analyticity does not explain how a priori knowledge is possible. Articulating the concept of a priori justification and explaining how a priori knowledge is possible require empirical investigation.

Bibliography

Ambrose, Alice, and Morris Lazerowitz. *Fundamentals of Symbolic Logic.* New York: Holt, Rinehart & Winston, 1962.

Anderson, C. Anthony. "Toward a Logic of A Priori Knowledge." *Philosophical Topics* 21 (1993): 1–20.

Armstrong, D. M. "Is Introspective Knowledge Incorrigible?" *Philosophical Review* 72 (1963): 417–432.

———. *Belief, Truth and Knowledge.* Cambridge: Cambridge University Press, 1973.

Audi, Robert. *Belief, Justification, and Knowledge.* Belmont, Calif.: Wadsworth, 1988.

Ayer, A. J. *Language, Truth and Logic.* New York: Dover, 1952.

Bealer, George. "*A Priori* Knowledge and the Scope of Philosophy." *Philosophical Studies* 81 (1996): 121–142.

———. "*A Priori* Knowledge: Replies to William Lycan and Ernest Sosa." *Philosophical Studies* 81 (1996): 163–174.

Benacerraf, Paul. "Mathematical Truth." *Journal of Philosophy* 70 (1973): 661–679.

BonJour, Laurence. *The Structure of Empirical Knowledge.* Cambridge, Mass.: Harvard University Press, 1985.

———. *In Defense of Pure Reason.* Cambridge: Cambridge University Press, 1998.

Broad, C. D. "Are There Synthetic *A Priori* Truths?" *Proceedings of the Aristotelian Society,* supp. vol. 15 (1936): 102–117.

Burge, Tyler. "Content Preservation." *Philosophical Review* 102 (1993): 457–488.

Burgess, John P. "Epistemology and Nominalism." In *Physicalism in Mathematics,* ed. A. D. Irvine. Dordrecht: Kluwer, 1990.

Butchvarov, Panayot. *The Concept of Knowledge.* Evanston, Ill.: Northwestern University Press, 1970.

Casullo, Albert. "Necessity, Certainty, and the A Priori." *Canadian Journal of Philosophy* 18 (1988): 43–66.

———. "Revisability, Reliabilism, and A Priori Knowledge." *Philosophy and Phenomenological Research* 49 (1988): 187–213.

———. "Causality, Reliabilism, and Mathematical Knowledge." *Philosophy and Phenomenological Research* 52 (1992): 557–584.

———. "A Priori Knowledge Appraised." In *A Priori Knowledge*, ed. Albert Casullo. Aldershot: Dartmouth, 1999.

———. "Modal Epistemology: Fortune or Virtue?" *Southern Journal of Philosophy* 38, supp. (2000): 17–25.

Chandler, Hugh. "Plantinga and the Contingently Possible." *Analysis* 36 (1976): 106–109.

Chisholm, R. M. *Theory of Knowledge*, 2nd ed. Upper Saddle River, N.J.: Prentice Hall, 1977.

———. *Theory of Knowledge*, 3rd ed. Upper Saddle River, N.J.: Prentice Hall, 1989.

Donnellan, Keith S. "The Contingent *A Priori* and Rigid Designators." In *Contemporary Perspectives on the Philosophy of Language*, eds. P. French, T. Uehling, and H. Wettstein. Minneapolis: University of Minnesota Press, 1979.

———. "There Is a Word for That Kind of Thing: An Investigation of Two Thought Experiments." *Philosophical Perspectives* 7 (1993): 155–171.

Edidin, Aron. "*A Priori* Knowledge for Fallibilists." *Philosophical Studies* 46 (1984): 189–197.

Evans, Gareth. "Reference and Contingency." *Monist* 62 (1979): 161–189.

Ewing, A. C. "The Linguistic Theory of *A Priori* Propositions." *Proceedings of the Aristotelian Society* 40 (1939/1940): 207–244.

Field, Hartry. *Realism, Mathematics and Modality*. Oxford: Blackwell, 1989.

———. "The A Priodicity of Logic." *Proceedings of the Aristotelian Society* 96 (1995/1996): 359– 379.

Firth, Roderick. "The Anatomy of Certainty." In *Empirical Knowledge*, eds. R. M. Chisholm and R. J. Swartz. Upper Saddle River, N.J.: Prentice Hall, 1973.

Frege, Gottlob. *The Foundations of Arithmetic*, 2nd ed. rev., trans. J. L. Austin. Evanston, Ill.: Northwestern University Press, 1974.

Geirsson, Heimir. "The Contingent *A Priori*: Kripke's Two Types of Examples." *Australasian Journal of Philosophy* 69 (1991): 195–205.

Giaquinto, Marcus. "Non-Analytic Conceptual Knowledge." *Mind* 105 (1996): 249–268.

Goldman, Alvin. "Discrimination and Perceptual Knowledge." *Journal of Philosophy* 73 (1976):771–791.

———. "A Causal Theory of Knowing." In *Essays on Knowledge and Justification*, eds. G. Pappas and M. Swain. Ithaca, N.Y.: Cornell University Press, 1978.

———. "What Is Justified Belief?" In *Justification and Knowledge*, ed. George Pappas. Dordrecht: D. Reidel, 1979.

———. *Epistemology and Cognition*. Cambridge, Mass.: Harvard University Press, 1986.

———. "A Priori Warrant and Naturalistic Epistemology." *Philosophical Perspectives* 13 (1999): 1–28.

Hale, Bob. *Abstract Objects.* Oxford: Blackwell, 1987.

Harman, Gilbert. *Thought.* Princeton, N.J.: Princeton University Press, 1973.

———. *Change in View.* Cambridge, Mass.: MIT Press, 1986.

Hart, W. D. "Review of Mark Steiner, *Mathematical Knowledge.*" *Journal of Philosophy* 74 (1977): 118–129.

Hempel, Carl. "Geometry and Empirical Science." In *Readings in Philosophical Analysis,* eds. Herbert Feigl and Wilfrid Sellars. New York: Appleton-Century-Crofts, 1949.

———. "On the Nature of Mathematical Truth." In *Necessary Truth,* ed. R. C. Sleigh. Upper Saddle River, N.J.: Prentice Hall, 1972.

Hilbert, David. *The Foundations of Geometry,* trans. E. J. Townsend. La Salle, Ill.: Open Court, 1950.

Jeshion, Robin. "On the Obvious." *Philosophy and Phenomenological Research* 60 (2000): 333–355.

———. "Ways of Taking a Meter." *Philosophical Studies* 99 (2000): 297–318.

Kant, Immanuel. *Critique of Pure Reason,* trans. Norman Kemp Smith. New York: St. Martin, 1965.

Katz, Jerrold J. "What Mathematical Knowledge Could Be." *Mind* 104 (1995): 491–522.

Kim, Jaegwon. "The Role of Perception in A Priori Knowledge: Some Remarks." *Philosophical Studies* 40 (1981): 339–354.

———. "What Is 'Naturalized Epistemology'?" In *Naturalizing Epistemology,* 2nd ed., ed. Hilary Kornblith. Cambridge, Mass.: MIT Press, 1994.

Kitcher, Philip. "Apriority and Necessity." *Australasian Journal of Philosophy* 58 (1980): 89–101.

———. "Arithmetic for the Millian." *Philosophical Studies* 37 (1980): 215–236.

———. *The Nature of Mathematical Knowledge.* New York: Oxford University Press, 1983.

———. "Aprioristic Yearnings." *Erkenntnis* 44 (1996): 397–416.

Klein, Peter. "Knowledge, Causality, and Defeasibility." *Journal of Philosophy* 73 (1976): 792–812.

Kripke, Saul. "Identity and Necessity." In *Identity and Individuation,* ed. M. K. Munitz. New York: New York University Press, 1971.

———. *Naming and Necessity.* Cambridge, Mass.: Harvard University Press, 1980.

Leibniz, G. W. *New Essays Concerning Human Understanding,* eds. and trans. Peter Remnant and Jonathan Bennett. New York: Cambridge University Press, 1982.

Lewis, David. *On the Plurality of Worlds.* Oxford: Blackwell, 1986.

Maddy, Penelope. "Perception and Mathematical Intuition." *Philosophical Review* 89 (1980): 163–196.

———. "Mathematical Epistemology: What Is the Question?" *Monist* 67 (1984): 46–55.

———. *Realism in Mathematics.* Oxford: Oxford University Press, 1990.

Malcolm, Norman. "Knowledge and Belief." In *Knowledge and Certainty.* Upper Saddle River, N.J.: Prentice Hall, 1963.

Manfredi, Pat A. "The Compatibility of A Priori Knowledge and Empirical Defeasibility: A Defense of a Modest A Priori." *Southern Journal of Philosophy* 38, supp. (2000): 159–177.

McGinn, Colin. "*A Priori* and *A Posteriori* Knowledge." *Proceedings of the Aristotelian Society* 76 (1975/1976): 195–208.

———. "The Concept of Knowledge." *Midwest Studies in Philosophy* 9 (1984): 529–554.

Mill, John Stuart. *A System of Logic,* ed. J. M. Robson. Toronto: University of Toronto Press, 1973.

Moser, Paul. "Introduction." In *A Priori Knowledge,* ed. Paul Moser. Oxford: Oxford University Press, 1987.

Nozick, Robert. *Philosophical Explanations.* Cambridge, Mass.: Harvard University Press, 1981.

Plantinga, Alvin. *Warrant: The Current Debate.* New York: Oxford University Press, 1993.

———. *Warrant and Proper Function.* New York: Oxford University Press, 1993.

Pollock, John L. *Knowledge and Justification.* Princeton, N.J.: Princeton University Press, 1974.

Polya, G. *Induction and Analogy in Mathematics.* Princeton, N.J.: Princeton University Press, 1954.

Putnam, Hilary. "The Analytic and the Synthetic." In *Mind, Language and Reality: Philosophical Papers,* vol. 2. Cambridge: Cambridge University Press, 1975.

———. "The Meaning of 'Meaning.'" In *Mind, Language and Reality: Philosophical Papers,* vol. 2. Cambridge: Cambridge University Press, 1975.

———. "What Is Mathematical Truth?" In *Mathematics, Matter and Method: Philosophical Papers,* vol. 1, 2nd ed. Cambridge: Cambridge University Press, 1979.

———. "There Is at Least One A Priori Truth." In *Realism and Reason: Philosophical Papers,* vol. 3. Cambridge: Cambridge University Press, 1983.

———. "'Two Dogmas' Revisited." In *Realism and Reason: Philosophical Papers,* vol. 3. Cambridge: Cambridge University Press, 1983.

Quine, W. V. "Two Dogmas of Empiricism." In *From a Logical Point of View,* 2nd ed. rev. New York: Harper & Row, 1963.

———. "Epistemology Naturalized." In *Ontological Relativity and Other Essays.* New York: Columbia University Press, 1969.

———. "Truth by Convention." In *The Ways of Paradox and Other Essays,* 2nd ed. rev. Cambridge, Mass.: Harvard University Press, 1976.

Quinton, Anthony. "The *A Priori* and the Analytic." In *Necessary Truth,* ed. R. C. Sleigh. Upper Saddle River, N.J.: Prentice Hall, 1972.

Russell, Bertrand. *The Problems of Philosophy.* Oxford: Oxford University Press, 1971.

Salmon, Nathan. "The Logic of What Might Have Been." *Philosophical Review* 98 (1989): 3–34.

Sosa, Ernest. "The Raft and the Pyramid: Coherence Versus Foundations in the Theory of Knowledge." In *Knowledge in Perspective: Selected Essays in Epistemology*. Cambridge: Cambridge University Press, 1991.

———. "Rational Intuition: Bealer on Its Nature and Epistemic Status." *Philosophical Studies* 81 (1996): 151–162.

———. "Minimal Intuition." In *Proceedings of the Notre Dame Intuition Conference*, eds. M. DePaul and W. Ramsey. Totowa, N.J.: Rowman & Littlefield, 1997.

———. "Modal and Other *A Priori* Epistemology: How Can We Know What Is Possible and What Impossible?" *Southern Journal of Philosophy* 38, supp. (2000): 1–16.

Stalnaker, Robert. "Assertion." In *Context and Content*. Oxford: Oxford University Press, 1999.

———. "Introduction." In *Context and Content*. Oxford: Oxford University Press, 1999.

Steiner, Mark. "Platonism and the Causal Theory of Knowledge." *Journal of Philosophy* 70 (1973): 57–66.

———. *Mathematical Knowledge*. Ithaca, N.Y.: Cornell University Press, 1975.

Summerfield, Donna. "Modest A Priori Knowledge." *Philosophy and Phenomenological Research* 51 (1991): 39–66.

Swain, Marshall. "Justification and Reliable Belief." *Philosophical Studies* 40 (1981): 389–407.

Swinburne, R. G. "Analyticity, Necessity, and Apriority." In *A Priori Knowledge*, ed. Paul Moser. Oxford: Oxford University Press, 1987.

Vihvelin, Kadri. "A Defense of a Reliabilist Account of A Priori Knowledge." *Pacific Philosophical Quarterly* 81 (2000): 90–97.

Zermelo, E. "A New Proof of the Possibility of a Well Ordering." In *From Frege to Gödel*, ed. J. van Heijenoort. Cambridge, Mass.: Harvard University Press, 1967.

Index